Moose Crossing

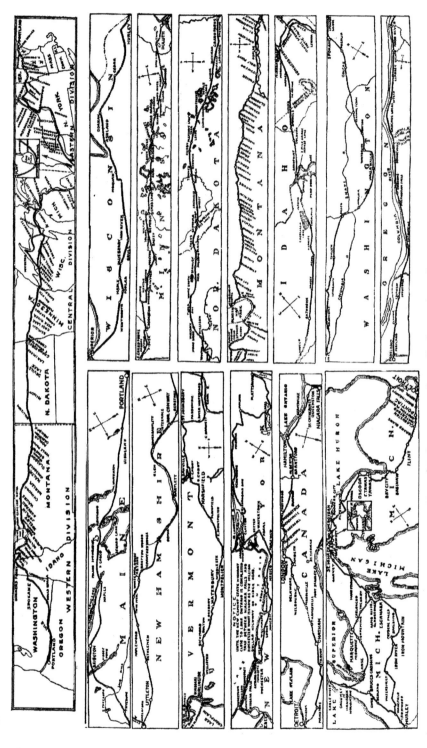

Map of Entire Route and Detail of Route in Each State
THEODORE ROOSEVELT INTERNATIONAL HIGHWAY
Portland Main to Portland Oregon

Moose Crossing

Portland to Portland on the Theodore Roosevelt International Highway

Max J. Skidmore

Hamilton Books
A member of
The Rowman & Littlefield Publishing Group
Lanham • Boulder • New York • Toronto • Oxford

Copyright © 2007 by
Hamilton Books
4501 Forbes Boulevard
Suite 200
Lanham, Maryland 20706
Hamilton Books Acquisitions Department (301) 459-3366

PO Box 317
Oxford
OX2 9RU, UK

Library of Congress Control Number: 2006935662
ISBN-13: 978-0-7618-3510-3 (paperback : alk. ppr.)
ISBN-10: 0-7618-3510-5 (paperback : alk. ppr.)

Table of Contents

Foreword

January 15, 2000

MILETA FARM

Dear Max:

Your magnificent journey has reached its destination at last. You have crossed this vast country of ours from Portland, Maine to Portland, Oregon and re-identified the Theodore Roosevelt Memorial Highway from coast to coast—an adventure in which, I am sure TR himself would have joined with enthusiastic vigor. You have followed that same star as have other intrepid explorers in the past. . . . .

Today, as we greet the dawn of the 21st century, you have brought to life once more the man who led us so boldly and confidently into the 20th century, one hundred years ago.

A bully job, Max Skidmore, and I salute you!

Edith Roosevelt Derby Williams
[Theodore Roosevelt's Granddaughter]

There! I have written the foreword.

Acknowledgments

The University of Missouri-Kansas City awarded me a Faculty Research Grant that helped to make my research for this book possible. I wish to express my gratitude to the University. In any work of this magnitude, there are multitudes of people who contributed. This is especially true of *Moose Crossing*. Countless numbers of librarians, scholars, public officials, and others—many along the more than four thousand miles from Portland to Portland—helped in ways that ranged from small to enormous. They were there to assist when I conducted research and when I journeyed along the Theodore Roosevelt International Highway. They provided encouragement; often even inspiration. Without exception, they were enthusiastic. Among the most enthusiastic was Dr. Ray Browne, the pioneer scholar of popular culture. He recommended the book to the University of Wisconsin Press, which was to have published it years ago. Poor funding, though, caused the Press's director to resign, and brought cancellation of contracts. Happily, Hamilton Books stepped up to become *Moose Crossing*'s publisher.

Many of these good souls will find their names in the book; many will not. Most will recognize their contributions; some likely will not. Regardless, I am in their debt.

I am happy to dedicate *Moose Crossing* to them all, even if I can mention only those within my family who always do so much. I especially thank them: my wife, Charlene, for her ideas, her support, and for thinking of the perfect title; our daughter, Trish, for her bubbling enthusiasm and suggestions; our sons Joey, who supplied his eagle editorial eye, and Alan Campbell, who went above and beyond the call of duty in suggesting that I should take the journey in his beloved truck.

Illustrations

All photographs are those that I took in connection with my journey along the Theodore Roosevelt International Highway. Most are scenes along the route.

The map that is the frontispiece originated with the Theodore Roosevelt International Highway Association in 1921. The Association published detailed guides to the TR Highway for each of five states. The guides for New Hampshire, Minnesota, and North Dakota included the detailed map on a fold-out page. The remaining guides, those for Vermont and Montana, did not include the map.

Because the guides are so rare, I was able to work only from photocopies. These had smudges and fold marks, and were far too poor to serve as illustrations. Ms Alli Kurtz came to the rescue with her computer skills.

Without Alli Kurtz, *Moose Crossing* could not have included these valuable maps that reveal the TR International Highway as it was nearly a century ago.

Chapter One

Introduction:
The Century, the Journey, the Book

America was mired in the mud—never mind that the new twentieth century was beginning. Never mind that the young Theodore Roosevelt soon would assume the presidency and become its most vigorous occupant ever. America's roads, or what passed for roads, fell far short of the standard set by the Roman Empire millennia before.

Like its president, America was bursting with energy. Its people already had conquered the continent, and now they wanted to explore their own vast country. Trains were available for those who could afford them, but in most cases there were no practical alternatives to rail.

More often than not the country's primitive paths were challenging even for horse-drawn wagons. Few people in any case wanted to waste valuable time plodding along for great distances in a nineteenth-century conveyance. The Machine Age had arrived.

For that most compelling of new machines, the automobile, roads in the United States were much worse than for wagons. Much of the time they were completely useless. That meant to restless Americans that the situation was impossible. Progress was movement. "Impassible" meant "unacceptable."

The automobile sounded a new call to roam. It was the loudest call yet, but however loud that call, there were few places the marvelous machine could go. It made the attraction of the road harder to resist, but the roads it needed were mainly in the future.

Few people now living can remember how challenging cross-country travel was in America until well into the twentieth century. Railroads and boats were acceptable if you happened to be going their way and could afford them. If you weren't or couldn't, you were out of luck unless you were adventuresome, and hardy as well.

The nineteenth century began with a zeal for road building, but interest dwindled when trains—providing comfort that no wagon or stagecoach could match—became available. The desire for roads had returned by the time the first automobiles began the long outpouring of love from Americans for their cars. But the country had lagged far behind. To impatient Americans, it seemed as if cross-country routes would never rise much above the primitive trails reminiscent of colonial times.

Outside of cities and their surroundings, roads of any quality at all remained rare until well into the 1920s. West of Chicago, even gravel was a welcome treat. The country raced its collective engines, but eager motorists often bogged down as soon as they left the city. One explorer kept a diary of his trans-continental trip in 1925, and recorded nineteen flat tires—in one day.

Drake Hokanson, in his excellent study of the first transcontinental road, *The Lincoln Highway*, reported that the first automobile crossing of the continent was in 1903. A fine PBS documentary, *Horatio's Drive*, with its companion volume of the same title by Dayton Duncan and Ken Burns, have dramatically presented that first courageous road trip to modern Americans. Dr. Horatio Nelson Jackson, a physician from Vermont, on a $50 bet, impulsively drove from San Francisco to New York with his mechanic, Sewell K. Croker. The journey took them sixty-five days.

At that time, and for years later, "improvement" generally meant little more than grading, or perhaps spreading some gravel. Roads were entirely the responsibility of local jurisdictions. Ordinarily, they levied a road tax that men could work off with shovels.

Still, in spite of the hardships and actual dangers—or perhaps because of them—the restless American desire for speed and adventure meant that opportunities were waiting. The open roads at first were more imaginary than real, but they were a dream that generated pressure for the real thing. This is not to say that the demand for roads came only from a romantic desire to roam, or that it affected only the wealthy who had become bored with their local surroundings. There also were practical reasons for good roads, as farmers discovered when their Model Ts made trips to their markets so easy in dry weather.

The year 1913 saw the first of the transcontinental routes—or at least the first feasible road that aspired to be transcontinental. That was the Lincoln Highway. The New York to San Francisco route was the brainchild of Carl Fisher, who had built the Indianapolis Motor Speedway. He proposed a "Coast-to-Coast Rock Highway." Within a month he had accumulated a million dollars in pledges. He failed, however, to receive the support of the man most important to the project, Henry Ford.

Although it may seem that Ford would have been eager to endorse the idea, he opposed it. His reason, in contrast to many of his other views, was uncommonly enlightened. "As long as private interests are willing to build good roads for the general public," Hokanson quoted him as saying, "the general public will not be very much interested in building good roads for itself. I believe in spending money to educate the public to the necessity of building good roads, and let everybody contribute their share in proper taxes."

Instead of Ford, Fisher found his supporter in Henry B. Joy, President of the Packard Motor Car Company, and in 1913, the Lincoln Highway project began. Hokanson noted "a total of nine named transcontinental highways in some way deserving of the title, including the Lincoln," by 1922. The Theodore Roosevelt International Highway was the only one of these with an international component.

The emergence of named highways did not mean that travel had become simple. In 1915, Emily Post—later to become this socially insecure country's most prominent authority on manners and etiquette, a stuffy precursor of the lively Miss Manners—attempted to drive the Lincoln Highway's length. Her son, Ned, taking a leave from his studies at Harvard, was at the wheel of the enormous hand-built European car piled high with steamer trunks; a cousin, Alice Beadleston, was also crowded aboard. Post had determined that under no circumstances would she be roughing it. She would spend each night at a comfortable hotel. Furthermore, each afternoon at tea time the party would stop by the side of the road. There, the women would brew tea, and serve it from an elaborate silver tea service.

In the Arizona desert, not only far from the Lincoln Highway but also far from whatever beaten track there may have been, she gave up. The party loaded the car on a train, and set off for California by rail. Her journey, and its travails, were well-reported. *Collier's* magazine had commissioned her trip so that she could provide its readers with vicarious thrills from tales of transcontinental adventure.

Undaunted by Post's experience, in 1918 a divorced woman in her 40s, Viola Stewart, accomplished the unthinkable. She drove alone in a Model T from Pittsburgh to the Twin Cities, demonstrating that it could be done. Along the way she camped, cooking all her own meals. She even brought along a portable oven, which she used to supply herself throughout the trip with freshly-baked bread. Much of her route was along the Lincoln Highway. She was a cook, not a writer, but even so, she missed a great opportunity in not having written of her triumph for publication.

Daredevils of another sort began to set records for coast-to-coast drives. Newspapers eagerly reported their results. Articles describing a mere journey from one coast to the other could bring fat fees from magazines whose readers devoured their tales of adventure on the open road. A common ritual involved dipping the auto's tires in the Atlantic, and then at the other end, in the Pacific—although the tires were not the same ones that had begun the trip.

Speed records kept falling until legal limits and law enforcement discouraged the efforts. Hokanson outlined the contests, which auto companies generally sponsored as promotions. Packard President Joy took twenty-one days to drive from Detroit to San Francisco in 1915. Only one year later, by contrast, Bobby Hammond drove there from New York in six days, ten hours, and fifty-nine minutes. The transcontinental record had fallen by 1925 to four days, fourteen hours.

Louis B. Miller, a 51-year-old X-ray salesman, determined that he could do better. Breaking speed records was his hobby. He and companion C. I. Hanson departed from the Western Union office in Jersey City at 1:00 am on the 14th of July, 1925, when the telegrapher gave the signal. They were in Miller's Wills Sainte Clair roadster, the "Gray Goose." They telegraphed their progress to C. H. Wills, president of the Wills Sainte Clair Company, although the company had not sponsored their run. Motorcycle police escorted them through some cities, members of civic clubs through others. Four days, six hours, and forty-five minutes later they arrived in Oakland.

Miller had lost six pounds, Hansen twenty-four. Rain had delayed them in Nevada, causing them to miss a ferry. It cost them, Miller believed, a full day. Nevertheless, there was a new record.

One year later, he tried again in the same car, traveling alone. He did cut nearly a day from his previous time. As Hokanson described it so well, Miller "was never the same again; he couldn't forget the addictive effect of sleep deprivation, speed, and fame." In 1927, he attempted something even more ambitious, a non-stop round trip from San Francisco to New York. He halted in New York City for exactly one minute, and completed the round trip precisely in one week—minus that minute.

Drivers even now would be hard-pressed to duplicate the coast-to-coast round trip times of these intrepid pioneers, today's high-speed automobiles and Interstate Highways notwithstanding. Certainly it would be difficult to match them legally. The speed-demon era, though, was brief. Except for remnants on race tracks, restricting laws and the new fascination with an even faster machine, the airplane, transferred most speed contests to the sky.

Speed records show that it was possible to drive coast-to-coast quickly. They do not demonstrate that it was easy, or that the average motorist could manage it. In 1919, for example, no less formidable an institution than the U. S. Army discovered just how rigorous cross-country travel on America's roads still was.

In order to test army vehicles and train its men, the first Army Transcontinental Motor Convoy set off from the White House heading for San Francisco. The convoy, stretching two miles, headed for the Lincoln Highway, and struggled on west. The 3,310-mile trip took sixty-two days. Along the way, the heavy vehicles fell through one hundred bridges, which the army rebuilt, no doubt improving the Lincoln Highway considerably.

A quick summary of the broken vehicles, physical and mental challenges, injuries, and fatigue does no justice to this almost-forgotten feat. It remained for a British writer, Pete Davies, to fill the void. In 2002 he brought a novelist's skill to the subject in his superb book, *American Road*. His subtitle is no exaggeration: *The Story of an Epic Transcontinental Journey at the Dawn of the Motor Age*.

The poor state of the country's highways indelibly impressed one of the members of the convoy, and thereby influenced American history. Captain Dwight D. Eisenhower was appalled at the state of national readiness, and the difficulties in moving troops and equipment across the United States. In January 1953, almost three and a half decades later, he took office as President. He had not forgotten the army's 1919 experience. In 1956, the Eisenhower administration sponsored and began to implement the most ambitious highway-building program in human history. It was Eisenhower's program that connected the entire country with a network of modern, high speed, roadways making it possible to drive from coast-to-coast without encountering a stoplight. America's automobiles (and its trucks) at last had their Interstates.

Long before the Interstates, though, attitudes had matured, and roads had become utilitarian. They developed steadily, and they brought unprecedented freedom and mobility. At the time, they seemed all to the good, but along with them came other consequences that hardly anyone anticipated—unwanted consequences. All the while they were opening the West for mass travel, they were closing that West as Americans had known it.

With all their contradictions, it seems especially fitting that one of the major arteries emerged as a memorial to Theodore Roosevelt. This is the story of that highway, of the President whose memory inspired it, and of the memories that the highway itself has left. It also is an account of the experiences that the highway continues to offer, despite having lost its identity, and a justification for re-kindling memory of that highway as a whole.

Until the spring of 1996, I had never heard of the TRIH. I was driving across the Continental Divide near Glacier National Park and noticed a roadside area containing a 60-foot obelisk. The monument was dedicated to Theodore Roosevelt, commemorating his contributions to conservation, and also the completion of the final link in the TR International Highway. According to a sign, "The Theodore Roosevelt International highway extends 4,060 miles from Portland, Maine, to Portland, Oregon, by way of Ontario, Canada."

That got my attention. As a child in a small city in the Ozarks—Springfield, Missouri—I had been fond of reading. Tales of exploration, the exotic Arabian Nights, and travel of all sorts intrigued me. As an adult, I completed a Ph.D. in American Studies and became a professor of political science.

I am privileged to have journeyed widely around the world, and as a Fulbright scholar to have lived in India and later in Hong Kong. I have associated with people from various cultures and from a range of stations—the very poor, high government officials, outstanding journalists, scholars, authors, farmers, artists, Asian and American martial artists, airline pilots, manual laborers, military officials from enlisted ranks to generals, and so on. My background has helped me to appreciate the manifold expressions of humanity in general, and to savor the variations within my own land.

Early in my life I developed an interest in highways as a means of exploring my own country. For some reason I had never pursued that interest in any organized way. Discovering the TRIH compelled me to introduce some system into my American travels, and to join the authors who use the open road as the basis for their creative works.

With the coming of the auto, the "road book" became a recognized genre, and it continues. Witness the affection Americans displayed for Charles Kuralt's sensitive television portrayals of his journeys, and the popularity of his many books.

The first of the auto road trip books probably emerged in 1916, when Theodore Dreiser wrote in *A Hoosier Holiday*, of his trek from New York to his hometown in Indiana. He started something. Of the many that followed, some are recognized classics. Henry Miller's *An Air-Conditioned Nightmare* and Jack Kerouac's *On the Road* spoke to generations of Americans as well as to teachers of literature.

In 1961, John Steinbeck's *Travels with Charley* gripped me as few books have. I recently read it again, and found it somewhat disappointing; but perhaps I expect too much. At any rate, its effect when it leaped into print clearly justifies its reputation as a classic. It may be simply that I find it suffering in comparison with William Least Heat Moon's *Blue Highways*.

There have been enough road books to form a library; many are excellent. Several by Jonathan Raban stand out, as does one (in addition to his *Horatio's Drive*) by Dayton Duncan. In 1987 Duncan related his journeys along the Lewis and Clark Trail. His *Out West* came out long before Stephen Ambrose published *Undaunted Courage*, the definitive history of Lewis's travels, but actually captures some of the same spirit. Ambrose wrote history while Duncan wrote of personal experiences, but his book is equally compelling.

As the 21st century neared, there was a new addition to the ranks of travel literature, highly (if briefly) advertised as a road book. James Morgan in 1999 published *The Distance to the Moon*, an account of a cross-country trip beginning from Florida in a brand new Boxster on loan from Porsche. The title comes from John Updike, who wrote that the average American male drives an equivalent of the distance to the moon every seventeen years. I enjoyed Morgan's title.

His book, though, is more a discussion of his reaction to cars than it is a road book. He did travel, but in a volume of fewer than 300 pages, he took until page 109 to cross Florida's state line. By the next page, he was all the way to Memphis. Much of his narrative dealt with telephone quarrels with his wife caused by admittedly insensitive comments that he was unwilling to retract. It was not to my taste.

Howard Frank Mosher's *North Country*, on the other hand, seizes the imagination. In 1997 Mosher recounted his journey along the border between Canada and the States. His trip was not a journey along the TR Highway, but he went through much the same country and was never very far from it. Mosher is thoughtful, his superb writing weaves words into intricate pictures, and his book is beautiful and poetic.

Dean Lawrence shared the typically American urge to travel in some unusual way and then write about it. He satisfied his urge no less than other authors. In *Travels with Peppy*, he recounted his motorcycle trip of more than 10,000 miles through 42 states in 36 days, accompanied by his dog, Peppy. His 1994 book is on a much different level from the others. In some ways it is a written equivalent of less polished expressions of folk art, but his journey obviously was exciting and his publication fulfilling.

Of the many other books, some should be better known. Geoffrey O'Gara, in 1989, wrote *A Long Road Home: Journeys through America's Present in Search of America's Past*. His excellent title describes his book perfectly. In a class by itself is *Diary of an Unknown Traveler*. The title is literal. Mary Harris found a diary discarded in items donated to the Salvation Army where she worked. Some forty-six years later she finally edited and published it. It chronicles a road trip that took place in 1928. Polished literature it is not, but it reveals the America of the time in a way that few other sources can.

My discovery of the TRIH gave me the opportunity to contribute to the literature. It re-kindled my interest in following a historic road that would take me through a great variety of regions. I set out to learn all I could about it—its history, its route, the politics behind it—and found that I had to dig deeply.

I wrote to highway departments and historical associations in all the relevant states and Ontario, to the Federal Highway Administration, the National Park Service, and the Forest Service. I telephoned libraries and automobile associations in the US and Canada, and visited archives, museums, and libraries in many locations. Bit by bit I managed to uncover pieces of information and useful items. Among the most valuable of these were 1920s road maps, and publications of the Theodore Roosevelt Highway Association.

The 1921 map was among the first ever produced, probably *the* first. It detailed the Highway's route across the continent from Portland to Portland, and had a separate segment for each state plus Ontario. This invaluable map was part of the Theodore Roosevelt Highway Association's Guides to the States of North Dakota, Minnesota, and New Hampshire.

These were counterparts to the Guide for Vermont that I discovered in the State Historical Society's library in Montpelier, although Vermont's booklet did not include the map. I managed to get a copy of New Hampshire's Guide from the State Historical Society in Concord, and found a copy of Minnesota's Guide at the State Historical Society in St. Paul. There also was a Montana Guide, which the Montana Department of Highways has reproduced and put on the Internet. One copy of the original North Dakota Guide may still exist. Joseph Ashley, a geographer at Montana State University, found it in an antique store in Tacoma. He knew of my interest in the TR Highway and graciously sent me a photocopy. He also supplied one to the North Dakota Historical Society's journal, *North Dakota History*, in connection with an article I published there. I thank him here for his thoughtfulness. Sadly, though, he later lent the original to someone who had been highly recommended. That person vanished, along with the only known original copy.

When I managed to reconstruct the Highway's history, as mentioned above, I discovered that it was the northernmost of nine "trails" in the 1920s that were, or aspired to be, transcontinental. I was surprised to discover that the TRIH had its genesis not in the east or west, but in Duluth, Minnesota. In February, 1919—barely a month following TR's death—a group of civic leaders under the leadership of a local auto dealer, E. A. Filiatrault, met in that Lake Superior city with "good roads" enthusiasts from many states to plan the roadway.

I found that it was a major artery with great significance to the development of ground transportation in the United States. Its international segment gave it an added dimension. In addition, the TR Highway was the largest memorial to the man who without doubt was the most dynamic President in American history. It deserves to be remembered on all these counts.

This, then, was the appeal. Rather than following a well-known route, however interesting that might be, I would be uncovering something of true historical significance that had been nearly forgotten through the years. So I turned my attention to the Highway, and also to the man whose name it bore. I discuss his presidency and his outstanding life in the final chapter of this book.

There is one other question that I should anticipate and answer. How did I select the title, *Moose Crossing*? TR, of course, was so identified with his repeated statement that he felt "as strong as a bull moose," that his race to regain the presidency in 1912 under the banner of the Progressive Party came to be known as his "Bull Moose campaign," and the Party members as "Bull Moose Progressives."

There are "Deer Crossing," or "Cattle Crossing" signs all over the country, usually with silhouettes of the animal, rather than words. The most unusual such signs that I had seen were in Australia, with the silhouette of a kangaroo. On the TR Highway, from New England westward I encountered occasional signs whose silhouettes warned "MOOSE CROSSING." Hitting a deer is bad enough for a car. Hitting a moose would likely be worse—worse, that is, for the car; equally bad, no doubt, for deer or moose. I mentioned the signs to my wife, Charlene, when I returned from the trip, saying it was symbolic that I kept seeing signs warning of moose on the Highway named for Theodore Roosevelt. "That's it," she said, "that's your title!"

She was right.

Chapter Two

Setting Out from Maine

PRELUDE

I stood looking west from Longfellow Square in Portland, Maine, at the beginning of the Theodore Roosevelt International Highway. Often, its earliest years, it was known simply as the "Roosevelt Trail." It took digging to discover just where it began, so I was especially happy finally to find that the setting was right.

I thought it appropriate that the seated figure of Henry Wadsworth Longfellow, a monumental rendering of one of TR's favorites, presided over the Maine end of the Highway. Longfellow gazes out upon it, relaxed, with his right arm resting on the arm of his chair, and the left in his lap. He has a good vantage point, atop a large marble pedestal above the heads of pedestrians.

I was pleased to discover that the precise starting point was in front of Cunningham's "OLD & RARE" and "OUT OF PRINT BOOKS." I was less pleased, although not surprised, to find nothing indicating the Highway. I turned my attention to Cunningham's. Where else would I be more likely to find information? My hunch paid off, but only in a modest way. I enriched my collection slightly with a paperback, *State 'O Maine Facts '66–'67*, which lists the TR Highway as a Maine attraction.

It says the "Theodore Roosevelt International Highway starts at Portland and follows Route 302 to the New Hampshire border," and mentions that "the road travels through historic areas of Cumberland County and leaves Maine at Fryeburg which is in Oxford County." It gives the length in Maine as 55 miles. The information was slim, adding nothing to what I already knew, but I was glad to find a relatively recent source that mentioned the TRIH.

I found out from the publisher, the *Courier-Gazette* of Rockland, Maine, that there were no files relating to the book, and no back copies of other issues. It had sold *State 'O Maine Facts* years ago to another company. That company searched its records, but found nothing. The book no longer is being published.

The proprietor at Cunningham's was interested to discover that the TRIH had begun in front of her shop. "I guess I should have known," she said, "but I didn't. I really think there should be a commemorative plaque in the Square." As I left, she said that she would suggest it to the Historical Society.

Longfellow Square, Portland, Maine—Longfellow Statue, Cunningham's Books

The two Portlands were perfect choices for the Highway's ends. More than the distance of a continent separates them. Despite sharing a name, they could hardly be more different, but still they are connected. The younger, more vigorous, and now much larger city in Oregon took its name from the older, more cautious city in Maine. Of course the Highway connects them physically, as well, but that link now is merely a thread. Two-lane travel is out of fashion, but there remains much to see and learn away from the Interstates.

The traveler along the length of the TRIH experiences some of the world's most striking scenery. Cities range from small to huge, from slow-paced to bustling, from the familiar to those suggesting Europe. There is the New England countryside with its lanes, villages, covered bridges, curiosities, and mountains—including views of the awesome Mount Washington, where some of earth's fiercest weather creates a true timber line at around a mere 4,000 feet, instead of the 10,000 feet or higher required for one in the Rockies. There is the Great Lakes country, a touch of Canada, the Upper Midwest, and the Great Plains—surprising because of their scenic variation, their friendly welcome, and their lack of monotony. In the Rockies, America boasts some of the most impressive mountain views in the world. The Pacific Northwest has a special magnetism of its own. The long tour is worth it for its aesthetic appeal alone.

But a trip along the TRIH can encourage understandings that are even more important than aesthetics—at least to an American in these days of fragmented, and even fractured, views of ourselves. The traveler can easily see, when proceeding west, how America developed. So a sense of history rides along as a companion. And, although there are clear differences from one place to another, one who truly looks will be compelled to recognize how very much Americans share, wherever they are, and whoever they are. A perceptive TRIH traveler will begin to understand how it is that the country remains united and cohesive, and surely will come to appreciate the remarkable achievement that incorporates diversity but retains a core identity.

The area around Casco Bay where Portland is situated has been settled since about 1632. By 1770 it had come to be called Falmouth. According to the Northern New England section of *The Smithsonian Guide to Historic America*, by Vance Muse and Paul Rocheleau, the early French and English settlers fought with one another, with Indians, with pirates, and "with the brutal winters." John T. Faris wrote that "jealous neighbors" had destroyed Falmouth in 1699, but that it was "rebuilt very soon."

Around 1715 settlers began arriving from Massachusetts Bay—the entire Maine area actually was part of Massachusetts. Portland became distinct from Falmouth on the 4th of July 1786. Faris said it occurred when Portland became the "commanding city of the neighborhood," and that the name "Falmouth was taken by a picturesque town close at hand." Massachusetts eventually relinquished the territory of Maine, which became the 23rd state in 1820 as part of the Missouri Compromise. Portland then served from 1820 to 1831 as the new state's capital.

Faris made his comments about Portland in his 1931 book, *Roaming America's Highways*, reporting briefly on his journey across the entire length of the TRIH. He was a writer who traveled widely in the late 1920s and early 1930s when ground travel in the United States, except by railroad, still presented a major challenge. Faris was popular for his dozen or so travel books rather than for any expertise in history.

Today, the first view of Portland from its outskirts is pleasant, but not distinctive. There are, of course, the same motels, fast-food restaurants, and roadside businesses that dominate all American cities and even much of the world.

But quickly the city's character began to present itself. There is a sense of assurance and stability. After crossing the city limit, I found myself downtown almost before I knew it. The distance isn't great, and traffic flows easily.

As I prepared to take the forgotten route across the continent, I was careful to take a good look at the city and the state where it had its beginning. Several interesting items in the *Press Herald* that morning in May reflected the individualism in which "Mainers," as they call themselves, take pride.

"Governor Signs Gay-Rights Bill into Maine Law," read the page-one headline. Four years earlier another governor had vetoed such a law, but on Friday, the 16th of May 1997, Governor Angus King signed into law a ban against discrimination on the basis of sexual orientation. The article said that made Maine the tenth state with such civil rights protection. The paper quoted the Governor as saying "You have been ridiculed, hated, discriminated against . . . hunted down and systematically murdered, not for what you choose, but for what God's nature made you. Not for something you had control over, but for what you are."

An opposition group was gearing up to run what it called an "honorable and positive" repeal effort.

[Footnote: spearheading the opponents was the "Christian Civic League of Maine," known according to the *New York Times* for campaigns against pornography and against shopping on Sundays. The local organization received immediate assistance from the

Christian Coalition. In a low-turnout election following devastating ice storms, just a few months after the act became law (right before Valentine's Day, in fact), Maine's voters narrowly repealed the new law. They were enlightened by television ads in which men testified that they had been homosexual, but "Jesus had cured them."]

Brief items inside the *Press Herald* included a report of a legislative committee's narrow rejection of "a plan to create a village at Biddeford Pool." The plan originally had been suggested to head off outright secession of a "disaffected coastal neighborhood of 270." In the very next column was news of yet another thwarted secession. Frye Island had sought to secede from Standish and become an independent town. The legislative committee reviewing the request killed it, because members thought the population of "30 year-round residents" was simply too few to form the "critical mass of people needed to form a town." Although the 1000-acre island in Sebago Lake has 372 homes, the item said, and in the summer has a "couple of thousand people," in the winter the summer colony shuts down "when its ferry stops running and the lake freezes over."

The Portland in Maine is small and deeply rooted in the past, and it offers much of the appeal of its overgrown sisters farther south. Along with those sisters—especially Boston, Philadelphia, and Baltimore—it offers a sense of coastal history (even if Philadelphia and Baltimore are not really coastal); of America when it was young. What it does not offer is their congestion, their pollution, and what much of the country would interpret as their Eastern, urban pace. But Portland *is* Eastern—Northeastern, as its lobstermen, monuments, architecture, and general culture make clear.

Street Scene, Portland, Maine

The Old Port Exchange is a refurbished district retaining the flavor of previous centuries, yet offering modern shopping and entertainment. Old warehouses and other buildings house upscale restaurants and shops. The district is near the water, but not directly on it. The number of houses with historical significance that have been preserved and are open to the public is impressive. The Joseph Holt Ingraham House and the Richard Hunnewell House on State, The Tate House on Westbrook, the McLellan-Sweat House on Spring, the Libby-Morse House (or the "Victorian Mansion") on Danforth, and the well-preserved Park Street Row, from 88 to 114 Park Street, are fine examples. The Eastern Cemetery, the Mariners' Church, the Customshouse, and the Portland Fire Museum are also points of historical interest. Fortunately, the huge fire that destroyed a third of the city on the 4th of July 1866 spared the older residential and waterfront areas.

Portland, Maine's largest city, is the largest city in New England north of Boston. It contains about a third of the people in the lightly-populated state. Although Maine contains about the same area as the other five New England states combined, it has only about a tenth of New England's population. Portland has remained rather stable in size. The 2000 census lists it as having nearly 65,000 people, about the same number as in 1990, but somewhat fewer than the 70,000 or more that it had in the 1930s. Although it has lost population to the surrounding towns of Cape Elizabeth, Cumberland, Falmouth, Gorham, Westbrook, and Yarmouth that are still growing, it has avoided much of the urban decay common elsewhere. It has some of the same troubles that any city faces, of course, but they don't seem overwhelming, as they do in other places.

Despite its small size, Portland boasts urban attractions, including a superb City Hall, an outstanding new public library, and an art museum that alone makes a visit to the city worthwhile. It is the center for trade and distribution for a large area, and is a major seaport. Portland seems larger than it is, and is every bit a city in the best meaning of the word, especially regarding cultural activities. Here Portland is most impressive.

The Portland Museum of Art is housed in a distinctive building. Its architect was Henry N. Cobb of I. M. Pei. The Museum's extensive collections include the works of outstanding artists such as Winslow Homer, Edward Hopper, and Andrew Wyeth, all associated with Maine. There are numerous art, literary, and drama groups, and the locals say concerts of the Portland Symphony attract larger audiences than boxing and wrestling matches.

Portland's architecture—often eighteenth and nineteenth century and including that of its churches—makes many of its street scenes especially attractive. The imposing hexagonal, tapering, tower of the Portland Observatory, built in 1807, dominates one section. The Eastern Promenade provides superb views of Casco Bay all the way to the Atlantic, and of well-preserved, stately, and beautiful Victorian homes.

It is apparent that poet and native son Henry Wadsworth Longfellow, is a source of local pride. The Longfellow House of his childhood is a tourist attraction. The Longfellow Square at the beginning of the TRIH could have been named for some other Longfellow—the family was well-established in New England—but it was not. How many American cities choose to honor poetry in such a fashion? The Appalachian Range ends elsewhere in Maine, in Baxter State Park in Piscataquis County, where Mainers call the end of the chain the "Longfellow Mountains," again, named for Henry Wadsworth.

The unfavorable reaction of modern critics to Longfellow's poetry isn't reflected in Portland, which appears to share the more favorable attitude of the nineteenth century. Perhaps the city is more perceptive than the critics. Children in schools across the country probably still absorb the myths of America's past from "Paul Revere's Ride," and other Longfellow poems. Tastes not only differ, but they change, and taste is a major element in criticism, despite the critics' professed objectivity.

Certainly, much of Longfellow's work is sentimental and uninteresting to 21st century sensibilities, especially "postmodern" sensibilities. Some is subject to parody—but is there anything, no matter how great, that isn't? Such poems as "The Skeleton in Armor," "The Arsenal at Springfield," and "The Wreck of the Hesperus" can hold their own in any company. For what it's worth, Longfellow's bust was the first of an American poet to be placed in the Poet's Corner in Westminster Abbey (unfortunately for him, posthumously), and, as TR's biographer Edmund Morris, notes, Longfellow's "Saga of King Olaf," was TR's favorite poem. Morris, in fact, used lines from "King Olaf" to serve as epigraphs at the beginning of each chapter of *The Rise of Theodore Roosevelt*.

Longfellow Square is only one of several attractive squares, and numerous statues in public areas throughout downtown Portland. One that captures the flavor of the area is another public square with a statue "Maine Lobsterman" in its center. Sculptor Victor Kahill created the work for the 1939 World's Fair. Later the Portland City Council purchased it, placing it in the square in 1977. A monumental Civil War Memorial near the Public Library and the First Parish Unitarian Universalist Church reflects Portland's sense of history.

But Longfellow Square is unique in being the point where the TRIH begins its long course west. I was fortunate in being able to pinpoint the position, because maps and descriptions of the Highway generally show it or describe it simply as starting in Portland. Even with considerable help from the librarians in the Portland Room, where I reviewed local materials, I could find nothing relevant in the Portland Public Library, but I had located the beginning in Longfellow Square before I set out for Maine. After a great deal of searching, help had finally come from the New Deal of TR's distant cousin, Franklin D. Roosevelt.

During the 1930s, the Great Depression threw huge numbers of Americans out of work, and there were no other jobs. Roosevelt's WPA gave them employment. While doing so, it created over 650,000 miles of roads, constructed dams, built over 100,000 schools, post offices, and other buildings, and improved or built some 800 airports. It provided public works projects to communities all over the United States, and gave purchasing power to the workers. Both workers and public benefited. The WPA—recognizing the importance of the arts, and assuming that writers and artists needed work too—also had a Federal Art Project, a Federal Writers' Project, and a Federal Theatre Project.

The Arts Project did many things, often very well. It caused some 10,000 works of art to be created and placed in public buildings. They included sculptures, paintings, and huge murals in public buildings—especially post offices—throughout the country. The Project also sponsored some 4,000 musical performances a month. In days before television, when many people could not afford records or a radio, these were often their only exposure to music outside of church.

The Theater Project encouraged experimental theater, and helped invigorate the dramatic arts. Equally important was the production of plays for residents of isolated villages across the United States. Often these plays gave citizens in remote areas their first experience with any sort of theater.

The Writers' Project in its American Guide Series generated a guidebook for every state in the Union, and also some regional works. Each guide included detailed descriptions of the state, including automobile routes and recommended trips. When John Steinbeck traveled with Charley, he said that he would have taken all forty-eight volumes with him—if only he had had the space.

Steinbeck said that the best writers in America produced the guides, but that FDR's opponents "detested" them so much that "the result was that in some states the plates were broken up after a few copies were printed." That, he wrote, "is a shame because they were reservoirs of organized, documented, and well-written information, geological, historical, and economic." In fact, he said, the "complete set comprises the most comprehensive account of the United States ever got together, and nothing since has even approached it."

That was in 1961, and it remains true. The WPA guides remain the only such comprehensive sources for most of the states. They have enduring value. They also located the precise beginning point of my journey.

The Maine volume of the *American Guide Series* came out in 1937, titled *Maine: A Guide "Down East."* Its editor, Dorris Isaacson, was at the center of many of Maine's cultural activities for decades following, and brought out a revised edition in 1971. Among others, The *Guide* recommended a tour from Portland to the New Hampshire line along the Roosevelt Trail, US 302. It described the road at that time, as two-lane "cement or macadamized." Most important, it located the beginning of the Roosevelt Highway as Longfellow Square in Portland, at the junction of US 1, State 25, and State 26.

US 1 and the state highways have been re-located within the city, but not Longfellow Square. The intersection is the same as ever. For purposes of following the TRIH, Isaacson's *Guide* is most valuable of all the state guides.

MOVEMENT

After a few days in Portland, I was eager to experience the Highway. I started at dawn, quickly scanning the morning's *Sunday Telegraph* before leaving. The "Travel Monthly" section devoted its full first page to the Pacific Northwest. The four articles included one on Seattle micro beers, one on the city of Spokane (a major point on the TR Highway), and another on the theater festival in Ashland, Oregon. The lead article dealt with cruising on the Columbia River aboard a ship, not a mere riverboat, with a ship historian to add discourse to the scenery. The route paralleled the TRIH which runs alongside the River for quite some distance. The article's dateline was Portland, Oregon. It was a nice way to begin the first day of my journey.

I drove to Longfellow Square to be as authentic as I could, and started my trip precisely at the Highway's beginning, the intersection that formerly was the junction of US 1, State 25, and State 26. It is no longer possible to start off exactly as drivers did in the 1920s. The original route of State to Forest is unavailable, because State now is a one-way street, and goes the wrong way. The next most direct route, Congress to Forest, initially appears to be the best substitute, but is not because of a "no-left-turn" sign at Forest. The way to go is to proceed on Congress and turn left on High, which soon (at six-tenths of a mile) runs into Forest. Forest is US 302, which the Roosevelt Highway follows through Maine and most of New Hampshire.

The original travelers, according to the WPA's *Guide*, passed a turnoff for Duck Pond at 8.3 miles from downtown Portland. The turnoff would have been onto a dirt road, and the motorists would have been driving on a "two-lane cement or macadamized roadbed," which would have continued throughout the state. The only thing different now is the smoother road surface on US 302, and the turnoff which no longer is dirt, but is paved.

Just beyond the Duck Pond turnoff I came upon the first solid indication of the existence of the TRIH. Near the village of Foster's Corner there is the "Roosevelt Trail Flea Market." The proprietor was helpful, but knew little about the TR Highway. She did help me locate a 1940 road map of Midwestern and Western states, which I bought. At about ten miles from my beginning, I came upon the first of what would be many curiosities. This was "Dick's Place," shining in the bright morning sunlight.

Roosevelt Trail Flea Market, Maine

It is a small building surrounded by junk and totally covered with hubcaps and wheel covers—tacky without doubt, but certainly eye-catching.

The drive was pleasant, and the traffic that Sunday morning wasn't especially heavy. There were many residences and businesses along the way, and at no time throughout Maine does the route go through an isolated region. Still, there is beautiful lake and forest scenery—enough to be a reminder that nearly 90 percent of the state is covered with woods.

Fortunately, the Highway avoids those areas that Maine also has in abundance: clear-cut expanses that assault the eye, while providing feed to the numerous paper mills assaulting the nostrils.

I decided to stop for a cup of coffee, and pulled into a small gift shop and cafe advertising maple products. The first thing that caught my eye was a display of maple-sugar candies, packaged in clear plastic—sugar pressed into the shape of maple leaves. The sign said, "Maple Sugar." The ingredients listed on the package, though, included only a tiny amount of maple sugar. The "Maple-Sugar Candies" were almost entirely cane sugar and corn syrup. I replaced the package, and proceeded on down the road, pausing to admire more local color, a large moose—a sculpture of sorts—standing outside an art gallery.

The moose is symbolic of Maine as well as of TR. More than once he remarked that he felt "as strong as a bull moose," but these days the mighty Maine moose is at the center of an international controversy—admittedly one set quite a bit to the north of the Roosevelt Trail.

Maine shares a rugged, wooded, border with Quebec. The area is so isolated that hundreds of square miles contain only dirt roads and tiny logging settlements. Authorities advise outsiders not to travel in the area without two spare tires—much like the original TRIH—and to be prepared to pull out of the way quickly when enormous, overladen, logging trucks suddenly appear to claim the road that they career along as if it were their private property.

The wildlife is plentiful, at least on the American side. In Quebec, the area is much more developed, with quaint little towns, manicured farms, and paved roads. This encourages wildlife—especially moose—to stay in Maine and avoid international travel. There's no danger of missing the border itself. Canada sits on the other side of a clear-cut swath some 50 feet wide.

Also on the Canadian side are hundreds of crude shacks on stilts. They exist for only one reason—hunters hide in them to shoot moose. Almost always, that means Maine moose. Americans might be shocked to know that, despite the history of peaceful relations between the U.S. and Canada, every year hundreds of Canadians shoot into the United States!

If a moose does wander into Quebec during the season, it becomes a legal target, of course. But in Maine, the majestic animal (which *State 'O Maine Facts* describes under the heading "Moose Monarchs of Woodland Areas of Maine" as "symbolic of the state's rugged and vast terrain") is no longer a game animal. *Facts* says that it became necessary to prohibit moose hunting in 1936. It still is virtually impossible even for a Maine resident to get a permit to hunt the state's moose, so there's no way at all a Canadian can do so.

The trouble is that these hunters are nonchalant about Maine permits. The region is so remote that they shoot across the border, roar across it into American territory in their all-terrain vehicles, hook their kill to their ATVs within a couple of minutes, and race back into Quebec long before American authorities can apprehend them.

In the rare cases in which an officer is near enough to make an arrest, the penalty is a fine of $1,000, or three days in jail. The hunters risk no jail time. They come prepared, pay their $1,000 in cash, and return to their shacks to wait for the game wardens to leave and the moose to return. The odds are against the Americans, but the officials live for the times in which they are able to apply the slap on the wrist. How often does that happen?—something like a dozen times in more years than that. It's a long wait.

For the moose who wanders within gunshot range, there are no odds. He or she is (quite literally) dead meat.

[Note: Terrorists, of course, could easily charge across the border, also. They, no doubt, would continue on into the United States, whose leaders seem to think all is secure if elderly women take off their shoes in airports, if officials listen in on citizens' conversations, or if the Justice Department hunts citizens who view pornography.]

When I drove through North Windham, I was pleased to find that its street name for US 302 is officially "Roosevelt Trail." Many of the businesses have signs bearing that name, and I enjoyed seeing "102 Roosevelt Trail," "209 Roosevelt Trail," and the like. Because of this, there are more reminders of Theodore Roosevelt in this part of Maine than on any other portion of the Highway across the country, except for the section through the Marias Pass in Montana. North Dakota as a state retains the strongest connection to TR, but the connection is rarely associated directly with the Highway.

I stopped at a crowded roadside restaurant with scents wafting throughout reminding me of my grandmother's kitchen on Thanksgiving Day. Two Maine Highway Patrol officers were having breakfast at a table squeezed into a small alcove, and they graciously shared their space with me for a time. They knew nothing about the TRIH, but they were aware that sections of US 302 were the "Roosevelt Trail."

They introduced themselves as Angela C. Platts and Lance McCleish. There was no original marker remaining anywhere from Portland to the New Hampshire line, but they offered to keep on the alert for anything of significance.

As I neared New Hampshire, I noticed that the area continued to be populated enough so that it isn't always easy to tell one town from another. A few miles beyond North Windham is Raymond, located on Sebago Lake. There is a bridge and an attractive picnic site near the town.

Not far beyond Raymond is Pulpit Rock, which the WPA *Guide* described as being "about 50 feet up from the highway." It described it as "a smooth projection 5½ feet high and equally wide, on which, it is said, the Devil used to stand when preaching to the Indians. During one of his discourses," the *Guide* continued, "according to legend, a rash young chief had the temerity to laugh in the Devil's face, whereupon the Evil One rose in a passion and, stamping his foot, caused the ground in front of the pulpit to drop 50 feet." Such is the stuff of New England. Nathaniel Hawthorne, says the *Guide*, was especially fond of the rock, and spent many hours there reading.

Passing through South Casco, a scenic location on the north shore of Sebago Lake, I proceeded onward to Naples. The public library there was closed, but it is in an especially attractive 1907 Victorian house, the historically-preserved "Locust House." Naples and the nearby vicinity offer several noteworthy sights. The Perley Farmhouse dates from 1809, and the Songo Lock from 1830. The Lock was important to the Cumberland-Oxford Canal connecting with the Songo River when trade flowed to Portland, and logs floated to sawmills. Now that the state, for environmental reasons, no longer permits logs to float down rivers, the traffic consists of pleasure boats.

I detected no evidence of the sharp political division that the WPA *Guide* mentions as having split Naples not long before its 1937 publication. I cannot say that the split no longer exists, because I spent too little time there and spoke to no one except superficially. Sunday morning was not the time in Naples for a stranger to find good conversationalists.

Whatever the situation now, the antagonism between the parties at one time was quite bitter. The emotions were so extreme as to require separate entrances for all public buildings, one for Democrats and the other for Republicans. Inside, the seats were arranged so that members of each party had half of each room. Feelings were so strong, the *Guide* reported, that even classrooms in schools were divided similarly, with children from Republican families on one side of the room, and those with Democratic backgrounds on the other. "The climax came," the *Guide* said, "when it became necessary to assign two teachers to each room to satisfy the rabid feelings of the parents." At the time of publication, 1937, the *Guide* said that the fierce partisan feelings had lessened considerably, but still were strong.

Beyond Naples is Bridgton, a pleasant community established in 1768 where the Highway turns west toward New Hampshire. One of Bridgton's most eye-catching sights is The Craftworks, in an old church right by the side of the Highway. Despite its small size, the town has a newspaper, the Bridgton *News.* Its editor, Wayne Rivet, was delighted to hear about the Theodore Roosevelt Highway and about my journey. He offered to publish an article about the trip, and to request that any reader with relevant information get in touch with me.

US 302 in Bridgton, as in North Windham, is called the Roosevelt Trail, and it is in Bridgton that a westbound traveler sees the final use of "Roosevelt Trail" as a street name. Conversely, of course, Bridgton would be the first point where a TR Highway traveler going east would see it mentioned. That landmark point is the Roosevelt Trail Professional Building, 302 Roosevelt Trail, on the north side of the Highway in the western part of Bridgton.

The Roosevelt Trail Professional Building houses several businesses, including Packard Appraisal, Inc. The company consists of two men, Phil Harmon and Fred Packard, who own and who named the building. They were a great resource, and know a good bit about the Theodore Roosevelt International Highway. As real-estate appraisers, they are familiar with deeds and real estate in the area going back to the early century. They said that it is common in that location for deeds to locate property by specifying its distance north or south of the Roosevelt Trail—and Roosevelt Trail throughout its course in Maine is US 302.

Beyond Bridgton, the first great mountains come into view at about forty-one miles from Longfellow Square in Portland. The WPA *Guide* reported that Pleasant Mountain "looms up ahead" at just beyond that point. Next it cited "Jockey Cap," which it described as "a gigantic 200-foot boulder near the roadside."

The final community along the TRIH in the State of Maine is Fryeburg, as my *State 'O Maine Facts '66-'67* noted. Fryeburg is on the Saco River Plain, and the fertile soil attracted English colonists in early colonial times. The Northern New England volume of *The Smithsonian Guide to Historic America* mentions that Fryeburg has two especially noteworthy sights. Two of the oldest residences in the town served as bases for newer structures. One, the Squire Chase House on Main Street, "incorporates the ca. 1767 home of one of the first settlers, Nathaniel Merrill, moved from its original site in 1824." The other, the Benjamin Wiley federal-style House on Fish Street, "also contains an earlier structure, dating from 1762."

The *Guide* listed the distance on the Theodore Roosevelt International Highway from Longfellow Square in Portland to the state line as 58.1 miles. *State 'O Maine Facts* listed it as 55 miles, which I found to be closer to the actual mileage. Although the road always was rather straight, it no doubt has been straightened slightly in spots, which would have shortened the distance.

I never did get to Frye Island. I wonder what I would have learned from the would-be secessionists there.

This brief jaunt, even with traffic and low speed limits, going through, not around, villages, could be driven in not much more than an hour. Of course I was driving slowly and stopping frequently, so I took longer than that to cover the Maine portion of the TR Highway. I intended it to—I was enjoying the first portion of my journey.

Back in 1921, A.W. Tracy, the General Secretary of the Theodore Roosevelt Highway Association, urged motorists to follow the route as it leaves "the eastern coast at Portland, Maine. It will take you up through the hills and mountains of Eastern Maine," he said, "through the very heart of Maine's wonderful scenic and touring regions. Circling around beautiful lakes, touching many celebrated summer resorts, it passes into New Hampshire at the edge of the White Mountains."

As I drew near to the New Hampshire state line, I remembered Tracy's description. Despite the passage of more than three quarters of a century, it is as valid today as when he wrote it.

Chapter Three

Rugged New Hampshire

Crossing into New Hampshire, I felt the full force of the Granite State. It's small, every New England State south of Maine is, but its terrain commands respect. Many places are called "notch," the local word for mountain pass. That's no exaggeration. The speed limits are low and in any case the geography mandates prudence. Forget about fast driving until New Hampshire is well behind you, even though its short distances sometimes seem greater than they are.

New Hampshire's volume of the WPA's Guide series described the tour along the Roosevelt Highway from Maine to Vermont. The route, it said, "known as the Theodore Roosevelt Highway . . . follows the Saco River Valley from the State Line to its source in the Crawford Notch, passing through the summer resort section of North Conway and Crawford Notch to Bethlehem, Littleton, Woodsville, and the Vermont Line." The Saco River that gives the region its name, the Guide noted, drew its own name from the language of the original Indian inhabitants, *Skok-kooe*, "snake-like stream running midst pine trees."

The state is heavily industrialized, but along the TRIH the impression is one of wilderness and small villages. A sense of place and tradition is as strong here in New England as it is in the Deep South, but the conservatism is different. It has no trace of the abrasive defensiveness that sometimes has been such a prominent Dixie characteristic. Certainly, lacking a heritage of slavery and defeat is an advantage.

Of course, the state has its own share of oddities. For many years, one of these was its leading newspaper, the Manchester *Union-Leader*. Under the long dominance of the late William Loeb, it had little if any competition elsewhere in American journalism for pure venom. During Richard Nixon's presidency, it did more than hint that the President—Nixon!—might be a communist agent.

However reasonable, however hysterical, whether kept to oneself or published statewide, New Hampshire respects the right to personal opinion, even the most eccentric. Rugged New Hampshire individualism—the state's motto is "Live Free or Die"—continues to characterize the population of this beautiful little corner of America with its harsh landscape. The people maintain one of the largest legislative chambers in the world. There are some four hundred state representatives. All members of the legisla-

Mt. Washington Cog Railway, New Hampshire

ture, the "General Court," both representatives and senators, serve two-year terms. Frugal New Hampshire avoids some of the high cost of a large legislature by paying its General Court members only $200—not $200 per year, but $200 per two-year term! The state's constitution dates from 1784, five years before the U. S. Constitution.

I shared the region's feeling of self-sufficiency as I entered the first settlement shortly beyond the state line, Center Conway. Like a turtle, I carried my shelter with me. I was driving a Ford F150 pickup truck with a secure watertight cap. I could sleep in the truck if I chose to, but I also had a small tent to let me come closer to the experiences of the route's early travelers.

The truck belonged to my stepson, Alan, who volunteered it. It was ideal, offering comfort for the night should I ever needed to use it. In the back, I could stand bending over, and windows with screens let fresh air in, but like the tent kept out mosquitoes and even the smallest gnats.

The truck was to perform flawlessly for some 15,000 miles as I continued relentlessly on through heat, rain, and even snow. I was to backtrack, explore points of interest near the Highway, and hunt for previous segments of the route that the modern road passes by. I was able to go places where a car shouldn't—or even couldn't. Eventually, I covered the TRIH in both directions.

Certainly my experience was different from that of the early travelers. Alan's truck would never so much as hiccup. Flat tires and car trouble, routine in the early days, happily were absent.

I planned to vary my accommodations according to circumstances. In Portland, simply for convenience I stayed in a downtown hotel. When there was nothing of special significance to the TRIH, I intended to find an inexpensive motel, or put up a tent in a campground. When an outstanding bed and breakfast or a notable hotel added character to the trip or was especially appropriate for the Highway, I would stay there. As much as I could, I wanted to feel what the early traveler might have felt.

A few miles beyond Center Conway the road crosses the Saco River. Despite the picturesque scenery, I proceeded on to Redstone, past the turnoff on the left to Conway, and then to North Conway where I stopped at the library. It was closed.

As I crossed the Mount Washington Valley, the vista reminded me that almost everywhere in New Hampshire the view includes a peak. Today, just as when Tracy wrote his description in 1921, The TRIH "curves through passes, giving an opportunity to see some of the most wonderful scenery in the New England states." It does not, however, include the state's 18-mile seacoast, nor does it go by New Hampshire's largest lake, Lake Winnipesaukee. Each is accessible with relatively brief side trips, and both of the trips are worthwhile. On this journey, though, I found the mountains so beautiful that I had no thought of digressing to lake or ocean.

I began to notice how many small cemeteries I had been passing. For quite some distance they had been a major part of the scenery. This seemed to be clear evidence that settlement by Europeans had begun long ago. In fact, Martin Pring had explored territory in what is now New Hampshire as early as 1603, and the first settlers arrived almost as soon as the Pilgrims landed at Plymouth Rock. Captain John Mason, the holder of the land grant from the King, named the area at about the same time that the Puritans were arriving in Massachusetts Bay. So it should have been no surprise that over a period of four centuries, quite a few cemeteries had accumulated

Beyond the first striking view of Mount Washington, past the "Road Kill Café," The TRIH continues through Glen on U.S. 302. It's worth digressing a few minutes north from Glen through Pinkham Notch—named for Daniel Pinkham who the locals say arrived in the late eighteenth century on a sled pulled by a pig—to the Mount Washington Auto Road.

The Pinkham Notch Camp, on the way, is also worth taking the time to visit. It has a cafeteria, and a hostel for hikers, especially for those hiking along the Appalachian Trail. It's a popular spot for motorists, and even more so for the foot traffic. The Appalachian Mountain Club operates a trailhead facility there throughout the year, and is the best local source for information. It provides maps, weather forecasts, and notes on trail conditions. There are showers available, and a small store has camping equipment for sale.

The Mount Washington Auto Road is open only from the middle of May to late October, and then only when weather permits. Weather on Mount Washington, whatever the season, often declines to grant a permit. The road itself dates from as far back as 1861, and supposedly is the "first man-made attraction in the United States!" That depends on the definition of attraction, of course, but it is impressive that it was possible to build a road at all up such inhospitable terrain with nothing but Civil War era technology.

Most of the road is paved, but the grades, averaging 12%, are extreme. With constant switchbacks, the distance to the top is eight miles—eight very long miles. There are strict regulations regarding vehicle size, and towed vehicles. Anyone who is nervous about driving mountain roads can join a tour and go up in a van. Mount Washington's weather not only rates among the world's most harsh, it also can change abruptly. Even in a car it pays to be wary, but it is vital for anyone deciding to hike anywhere around Mount Washington or elsewhere in the Presidential Range to get advice from the locals. It is entirely possible anywhere in the vicinity to set off on a warm—even hot—cloudless day, and within an hour or two to face blizzard conditions at the same time that other hikers two or three miles distant remain in the warm sunshine.

The views from the peak, in or around the visitors' center, are splendid, of course. For anyone visiting the first time, though, the surprising thing may be how interesting the mountain itself is. In hardly any other region is there a timberline at such a low altitude. Almost nowhere else is there such consistently high wind and often other violent weather, even on the mightiest spires in the Rockies. It is exhilarating—and without shortness of breath! The summit is the top of New England. Its altitude of 6,288 feet cannot match peaks in the Rockies and elsewhere, but it seems to be the top of the world.

Back on U.S. 302, I continued west. At Bartlett, I came upon a covered bridge. The highway now bypasses it, but there is a clear view from the road, and space nearby for parking. Covered bridges were practical in their time, and served their purposes well.

Covered Bridge, Bartlett, New Hampshire

They now reflect a vanished tradition. The original TRIH traveler would have crossed several throughout New England. Bartlett's attractive bridge had been preserved, and has become highly practical for modern times as well—it has been converted into a shop.

Beyond Bartlett, the TRIH continues through especially scenic terrain into the White Mountain National Forest. The Forest covers much of this part of the state, but until this point according to the map the road has been surrounded by a narrow strip of land outside the Forest. After a few miles the road crosses Crawford Notch, and again emerges from federal land.

Road signs warned me that I now was in a "Moose Crossing" area. Moose are plentiful in New Hampshire and there had been warnings on the way to Mount Washington, but this was the first sign that I encountered on the Roosevelt Highway itself. Moose are a hazard. Not only are they likely to weigh more than 1,000 pounds, they are so tall that a car's headlights may shine right between their legs, and miss their reflecting eyes. When an auto's hood goes under the moose's high body, the windshield hits it—a tragedy for both moose and driver. When threatened, moose may stand still, dart away in any direction, or attack.

Just beyond the beginning of Crawford Notch, I came upon a picturesque footbridge over a low dam, creating a rushing waterfall. The WPA Guide put it well. The traveler has hardly left Bartlett behind when "the Saco turns northward, and beyond Sawyer River the mountains begin to close in on the highway." It might have added they begin to close in on the river as well.

Roadside View of Moose Crossing, New Hampshire

It was all so inviting that I would have felt ungracious not to stop and enjoy the surroundings. I walked across the short bridge over the Saco and back, taking in the soothing sound and sight of rushing water. On the other side of the highway was a store selling ice cream and souvenirs. The area is surrounded by sharp peaks close enough to cause at least a hint of discomfort to anyone who might be claustrophobic. To me it was stimulating. It is the kind of scene that can lead the imagination to run away with itself.

Still, the awe the landscape inspires is not based totally on imagination. The surroundings are peaceful, but convey a potential for something quite different. It requires no special perception to recognize at least vaguely that the mountains are unusual, that they might present a real threat.

This was the site of an 1826 tragedy that emphasizes the potential power of New Hampshire's jutting angles and elevations. Although the "Willey Slide" is famed among natural disasters, I had never heard of it before.

This part of the road had been the scene of wagon traffic since 1803, more than a century earlier. Use of an existing route enabled the Roosevelt Highway to be ready for use almost as soon as its Duluth originators proposed it. *Good Roads* magazine reported on July 28, 1920 that New Hampshire's State Highway Commissioner Everett had completed marking the state's portion of the Highway, which, it said, was "one of the best in the state."

The New Hampshire Good Roads Association reported a month later, on August 25, 1920 in the same magazine, that "Frank A. French has just returned from an inspection of the marking of the Roosevelt International Highway in its course through this state and reports completion of the trail markings." The Association noted that the wide red band with the letters "T.R." were to be seen "all the way from Portland, Ore. to Portland, Me., and already," it said, "tourists are making portions of the tour and some this season will take the entire route for their vacation trip."

The route in New Hampshire, the Association said, "covers a most wonderful section of the state, entering from the west at Littleton and passing out into Maine at Conway. In this course the tourist sees our whole cross-section with the big range of mountains and including the marvels of Crawford Notch." The praise included the entire T.R. Highway, not merely New Hampshire's section. "As the highway keeps to the northern boundary of the United States all the way from coast to coast, it seems quite appropriate to accept the slogan . . . through 'America's playgrounds'."

The Roosevelt Highway's path brought it to what was then even more than now an isolated stretch of fifteen miles through what local people called simply, the "The Notch," or sometimes "The Pass of the White Mountains." A hunter, Timothy Nash, had discovered Crawford Notch in 1771 by accident. According to Muse and Rocheleau's *Smithsonian Guide to Historic America*, he stumbled upon it while tracking a moose. (What better beginning could there be for a segment of the TRIH?)

Then in 1825, Samuel Willey, Jr., of Bartlett, moved into a farmhouse in the Notch. His friends in Bartlett had convinced him that The "Notch House," as it was called, would be a good investment. Weary travelers through the Notch surely would welcome it as an inn.

Local historian Floyd Ramsey found that the house had been built in 1792 directly on a mountain rising 4,260 feet behind it. In 1845 that mountain became Mount Willey. In front of the house, across the now dammed river, and beyond a small meadow, rises Mount Webster, at 3876 feet.

The house was run down but Willey thought it seemed promising. He and two hired men set about preparing it for the winter. When winter came, he complained that the raging winds, fierce snowstorms, and bitter cold were much worse than anything his family had experienced in thirteen years in Bartlett. Still, in spite of the storms, there was enough traffic that the Willeys prospered. They began to expand what people now knew as "The Willey House." By spring's end, they had made substantial progress.

That summer was exceptionally dry, and gave ominous warnings of the trouble to come. At one time a road crew took shelter in the Willey House during a sudden rainstorm. As they waited for the storm to pass, a small but powerful slide came within fifty feet of the barn. Within minutes, several hundred feet of the road were buried by mud and rubble. Another, smaller slide followed the first, and passed harmlessly. Willey and his family were alarmed, but decided that another slide was unlikely. They remained.

The summer, too, remained—hot and ever drier.

On Monday, the 28th of August, violent and lengthy thunderstorms unleashed huge bursts of rain throughout the Notch and into the valleys. Except for the rushing of the small river, which had risen 24 feet, things were calm after midnight. The next day there was flooding at both ends of the Notch, with devastated crops and drowned livestock. Seeking to save any animals that had survived, neighbors made their way through the pass along the remnants of the road, which had washouts a full twenty feet deep, to the Willey House.

They were relieved to see that the house was unharmed, but they were puzzled to find it empty. A huge landslide had rushed down Mount Willey, covering the landscape and sweeping all before it. It had spared the Willey House because a gigantic boulder had split the powerful stream for a short distance. The southern half passed by the house and attached woodshed, while the northern half annihilated the barn. Just below the house, the streams of hurtling debris had rejoined.

It appeared as if the Willey family had escaped. It was not until Thursday the 31st, that searchers discovered the bodies of the family and the other residents. Apparently, they had left the Willey House because of rising water. Ironically, the house that they fled turned out to be the only place that offered safety. As a further irony, the Willey House itself succumbed to a fire in 1899.

Ramsey recounted the episode in some detail in *Magnetic North* magazine (vol. 6, no. 2). His well-written piece has been reprinted as a pamphlet, "The Willey Slide," which I found for sale as I browsed through the store at the site. It was this interesting work that provided me with the details of the tragedy. I had been under no illusion about the potential for danger lurking behind the beauty of New Hampshire's rugged peaks, but when I stepped outside and walked to the truck, I viewed the surrounding mountains with even more respect than before.

Beyond the site of the Willey tragedy is Silver Cascade. It took no imagination to come up with the name. The white water does glisten almost silver as it cascades over and around boulders. There is space for parking, permitting photographs. That's good, because parking by the side of the highway where there is no parking area is illegal anywhere in New Hampshire, and is an invitation to have the car towed away—often far, far away.

A short distance from Silver Cascade I found myself in Bretton Woods, where travelers seeking luxury in Victorian surroundings may opt to stay in the huge Mount Washington Hotel. The famed Bretton Woods International Monetary and Financial Conference took place there in 1944. Bretton Woods, itself looked over by Mount Washington, now is a ski center.

More interesting today than the economic conference is the Mount Washington Cog Railway. It runs to Mount Washington's peak from Bretton Woods, on the opposite side of the mountain from the Auto Road. A short road climbs gently to the railway's beginning.

Snow began to fall as I drove upward toward the railway, and the temperature dropped sharply. In the few minutes I took to reach the terminal, there was snow on the ground. It stopped snowing as suddenly as it had begun, but the air remained cold. It became colder with each foot going up the mountain.

The Cog Railway has been chugging up the mountain since 1869. It looks its age, but has an excellent safety record. The small, green, steam engines with their flared smoke stacks are deceptive. They look hardly up to the task that they accomplish so well—and a severe task it is.

They must push their gaily-painted blue and white passenger cars straight up grades that reach 37.5%, allegedly the steepest in the world for a nonfunicular railway except for one in the Swiss Alps. Their boilers are tilted forward at a comic angle, so that the backward tilt will be less as they make their sharp ascents and descents. It takes them an hour to cover the three-mile stretch to the top. The engines burn a ton of coal for each round trip.

It is fascinating to watch from the train's window as the engine puffs its way up to the peak. The steepness of the track makes vertical structures nearby appear to jut out at an angle. Trees become smaller and smaller until they disappear completely. The tundra above the treeline is more characteristic of Alaska than of the other forty-nine states, and that also is true of Mount Washington's weather. It is easy to imagine yourself a thousand miles to the north.

The railway operates roughly the same dates that the Auto Road, on Mount Washington's opposite side, is open for travel. Of course they both reach the same visitors' center, which includes a restaurant, a museum, and a gift shop.

Back in Bretton Woods there was no trace of snow and the air had warmed considerably, although it still was cool. The TRIH continues on through the Hamlet of Fabyan. Once again the road briefly penetrates the White Mountain National Forest, leaving it permanently just before reaching the village of Twin Mountain, which is in the larger Town of Carroll. The Carroll Town Hall at Twin Mountain is a well-preserved example of a large New England Victorian mansion that has been expanded for public purposes.

A short digression from the TRIH south from Twin Mountain on U. S. 3 brings the traveler to the Franconia Notch area, a premier tourist attraction. There are many places to stay, often showing their advanced age but offering unparalleled views. Several working farms scattered about offer food and lodging.

The Frost Place offers something unique: poetry readings by a poet-in-residence, and a mile-and-a-half walk along a "Poetry Trail." Robert Frost, the poet New England claims for its own, lived there for some eleven years, and an exhibition includes many of his possessions. Although certainly the San Francisco-born Frost was more a universal than a regional poet, he did provide powerful experiences of New England to readers who would never come near America's Northeast.

One of the most photographed spots was "The Old Man of the Mountains," a natural rock formation resembling a face jutting out from a stone cliff. Sadly, in 2003 the ancient formation vanished in a rock slide. Its image remains on New Hampshire's commemorative quarter coin, serving as a frequent reminder of the persistence of change.

Returning to the TRIH, I continued west on U. S. 302, passing through the small settlements of Pierce Bridge, Maplewood, and Bethlehem. Abruptly the Highway enters marshy countryside. Soon, stone walls picturesque enough to have been inspiration to Robert Frost himself, close in on the roadway. Just ahead lay Littleton.

After so many tiny villages, Littleton's Main Street has almost an urban feel. The settlement dates back to the 18th century; the first town meeting took place in 1787, two years before the adoption of the U. S. Constitution. Littleton benefits from its location on Interstate 93 (no larger than it is, it has four exits from the Interstate) at the half-way point between Boston and Montreal. It has the bustling air of any commercial center, and offers good restaurants and excellent lodging.

There are numerous historic buildings, including the Littleton Opera House, the Community Center in a Queen Anne mansion, and the Littleton Public Library. Thayer's Inn, an attractive hotel on Main Street, dates from 1848 and receives acclaim as one of the oldest surviving inns in New Hampshire.

Just beyond Thayer's, however, is the Beal House Inn, a splendid bed-and-breakfast dating from 1833. It originally was a rambling farmhouse, and has offered lodging since 1938. I had stayed there on my way to Maine, and couldn't have chosen a better place, but I have not been there since new owners took over.

The Inn's address is 2 West Main Street, and it sits at the end of that street, just beyond a fork in the road, which is the juncture of two highways. U. S. 302 takes the left side of the fork and turns south. When it does so, here at this intersection, U. S. 302 takes permanent leave of the T. R. Highway.

The fork to the right is New Hampshire 18. That was my route, because at this point the T. R. Highway takes State Highway 18, and continues on, past the Beal House Inn on the right, out of Littleton, and soon out of New Hampshire.

I continued west. Within a few minutes, the TRIH, now still following New Hampshire State Highway 18, passes New England Power's Moore Station on the right. It then crosses the state line into Vermont.

Chapter Four

Vermont: New England Oasis

The Vermont state line seems much farther, but is just slightly over 120 miles from Portland. As New Hampshire State Highway 18 changes into Vermont State Highway 18, the TRIH enters its third state. The route already had ranged from the flatness and salty breezes of the Atlantic coast through crisp-aired mountains that command respect. From the urban east I had reached some of the most rural country in America.

Vermont is unique in that its "Official State Map and Touring Guide" still identifies the Roosevelt Highway. The various editions do, though, have an error: they designate U.S. 2 completely across the state as the T. R. Highway. But between the New Hampshire state line and St. Johnsbury—as David Scott, data and mapping engineer for Vermont's transportation agency verified—the actual route departs from U. S. 2 and follows State Highway 18. Another road map, the "Vermont Travel Guide," also identifies the TRIH, and lists it correctly as taking State Highway 18 southeast from St. Johnsbury into New Hampshire. Oddly, it gives a dual routing, also including the error; the publisher is The National Survey ("The Home of Fine Maps"), in Chester, VT.

In 1921, the Vermont Division of the Theodore Roosevelt Highway Association published *Glimpses Along the Roosevelt Memorial Highway in Vermont*. The Library of the Vermont Historical Society has an original copy—most likely the only one in existence. It lists the author as James Taylor Paddock, an error in cataloguing. The secretary of the Vermont Division of the Theodore Roosevelt International Highway Association in 1921 was James P. Taylor, probably the same James Paddock Taylor who was the pamphlet's author. I could find no reference anywhere in all the TRIH records to a James Taylor Paddock.

Taylor traced the route through the state. "The Roman made his roads level and straight and liked them so. Straight and monotonous," he wrote. "But the Vermonter, he is a poet. His highways have all the charms of by-ways." The pamphlet praised the Vermont pursuit of the loveliest, rather the quickest. Its author would have been startled and saddened by Vermont's eagerness in the latter half of the 20th century to copy Rome.

For over four decades, the safety recommendations of the American Association of State Highway and Transportation Officers, incorporated in their "Green Book," have

29

dominated road building in this country. As a result, roads have become wider, straighter, and safer for speeds well beyond the legal limits. They've also gobbled up land and neighborhoods.

Until recently, Vermont was as enthusiastic in its zeal to bring its highways up to Green Book standards as any state. This means that engineers and number-crunchers ruled. People concerned with scenery, community preferences, or even environmental considerations had only marginally more influence on highways than road kill did.

Cheryl Rivers was one Vermonter who cared, and acted. She lives in Bethel, a tiny village south of Montpelier. Bethel sits on lightly-traveled state road 12. The village had a small, scenic, one-lane bridge. Even though there was little traffic, the state decided to replace the little bridge with a huge forty-foot structure that could carry traffic faster than the roads that crossed it could. Green Book standards demanded it.

Cheryl Rivers fought. The "megabridge," wasn't needed, she said, and it wasn't safe to drive fast in the area anyway.

Rousing the Vermont spirit, she brought the engineers to a compromise. But she wasn't finished. She campaigned for the state Senate, and won election in 1990. As a senator she advanced the cause of the "asphalt rebellion," and introduced a reform law that brings back the attitude that Taylor praised. That law now allows Vermont to design roads and bridges according to intended use; not merely for speed.

Vermont returned to its roots. It became the only state in the country to permit alternatives to Green Book standards. It still has its Interstates and other modern highways, but can now balance the value of high speed against retaining some of its Green Mountain uniqueness.

Fortunately, the original route that I was following had been little affected by the state's infatuation with high-tech. The TRIH still reflects the charm that captivated Taylor so long ago, when he found joy in "the maze of Vermont's roads," and said lyrically that "the quick succession of angles and curves means infinite variety, ever some new picture."

I continued on route 18 past Lower Waterford. Presently I passed by the Stiles Pond Reservoir, and then East St. Johnsbury, to see Maple Grove Farms, a reminder of one of the area's major industries: it produces that delightful product, maple sugar. Vermont is the center of an extensive maple-sugaring region that reaches from coastal New England through parts of Canada and extends as far as the Midwest. The complex includes a Maple Museum, an old mill, and "The World's Largest Maple Candy Factory." It now is one of Vermont's most popular tourist attractions, but the very first travelers on the TRIH would have been able to visit it too. Maple Grove originated in 1915 when George Cary tried using maple sugar to flavor—of all things—chewing tobacco.

In another mile or so, the Highway crosses the Passumpsic River into St. Johnsbury over the Memorial Bridge, which dates from World War Two. St. Johnsbury is the first point, traveling west, at which the TRIH becomes U.S. 2. The two run together just for the remainder of the route through Vermont, and then diverge until the Roosevelt Highway reaches Michigan's Upper Peninsula.

U. S. 2—called the "Great Northern" after the railroad that it parallels in the West and Midwest for such a long distance, well over 1,000 miles—now forms the bulk of the Theodore Roosevelt Highway. But not in the East. The few people who remember the TRIH often think "it has been renamed U. S. 2," but Vermont is the only state east of Michigan in which U. S. 2 and the Roosevelt Highway ever coincide.

St. Johnsbury's population is under 10,000, but the small city contains bookstores, libraries, museums, and good restaurants. Its appearance reminded me of a Swiss village. At the intersection of Prospect and Main is the Fairbanks Museum and Planetarium.

Further along Main are the Athenaeum, Art Gallery, and a Public Library which has a collection of 19th-century American paintings. The route turns right at a statue onto Eastern Avenue. The Northern Lights Bookstore and Cafe suggests quite a cosmopolitan atmosphere for a small community in a rural area.

Not far west of St. Johnsbury is Danville (where the fiery Thaddeus Stevens, spokesman for education and for a hard line against the defeated South, was born) and then West Danville. At West Danville Joe's Pond invites a stop. A small dam holds the pond in check, and a short, narrow—44 inch wide—covered footbridge spans the stream. The bridge is wooden, weathered gray, with a wood-shingle roof. Although it appears ancient, it bears a plaque saying "Historic Site, West Danville Footbridge, 1977."

Flanking the walkway to the bridge is a statue on the left. On the right are a marker and a bench, each of stone. The marker bears a carved scene including a face captioned "Indian Joe, 1745-1819." The inscription reads "JOE'S POND" in large letters, with "MEMORIAL BRIDGE, 1977," in smaller capitals. It honors "all those who

Joe's Pond, West Danville, Vermont

have contributed to the spirit of this community." With no explanation, the bench is carved with the words: "DiLAURA MEMORIAL BRIDGE."

On the other side of the highway is Hastings Store, another touch of pure rural Americana. I could have selected from a wide variety of items, including fresh cider. The store doubles as a post office.

Joe's Pond reportedly bears the name of an Indian who warned early settlers of an impending attack by neighboring Indians. No sooner did I leave Joe's Pond and its air of tradition, than I came upon Molly's Pond and found anything but. Instead, there was Brookside Statuary. In full color, a team of concrete pigs pulled a sled. There were frogs, gnomes, gargoyles, fish, birds, Buddhas, deer, cats, dogs, rabbits, Virgin Marys and almost anything else that anyone might want in concrete.

The nearby Farmer's Daughter Gift Barn certainly isn't a natural wonder, either. As a curiosity in some ways it's almost as eye-catching as nature's works. It offers for sale a huge array of tourist-oriented items.

The eye-catching feature, though, is not the barn itself, the nearby duck pond, or the stationary steam engine located outside; it is a vividly-colored cutout of the back of a young woman holding up the "FARMER'S DAUGHTER GIFT BARN" sign. She has reddish-blond hair, is wearing a red dress, stockings, a black belt, high-heeled black shoes—and blue panties. Her dress is flipped up to reveal the top of her right stocking, and her blue-pantied cheek. For travelers going east, the sign is the same except that she is on the right, and her skirt is flipped up on the left. Such a colorful display stands out especially in Vermont, where there are no billboards. The visual clutter along highways, so common elsewhere, simply doesn't exist. (The striking sign obviously struck someone the wrong way. When I passed it again later, it had been defaced by spray paint.)

If I needed a reminder that I was still in New England, the Martin Bridge down the road provided it. There are covered bridges in other places, of course, but they still suggest New England to me. Madeleine Kunin and Marilyn Stout in 1976 co-authored an extensive guide to Vermont, *The Big Green Book*. They said that Vermont is especially associated with covered bridges.

Kunin and Stout cited Herbert Congdon's 1970 book *The Covered Bridge* to demonstrate how versatile such bridges could be. The structures date not from colonial times, but from the 19th century. They found use as shelters, drill floors for local militia, and even as sites for camp meetings. One, the Fisher Bridge in Wolcott, is even a railroad bridge with a "full-length cupola . . .[to provide] . . . a smoke escape." Vermont covered bridges became so common that they inspired tall tales. One described a drunken farmer who drove his team into a barn one dark night. He became enraged, bellowing, "Who in hell boarded up the end of this bridge?"

Kunin, by the way, went on to become Vermont's Governor. In a tribute to her that also reflected the progressive spirit of Vermonters, she served three terms. It was the first time in U. S. history for any state to elect a woman three times to its chief executive position. It also says something about Vermont's spirit that when it entered the Union in 1791 to become the 14th state, the first after the original 13, it entered with complete religious freedom, and with the vote for all adult males. In fact, when the Supreme Court in 1857 helped to bring on the Civil War by denying in its infamous

Dred Scott decision that blacks could be citizens, Vermont and its neighbor New Hampshire reacted with outrage. They immediately passed laws protecting the citizenship of their black residents.

Only in New England do governors' terms remain so short: two years. Vermont, along with New Hampshire and Rhode Island, are the only states that retain such brief terms.

Ahead lay Marshfield. At the Marshfield Village Store a wooden Indian stands guard. A traveler from the 1920s would easily recognize the immaculately maintained place. The three-story building dates from 1852. That traveler also would recognize many of the items for sale, but there is one that long after the 1920s would have puzzled all but Italians. "CAPPUCCINO," proclaims a red sign. I suddenly became aware that from Portland through New Hampshire to this rather isolated portion of Vermont, I almost always was close to someplace where I could get a cup of that sign of modern American culture, cappuccino! The word may be Italian, but not the brew that the small machines dispense—still, it doesn't have to be authentic to be pleasant.

Plainfield has the reputation of being a holdover from the 1960s. Nearby is Goddard College, which feeds that reputation. It's an interesting institution that has attracted many students who continue to do their best to represent the counter culture. Unfortunately, the College has gone through some periods of severe financial troubles in recent years.

As for Plainfield itself, I expected a touch of the atmosphere that lingers in Berkeley, Boulder, and even Missoula, but was disappointed. I suppose that some of the same free-wheeling spark may be there, but more than anything else the town just seemed a bit tired and rundown and not at all characteristic of what I had seen so far in Vermont.

There was nothing rundown about the rugged and impressive scenery that I encountered as I continued west, enjoying the mountainous view that included an especially beautiful waterfall. Also beautiful was the sight of Montpelier nestled in the valley before me, with the gold dome of the state capitol gleaming in the sunlight.

Montpelier, with a 2000 census of 8035, prides itself on being the smallest state capital in the country. It also is among the most interesting. Its location alone makes it one of the most splendid spots anywhere, and it offers a cosmopolitan atmosphere that many of its larger sisters would be hard-pressed to equal.

Appropriately, for the capital of a state with a decided French heritage and one in which many citizens still speak French, Montpelier bears the name of a French town. A short walk will take you not only to the seat of government, but to the Vermont Historical Society Museum and Library, to bookstores, the Hubbard State Park, coffee shops (selling cappuccino, of course, but there it is authentic) and bagel stores, excellent restaurants, and countless monuments and historical sites.

Montpelier is situated at the confluence of the Winooski and the North Branch Rivers. Although Vermont is the only New England state without a seacoast, its 341 square miles of inland water apparently were enough to inspire Admiral George Dewey. The Dewey House, where he was born, is one of Montpelier's historical sites.

Each state capitol building has its own characteristics. Vermont's is modest in size, fitting the state itself. Beneath its bright golden dome it sits a brilliant white, behind

Vermont State Capitol, Montpelier

and above a broad expanse of green bisected by a wide walkway leading to the capitol steps, also all white. The building sits before a forested ridge.

Vermont long was a Republican stronghold. Its opposition to slavery was unequaled and it continued its allegiance to the GOP into the Great Depression. In 1912 and 1936, the twentieth century's most disastrous electoral years for Republicans, Vermont each time was one of only two states to remain faithful to the Party. In 1912, along with Utah it voted for Taft, and in 1936 it joined with its larger New England sister, Maine, to become one of only two states to vote for Landon and against FDR and his New Deal. Thus Vermont voted against Theodore Roosevelt, then the Bull Moose candidate, and later also against his distant cousin Franklin D. Roosevelt—it was the only state to vote in both years for the Republican opponent of a Roosevelt.

Even in traditional New England, though, things change. Cultural and environmental issues weigh heavily in the Green Mountain State. The ban on roadside advertising illustrates the new spirit. Instead of billboards, Vermont places standardized markers listing the names of nearby businesses that provide lodging, food, fuel, recreation, and other services.

Visually, the billboard ban is dramatic. Vermonters have become equally willing to go against the mainstream in politics. Burlington set the tone by electing a socialist mayor, Bernie Sanders. In 1990, Sanders, by then one of the country's most successful mayors, won Vermont's sole seat in the U. S. House of Representatives. He continued to represent the state as the only Independent in the House, deciding instead to run for the U. S. Senate in 2006. Vermont had another independent in the Senate as well, when James Jeffords left the Republicans during the presidency of the second

Bush. He then represented Vermont in the Senate as an independent, caucusing with the Democrats, choosing to retire at the end of his term in January 2007. The sharp contrast between the state's politics and those of its conservative neighbor to the east, New Hampshire, leads to grumblings about the "People's Republic of Vermont."

The Vermont Historical Society's Library proved to be especially valuable. Barney Bloom, an excellent reference librarian, enthusiastically made materials available. It was there that I found Taylor's pamphlet on the TRIH, which Bloom helpfully photocopied.

The bearded Bloom—with his boots, jeans, flannel shirt, and green sweater vest—typified the Vermont nonconformist in dress and manner. He was professional and efficient, but in contrast to the stereotype, was friendly and relaxed. We stepped outside to enjoy the weather, and chatted briefly before I continued down the road pursuing my own westward movement.

After Montpelier, the road begins to follow closely along the route of Interstate 89. All the way across the state, it threads back and forth under the Interstate. The Interstate takes most of the traffic, but U.S. 2 continues to be valuable, and it provides access to numerous communities that the Interstate passes by. The road also parallels the Winooski River.

Just past the village of Middlesex is Camp Meade, an attraction for military enthusiasts that might have amused Theodore Roosevelt himself. Along with a military surplus store, it offers food and lodging. In a setting that during the New Deal of the 1930s was a camp for the Civilian Conservation Corps, diners can view various military vehicles and armaments, and debate the relative merits of camouflage tablecloths and a bomb suspended overhead. The fortunate few might even stay in cabins named for well-known military figures.

As a tourist attraction, though, Camp Meade loses decisively to the nearby Ben and Jerry's Ice Cream Factory. Befitting Vermont's modern atmosphere, the company is known for supporting progressive causes. It is also known for excellent ice cream, sherbets, and sorbets made from natural ingredients. Their names—such as "Cherry Garcia" and "Doonesberry"—alone would make them attractive. I've heard they have a special appeal to fans of the Grateful Dead. Children and teenagers especially enjoy the park-like surroundings. Picnic tables with superb views are a nice touch.

It soon became obvious that the TRIH was taking me into the mountains. The Winooski River that paralleled the road rushed more and more rapidly. Warm, fairly clear, weather wasn't far behind, but the temperature dropped suddenly, and an abrupt rainstorm gave way to huge flakes of snow.

The Interstate was elevated above my road and offered those who chose it a relatively level passage through the mountains. It had little effect on the world below, and its presence did nothing to disturb the atmosphere of isolation. If anything, the imposing surface high overhead supported by massive posts and pillars simply melded into nature's vertical landscape to emphasize the loneliness of the darker depths.

The snow increased, and I was almost startled as I rounded a bend to see the quaint settlement of Jonesville. I briefly took refuge there in the Country Store. I sipped a large cup of cappuccino (what else?), and asked the clerk if she knew of the TRIH. She referred me to Pat, saying that he knew everything about the area.

"Pat," it turned out, was the butcher, Pat Quinn. I found him at the back of the store, cutting meat. He was a small serious-looking man with slightly-tinted glasses, a white fringe of hair circling his head, a white neatly-trimmed mustache, and a closely-cropped white beard. Rather than an apron, he wore what looked to be a long lab coat. It also was white except for splashes of red. The folded paper and two pens in its breast pocket heightened the image he presented of a somewhat bloody, but nonetheless benign, surgeon.

"Do I know about the Theodore Roosevelt Highway?" he responded slowly without looking up. Then he raised his head, looked at me, and smiled. "I sure do. I remember it well. I've lived here all my life, and I'm in my seventies. Well, I've always lived here except for the time I was in the military back in World War Two. That's the Highway, right outside this door."

He looked back down and swung his cleaver—chop, chop. Then, he laid it aside. Except for fresh marks from the meat, his equipment and was scrupulously clean, as was every surface. He obviously took care in his work.

Wiping his hands, he walked over to me.

"The highway wasn't surfaced at all until after a great flood back in 1927 or 1928 washed everything away. That flood was something. I was real little at the time, but I remember it. They paved the road then for the first time when they built it back."

I told him that he remembered more about the Highway than anyone I'd met yet along the route. He asked how far I planned to go.

"I'm heading west all the way as far as the Highway went. It's over 4,000 miles from Portland, Maine to Portland, Oregon, and that's where I'm going," I told him.

"That's just fine!" he grinned. "All the way to Portland, Oregon, huh?' he said. "I knew it went all the way west, but I wasn't sure where it ended. Well, you're gettin' near the Lake Country now. Did you know that Roosevelt was there in the islands when he got the news that McKinley had been shot?"

"I have read about it," I admitted.

Driving through the Winooski River Valley past one dairy farm after another, I admired the red-winged blackbirds that busied themselves adding twin splashes of brilliance to the landscape. One landed deftly on a MOOSE CROSSING sign as I approached. It watched me proceed on to Richmond.

The Highway passes through Richmond's one stoplight. For an interesting diversion, you might turn left there and go south for a half mile or so to the Old Round Church. Five Protestant groups cooperated in 1813 to build the interesting structure, but the cooperation didn't last long. Turning the other cheek was not popular among the churched, and their bitter disagreements led them to abandon the building to the community, which converted it into a town hall. Now it's the pride of the local historical society.

Back on US 2, the route again goes under the Interstate, and comes to Williston. Only a few miles from Burlington, Williston is a suburb of sorts. It presents a neat picture of well-kept white frame houses and lovely maple trees.

Burlington itself is a large city by Vermont standards, the largest in the state. It may have fewer than 40,000 residents, but it stands out from the surrounding isolation as a bustling metropolis.

The city's mountainous setting reminded me somewhat of Denver's. Burlington's colors, though, are different. Denver's somewhat arid location emphasizes earth tones, while around Burlington the greens of the mountains and the deep blues of Lake Champlain dominate.

Taylor said that the best place to enjoy Burlington's sunsets is from Ethan Allen Tower in Ethan Allen Park. The park is on a hill where Indians once set signal fires. It honors Ethan Allen, known as a hero of the Revolution for his capture of Fort Ticonderoga from the British. Schoolbooks, though, sometimes are misleading. Allen had organized his Green Mountain Boys not to fight Britishers, but to fight New Yorkers.

During colonial times, the British had been vague about the boundary between New Hampshire and New York. Shortly before the Revolution, the governors of both colonies made land grants in the disputed area. To settle the resulting controversy, the British decided that New York had jurisdiction. Naturally, this infuriated those who held grants from New Hampshire, including Allen and other speculators.

Allen represented New England pride against New York, and created the Green Mountain Boys as a resistance movement. He led military action against New Yorkers and their courts in the region, which the rebels had begun calling Vermont. New York put a price on his head, but could never capture him. As the Revolution began, he turned his attacks against the British, and was a valuable ally to the Americans. Ultimately, the Green Mountain Boys became a part of Gen. P. J. Schuyler's force invading Canada—but not under Allen's leadership. The men had chosen as their head his cousin, Seth Warner.

Vermont declared its independence at Westminster in January 1777. In July, a convention in Windsor reaffirmed the declaration, and adopted a new constitution, the first in America that guaranteed the vote to all adult men. Because of New York's hostility, though, the Continental Congress refused to recognize Vermont as the 14th state.

Allen and his brothers had received large land grants along the eastern shore of Lake Champlain, and encouraged settlement in Burlington. They also established the University of Vermont, by the path of what came to be the TRIH. Taylor was to remark that it was especially appropriate that the Highway passes Morrill Hall on the campus—honoring Vermont Senator Justin Morrill who sponsored the act establishing America's great land-grant universities—and the home of Vermont Senator George F. Edmunds—whom Roosevelt as a young delegate to his first national convention in 1884 had supported for president.

For over a decade, Vermont operated as an independent country. During this period Allen even entered into unsuccessful negotiations to make it a Canadian province. This makes him perhaps the only Revolutionary hero honored today who demonstrated clearly that he was not committed to the American Union. Undoubtedly, though, he was firmly committed to Vermont, and the park demonstrates Vermont's affection for him.

Burlington is a special place, even in Vermont. In a state without a seacoast, it's a port of entry. It has grown into a thriving city, but more important, it shows that things can go well.

The city is a major industrial center. As recently as 1981, public beaches were polluted, affordable housing hardly existed, sidewalks were crumbling, streets seemed to
be more pothole than pavement, and snow removal became increasingly uncertain. A
local Democratic machine operated in collaboration with Republicans to resist
change.

In protest, the city's voters did something outrageous—at least by American standards. They elected a socialist mayor. Bernie Sanders won by fewer than a dozen
votes, but he won, and he was no stealth candidate. The voters knew exactly what they
were doing. Sanders not only campaigned calling for reform, but proclaimed himself
to be a socialist. Fortunately for the voters, and for Burlington, he was also a practical, shrewd politician, not an ideologue.

Sanders worked patiently for years to overcome the natural American prejudice
against the "socialist" label. More than a decade and a half later, he now is away from
Burlington, in Congress, and has received praise from Republicans and Democrats
alike. His party, the Progressive Coalition, remains in power.

In the meantime, repairs have put the streets in good condition, snow removal is
prompt and efficient (and includes sidewalks), a modern sewer system has removed
much of Burlington's pollution from Lake Champlain (the city is one of the few in the
country that even treats its storm run-off), there are new parks and bicycle lanes, and
there has been a housing boom, both luxury and low-income. In addition, voter turnout
has skyrocketed, people have become politically active throughout the city in local associations and councils, the arts are thriving, and there even are plans for light-rail
transit tying Burlington to the surrounding area.

Sanders reached outside the traditional framework of "public or private." At his urg-
ing, Burlington created non-profit corporations to deal with many of the seemingly-in-
soluble problems. It now has housing for the elderly, and accommodation for the home-
less. There are programs of micro loans for creation of small businesses, which have
helped to create many jobs. There is a Community Land Trust that builds houses for sale
and rent, selling them at below market value but requiring that, when sold, they be re-
sold to the corporation at a profit rate lower than normal appreciation. The Trust also as-
sists low-income residents who have financial difficulties. Developers must include affordable housing along with luxury units. A general property tax increase had been
threatened before Sanders became mayor, but he rejected it, and avoided harming low-
income homeowners by raising taxes on business and tourists instead.

Route 2—the TRIH—comes into town on Williston Road, passes through its center as
Main Street, and now turns north onto Winooski Avenue before reaching Lake Champlain. It can be confusing to try to follow the Roosevelt Highway's course through the
city, but Burlington's area, like its population, is modest in size. I soon was on my way
north, through Winooski and Colchester, the home of Vermont Public Radio. I still was
only about 215 miles from my beginning in Portland. Quickly I came to Chimney Corner, and proceeded through Sand Bar State Park and the Sand Bar Wildlife area. It was
a wild, marshy haunt for birds and small animals. Fish no doubt enjoy it too.

I was really in the Lake Champlain Island country, as I crossed over a long bridge
onto South Hero Island in Lake Champlain. The lake is large—over 100 miles

long—and lovely. If it applied for membership, the Great Lakes might accept it as a junior partner. Vermont has the eastern shore of Lake Champlain to make up for its lack of a seashore, and it does it well. Like the Great Lakes, Lake Champlain—with its 490 square miles—is so huge that it gives a feel of the sea. In fact, during the War of 1812 it enabled Burlington to be the target of a British naval attack. To put matters in perspective, though, Lake Champlain would be decidedly the junior partner. The Great Lakes range in area from Ontario's 7,540 square miles to the 31,820 of mighty Superior.

[Footnote: Congress, responding to pressure from Vermont, actually did pass an act declaring Champlain to be treated as one of the Great Lakes. President Clinton signed it into law on March 6, 1998. Vermont sought the designation to make the study of environmental threats to Lake Champlain eligible for federal funds. But I had been wrong. The Great Lakes decidedly did not welcome Lake Champlain, even as a junior partner. Fred Upton, a Republican U.S. Representative from Michigan—a state with shores on all of the real Great Lakes except Ontario—not only opposed the bill, but vowed to get the designation overturned. According to the newspaper reports, he had lined up support from some twenty representatives, both Democratic and Republican, from Michigan, Wisconsin, Ohio, and Illinois—all states on the Great Lakes—and, oddly, from North Carolina. Upton rumbled that he grew up around Lake Michigan and knew a Great Lake when he saw one. Anyone who thinks Lake Champlain is a Great Lake, he said, was "on thin ice."

It's a good story, but an aide to Vermont Senator Patrick Leahy who had sought the change, said that the whole situation was absurd. The Sea Grant Act didn't declare Lake Champlain to be a sixth Great Lake, it only treated it in the same way for the purposes of sea grants. He pointed out that various laws, including the Sea Grant Act, treated Puerto Rico and U.S. territories as states for certain purposes, but that doesn't make them states.

The explanation didn't help. The furor became so great that Leahy introduced a correction. Lake Champlain would be eligible for funds under the National Sea Grant program, but it specifically would not be designated a sixth Great Lake. Congress and the President approved the revision. It all seems to have been a tempest in a teapot—well, maybe something larger than a teapot, but certainly smaller than a Great Lake.]

On South Hero I stopped at the Sand Bar Inn on the left side of the road. The view across the highway over the water and toward the mountains was spectacular, so I settled in for the evening.

The Inn's cozy little pub was crowded with people from the area, but there was space at the bar, where I sat to eat. Several of the customers remembered the TRIH. Among them, to my right were Merlin Cox, and Leo and Joyce Pidgeon; to my left was a retired professor of civil engineering at the University of Massachusetts at Amherst, Dr. Charles E. Carver, Jr.

"The Teddy Roosevelt Highway came just outside this front door," they said. "Now it's called Highway 2, but there was a road here even before it was the Roosevelt Highway. That was back before the 1920s. It was a toll road with a lot of wagon traffic coming onto and off of the islands. Everyone says this building we're sitting in was the toll booth for the road."

I asked them if they knew of any Roosevelt Highway markers. Merlin, Leo, and Joyce all agreed that not long ago they had seen a sign marking the Highway in Burlington. It was where U.S. 2 crosses I-89.

The sun hadn't set, so there was still enough light for a good picture. I drove the short distance back to Burlington, but was disappointed. There was no sign of a sign.

The next morning I proceeded north. I was pleased at least to have found people who remembered the TR Trail. North of Grand Isle, I was stopped by a drawbridge. It was barely beginning to open as I neared. The morning was cool and crisp, and I sat with the engine off and the windows open. After about five minutes, two small sailboats passed through the open bridge, and it began to close. I enjoyed it, but the highway engineers would have been appalled — it was shamefully below Green Book standards.

With all their coves, inlets, and other hiding places, it isn't surprising that this area of the Lake Champlain Islands was a hotbed of smuggling activity during Prohibition. Rum runners could bring their wares by water from Canada, and count on finding shelter from pursuers. The "Carrying Place," on North Hero is a narrow strip of land separating the east from the west portion of Lake Champlain in the north, which for centuries permitted an easy portage for Indian commerce. Bootleggers using light boats put it to the same use, and brought a steady flow of liquor to thirsty New Yorkers on the western shore.

Old TR Highway, North of North Hero, Vermont

At several points along the way there were signs informing drivers of ferry service across Lake Champlain to New York. In the very earliest years of the TR Highway, the route involved a ferry crossing to Plattsburg, but as roads developed during the 1920s, the route was relocated to remain in Vermont somewhat longer, heading north.

At South Alburg, there was a turnoff to Isle La Motte, where Roosevelt was vacationing when he received news that President McKinley had been shot. I decided to keep on the main road and not take the side trip.

The final town in Vermont is Alburg. According to a promotional brochure, "Alburg, the northern boundary of the Champlain Islands, is one of the two pieces of land in the contiguous United States, other than an island, which does not touch any other piece of land in the United States." As I entered the village, I saw the "Islands in the Sun Senior Center." There were people there, so I stopped to chat.

The Center's president, Evelyn Dubuque, showed me an exhibit of her sketches of significant local buildings. They were being displayed for a local bi-centennial. She modestly disclaimed any artistic talent—too modestly, I told her.

She remembered the TRIH well. Her parting words were that she would check with her high-school history teacher, who might remember more than she does about the Highway. "She's getting along in years," she said, "but she's still sharp."

North of Alburg, Vermont lost its prosperous look. I passed a small, rather shabby, information booth that was closed, a cemetery, and a tumbled-down barn. I stopped for gas and at a convenience store just before I drove onto the long, high, Korean Veterans' Memorial Bridge, leaving Vermont and connecting it across Lake Champlain with New York.

Chapter Five

New York: Crossing T.R.'s State

Early travelers would have had to wait for a ferry to cross Lake Champlain, but the bridge permitted me to leave Vermont for New York on my own schedule. The day was still cool, and fog had begun to roll up from the Lake. Above me the clouds were heavy. They hung low, reaching down toward the road, which beckoned to the fog.

"New York" is familiar nearly everywhere because of New York City's heavy presence in the American movies and television that nearly the entire world watches. But that New York is only New York City.

It would surprise even many Americans to learn that the state itself is highly agricultural, with large expanses of parklands and rural areas. There are more acres of forested land in New York than in any state on the TR Highway's route until it reaches as far west as Montana. That means that there are more extensive forests in New York than there are even in Michigan, Wisconsin, or Minnesota—states noted for their "North Woods"—and only one of its cities is truly large.

The "Empire State" also has scenic wonders that rival those anywhere, but its population some time ago slipped behind that of the upstart, California. New York City remains the country's largest, but the state had to adjust to being number two in size. Worse yet, New Yorkers were only beginning to accept that insult when they were faced with a true indignity: they slipped again. New York State in the 1990s began to rank third in population, behind—of all places—Texas!

The TR Highway enters New York at the tiny settlement of Rouses Point, right at the end of the bridge. (The name rhymes with "cow," not "coo.") By then it gives up its brief eastern flirtation with U.S. 2, forsaking it for U.S. 11 instead.

The original route went across Lake Champlain farther south to enter New York at Plattsburgh. As it crossed the Lake, it passed the site of the Battle of Plattsburgh, a naval battle in the War of 1812 in which the Americans chased the British back into Canada. Although I did not digress to the Plattsburgh route on this trip, I came back a few months later to drive that segment, too, and compare them.

Plattsburgh is a small but engaging old city, with a look of genteel poverty, a river walk, attractive public buildings, a branch of the state university, and a sense of history. Near the river walk stands the Macdonough Monument, a stone eagle sitting atop a tall tower. It is an eye-catcher, and commemorates Commodore Thomas Macdonough's naval victory against greatly superior British forces. His feat remains one of the great naval triumphs in American history.

The earlier route proceeded northwest from Plattsburgh along what now are State Highway 374 and County Road 24 to Malone. That rugged route through the Adirondacks remained the TR Trail's course as late as 1923, but there were sound reasons to move it farther north, even though the scenery is less majestic. Neither route goes through a prosperous region, but the houses along the mountain trail tend to be run down, suggesting Appalachia.

Dilapidated real estate wasn't the trouble, though. The problem was the terrain. The same hills and valleys that stimulate the eye even today can create trouble for wheeled transport—and of course in the early days the challenge was even greater. So, years before the stock market crash of 1929, maps had come to agree upon a newer, less difficult, route. Entering New York at Rouses Point not only pointed the Highway through less daunting territory, but in contrast to the Plattsburgh entry, it required a much shorter ferry trip across Lake Champlain. The majestic lake narrows considerably as it approaches the Canadian border.

Both the country here and its people are far from fitting the stereotype of "New York." Still, there is a modern north-south freeway, and that does bring a break in the isolation. No sooner had I crossed that Interstate, than I entered the small settlement of Mooers. I found it to be a clean, rather quiet, place similar to those sprinkled widely throughout the country. It was typical small-town America.

On my left, was a white frame house. On the broad, bright green lawn, next to a "For Sale" sign, stood a crowd of life-sized cut-out figures. At first glance, they seemed to be made of metal, but closer examination revealed them to be cut from wood, and painted a flat black to resemble shadows or silhouettes, Each had a bright red bandanna tied about its neck, fashioned from plastic to withstand the elements. The group included bears, dogs, cats, running children, and men—several with pipes—each leaning against some object such as a fence or a tree.

The varied shapes—and their stark black, with the splashes of vivid red—against the brilliant green of the spring lawn added visual appeal to a morning that, even though the fog had lifted, was still gray. I complimented the proprietor, Cora Smith, who said that her brother-in-law made the figures. They have them displayed all summer, but remove them when the weather becomes harsh. She said they'd sold many to motorists from far and wide, and that a number had gone to Ontario and Quebec. I could expect to see them far from Mooers.

I had thought I was in the Village of Mooers, but Dave and Brenda Supernant of the Northern Tier Chamber of Commerce ("serving the towns of Champlain, Chazy and Mooers") told me that it no longer exists. It had dissolved itself shortly before, although the "Town" remains. The "village" was a smaller unit within the town—so much for the intricacies of local government, especially in the older sections of the country.

The Town of Mooers may no longer have a "village," but it does boast a historian, Carol Nedeau. She's a long-time resident and elementary-school teacher who supplied some fascinating and highly relevant information from within her own family. Her

Folk Art Sale, Mooers, New York

grandmother, Harriet Annis, had been at the Buffalo Exposition on that historic day in 1901. She was an eyewitness there—before high technology and tight security—on the 6th of September when anarchist Leon Czolgosz shot President McKinley. McKinley died on September 13, catapulting Vice President Theodore Roosevelt into the presidency.

Miss Annis was about 13 at the time. She was in the elaborate "Temple of Music" while the President greeted members of the public. His secretary, George Cortelyou, had argued that it was too dangerous, but McKinley shrugged off Cortelyou's warning, and insisted on appearing at the reception.

He was standing in the middle of the crowd, shaking hands with one person after another. One man had his right arm wrapped in what appeared to be a bandage—it turned out to be a large handkerchief. She watched as the man approached McKinley. In front of the astonished assembly and in full view of the young girl, the man suddenly shoved his wrapped hand toward the President. The cloth erupted in flame and smoke as a handgun concealed within blasted twice. She saw the President crumple into the arms of a Secret Service agent.

Ms Nedeau had heard the story from her grandmother in vivid detail. Without the event that her grandmother had witnessed, there might never have been a President Roosevelt. Almost assuredly, there never would have been a Theodore Roosevelt International Highway.

Leaving Mooers, I passed through the tiny settlements of Ellenburg Depot and Chateaugay. Chateaugay no doubt is a historic community—French Canadians settled it in 1796. My most vivid memory of it, though, is that of an enormous junkyard, even though there is a scenic bridge, high above the Chateaugay River.

Just down the road on the Salmon River is Malone, a small community settled in 1802. Although it has fewer than 7,000 residents, Malone has a daily newspaper, the *Telegram*. I picked up an issue. It presented a nice mix of news for a small paper. A front-page story discussed proposals for an open border between the United States and Canada (obviously, this was before the reaction to 9/11). Another described a controversy between the state and the Mohawk Tribe. New York was attempting to collect taxes on tobacco and fuel sold to non-Indians on Indian land, and the issue was complicated by a conflict between factions within the Tribe itself. The article warned of possible local uprisings similar to those it said had occurred near Syracuse, when "members of the Onondaga nation, joined by lone representatives of the Mohawk and Oneida nations, set tires ablaze on Interstate 81 last weekend, as a gesture of protest against the interim tax agreements."

The root issue here may have seemed technical, or even trivial, and it was merely a pale reflection of the fierce intercultural conflicts of the past, but it revealed the continuing tensions. Anyone who thinks the accommodation has been complete—here or anywhere across the country—doesn't understand the situation.

The TRIH extends from Malone northwest on State Highway 37, which for a time is built up several feet above the surrounding land. I proceeded almost to the Canadian border at Fort Covington, and then over rough and poor pavement, including bridges across the Salmon, Little Salmon, and St. Regis Rivers, into Mohawk land. An Indian store had a large sign advertising cappuccino. I continued on through Hogansburg, the site of the Akwesasne Cultural Center on the St. Regis Mohawk Reservation (the Center is devoted to the culture and history of the Iroquois). I continued on to Rooseveltown.

The name has nothing to do with TR. Rooseveltown is the site of a bridge crossing into Canada over the St. Lawrence, but the bridge wasn't opened until the 1930s. Throughout the heyday of the TRIH, the 1920s and early 1930s, the community's name was Nyando.

That changed in 1934. When The Roosevelt International Bridge became the namesake of Franklin Roosevelt, the community decided to do the same. The New Deal President had journeyed to Nyando to dedicate the new bridge, and the community changed its name in his honor.

There is hardly anything left. The road signs to the bridge didn't even carry the name Roosevelt, and except for some houses there is barely any sign of a town. What there is lies south of the road. A sign does point to "Rooseveltown," but there is little to indicate when you pass into, or out of, the community.

This northern portion of the state was settled later than most parts of New York. The WPA *Guide* remarks that "as late as 1813 Spafford in his *Gazetteer* called Franklin County 'the least valuable county in the State'." But now it's the location of some of the most attractive parts of the Seaway Trail, which, according to promotional literature, is the longest recreational trail for mixed usage in the United States.

The Trail's 454 miles follow the St. Lawrence River to Lake Ontario, around the southern shore of the Lake to Niagara, through Buffalo, and along the southern shore of Lake Erie to Ripley. Ripley is in the far southwestern portion of New York State, almost at the Pennsylvania line. That's far off the TR Trail's course.

Here at the Seaway Trail's beginning, though, it follows the Theodore Roosevelt Highway. The route is more than scenic. It also becomes interesting technologically. The Eisenhower Lock near Massena reveals the St. Lawrence to be more than a river. Modern technological achievements have turned it into one of the world's major waterways, with shipping flowing between the Great Lakes and the Atlantic Ocean.

I took a short diversion to the lock, and arrived at just the right time. The road goes into a round tunnel, above which, creeping through the lock, was a large freighter. From the road, there was no sign of water, merely the dramatic sight of a ship easing across an overpass.

In Massena I stopped at the Henry Warren Memorial Public Library. Finding nothing, I proceeded on to Ogdensburg. The Seaway Trail along the way gave frequent views of the St. Lawrence.

I found Ogdensburg to be full of reminders of the War of 1812. Its Greenbelt Riverfront Park contains a well-maintained Battlefield Walking Tour. It took some time for tempers to cool following the war. As late as 1837 Ogdensburg remained a hotbed of resentment against the English. It became headquarters for a group of Americans who sought vainly to seize Canada from the British in the brief so-called "Patriots' War."

I opted to spend the night in a motel, and the next morning drove around Ogdensburg again. The community is old, and most of the houses are small. The downtown area still has some mansions, generally well preserved. There is a palpable sense of the past, and a strong identification with Canada, just on the other side of the St. Lawrence.

I went to the Public Library, and arrived a few minutes before it opened. Rather than standing around or staying in the truck to wait, I walked across the street to take a picture of the building. A woman was sitting there in a car.

"It'll be open in a few minutes," she called over to me.

"Thanks," I said. "I'm just taking a picture and then I want to check the local history files."

"I can probably help you," she said. "I worked at the library for twenty-one years before I retired, and I'm the local historian. My name's Persis Boyensen. I set up the local history collection. I had to kick the DAR out of the library to make room for it. I put it in the room where they'd been for a long time. They're still mad at me. Huh! I'm a member myself, but they're a private organization. I don't see why they should expect taxpayer funding."

I explained what I was doing, but I drew a blank. She didn't know about the Highway, and was certain there was nothing about it in the library. To be sure I reviewed the files myself. She was right. Later, she joined me in the local history room, and we had an interesting discussion about Ogdensburg's past, about the importance of history, and about her own work, which was extensive.

She asked me if I had been to the Remington Museum, and I told her that it was my next stop. Frederick Remington moved to Ogdensburg from Canton when he was a boy, and Ogdensburg proudly preserves memory of its adopted son. The Frederick Remington Art Museum is at State and Washington Streets—right across the street from the library—in a three-story house built by David Parish, a local banker, in 1809.

The house has its own history, which is as colorful as the artworks it contains. In its own way, the legend is as sad as any painting or sculpture that Remington produced. By 1838, the mansion had come into the possession of Parish's nephew, George. That year, so the story goes, George played a high-stakes poker game against one John Van Buren.

The name may not be familiar now, but at the time it was. John was the son of Martin Van Buren, who then was President of the United States.

The younger Van Buren was losing heavily, and had run out of money. In desperation, he offered to bet his mistress, Maria Ameriga Vespucci, a descendant of Amerigo Vespucci, from whom America took its name. George Parish accepted, and won. He installed Ms Vespucci as his own mistress in the house at State and Washington, thus causing a major scandal throughout the staid community. Decent citizens of course, expressed their Christian charity by doing what was right—they scorned "Parish's fancy woman," refusing to have anything to do with her.

She lived there, reclusively. Parish never married her. After some years he moved to Europe, and left her alone. Ultimately, she returned to Europe, again alone.

The tale of the bereft Ameriga became the subject of a 1929 novel by Walter Guest Kellogg. Despite its overblown prose, it received favorable reviews in several newspapers, including the New York *Herald Tribune*.

Mrs. Boyensen questions the accuracy of some of the legend. She had reviewed the manifest of the ship that brought Ameriga to this country and found that Parish was also a passenger. Kellogg's novel does mention that they had met on the ship, but he still includes the fateful card game. He conceded in a forenote that he could not document the game, but he accepted it as valid because the story was current in Parish's time.

The museum itself is excellent. Some of the paintings in its collection would surprise those who think of Remington merely as an illustrator, or who associate him solely with action. His later work shows strong influence from the impressionists, certainly in style, but often in subject as well.

I left on a narrow, but smooth, road with fairly heavy traffic, but no congestion. The part of the state past Ogdensburg has a prosperous appearance, which was evident despite the heavy rain that had just begun. I passed Mater Dei College on the left, and Lt. Lawrence State Park on the right. The views there are excellent. In some ways, the ghostly appearance that the rain and fog added made them even more impressive.

At Morristown, the TR route goes off to the right and becomes State Highway 12. It passes Jacques Cartier State Park, with more superb views, and goes on through Chippewa Bay, a community dating from 1818.

At Alexandria Bay is the beginning of the Thousand Islands. When A.W. Tracy of the Theodore Roosevelt Highway Association wrote his praise of the Highway in

1921, he said that in driving across New York to the St. Lawrence River, "one of the first things that we see is the Ten Thousand Islands and the eastern shore of lake Erie with her many historical points and legends of pioneer days."

Whether or not Tracy ever actually journeyed the length of the TR Highway himself, he garbled his geography. The Islands are at the eastern tip of Lake Ontario, not Lake Erie, and they are the "Thousand Islands," not the "Ten Thousand." The only time the TR Highway ever came near to Lake Erie was in Ontario where it was close to the Lake's northern shore.

This name, though, is a rare instance of understatement. The many islands where the St. Lawrence joins Lake Ontario actually number closer to two thousand. They contain many parks and recreational areas, and also many extravagant houses dating from early in the century. TR travelers in the 1920s would have seen many of them across the water, and some remain in view today.

Boats now take tourists to one of the most interesting, on Heart Island. George Boldt, the owner of the Waldorf Astoria Hotel, began in 1900 to build a 120-room castle there for his wife, Louise. But in 1904, before it was completed, she died. Boldt ceased all activity on the castle and surrounding buildings, and in his grief never returned. After years of damage by vandals and the elements, the complex was restored, and finished. Boldt Castle and Yacht House now are major attractions.

They include—of course—a gift shop.

The Highway continues on through Clayton, which is known for its Antique Boat Museum, containing one of the world's largest collections of freshwater recreational boats. Boat rides in antique craft are available. More relevant to my trip was a fine little public library, the Hawn Memorial Library at 220 John Street, with a strong local history collection. I reviewed the materials in the local history files, locating nothing about the TR Highway until a Hawn History Room Volunteer, Mrs. Phoebe B. Tritton, found just what I wanted. She reproduced three sheets of a road map from the first volume of the 1927 edition of the *Official Automobile Blue Book*. She even went to the trouble of highlighting the route of the TR Highway from its beginning in Portland, across New England and New York, into Ontario at Niagara Falls toward Hamilton.

According to this map, in 1927—except for most of the length in the two tiny states of New Hampshire and Vermont—the road had some sort of surface all the way from Portland to Hamilton. The detail was good, and included each community on the Highway. It was the same the route that I had identified and followed. That was reassuring. With a minor exception it verified what I had found. The exception showed the Highway entering New York not at Plattsburgh (this was before the Rouses Point entry), but at Port Kent, just south of Plattsburgh and across Lake Champlain from Burlington.

Every other source that I have found placed the New York entry initially at Plattsburgh, and later at Rouses Point. The road from Port Kent to Malone would have been even more challenging than the one to Malone from Plattsburgh, and appears simply to have been an error. It is possible that travelers took one of several alternate routes before things had been clearly defined, but reports indicated that the TR Highway had been fully marked before 1927, at least in the US.

At any rate, I was happy finally to find some solid information in New York. Later, I was to find this map in the Library of Congress, along with others from various *Blue Books* throughout the 1920s. Mrs. Tritton's discovery, though, was my first view of the *Blue Books*.

From Clayton the route follows State Highway 12 to Watertown. With a population of some 30,000, Watertown is one of the larger cities in the region. It's a pleasant and attractive place, full of stop signs and red lights, and it has a good newspaper, the *Daily Times*.

The Black River runs through the city, and supplied power for its early mill industry. The Jefferson County Historical Society, located in an 1876 Victorian mansion on Washington Street downtown near the Roswell P. Flower Memorial Library, features an exhibit of water turbines from the old mills. Edwin Paddock, a local businessman, built the house, which itself is on display with gardens and period rooms.

It was in Watertown that Frank W. Woolworth, a young clerk from a general store, developed a powerful idea that would be a force in American retailing for a long time to come. In 1878, he set up a table with a sign, "Any Article for 5c," at a local fair. Everything sold almost immediately. The experience inspired him to open his first "five and ten cent store" in Utica. It was the first in a huge chain of "Woolworth's" that dominated a niche in American marketing for a century.

Just after I departed Watertown, a heavy fog had settled in on the area—again. I followed the TR route onto State Highway 3, which follows the shoreline of Lake Ontario. I passed by Sackets Harbor Battlefield State Park, Wescott Beach State Park, and Henderson Harbor, but the fog obscured the scenery. I decided to stop not far from Watertown, in a secluded campground in a forested area right on Lake Ontario.

I set up camp within ten or fifteen minutes—my tent goes up quickly. After a small dinner, I set up my laptop computer on the picnic table, but that didn't last long. The fog still was thick, and the night was chilly—the temperature had dropped probably into the upper 30s. After a few minutes, the chill got to me, so I moved into the tent where the laptop became literally a laptop—I sat in a low camp chair with the computer on my lap. I wrote until the battery gave out, secured everything, and crawled into my sleeping bag.

The chill of the night couldn't penetrate. I was warm and comfortable. Somehow, I always feel more alone in a tent than in a motel—but less lonely. The fog muffled every sound but one. Now and then I heard the mournful tone of a foghorn. I felt— experiencing the deep bass tones that were lulling me into a satisfying sleep—as if I were in a different world.

I awoke long before daylight, refreshed. Outside the tent, I found that the fog was even thicker than it had been the night before. I chose, after warming myself with a vigorous workout, to have breakfast in more comfortable surroundings. I took down my camp, got back onto State Highway 3, and found a nondescript place for a non-memorable breakfast.

After the fog had begun to burn off, I stopped at an overlook toward Lake Ontario, and enjoyed both the view, and the sight of a strange house off to the side. It had a squat, round, tower of sorts—probably for observation—with round, porthole-like windows in the side. Somewhat off the route on a side trip, I found Ray's Bay Lighthouse.

Despite the lifting of the fog, the day remained dark and heavily overcast. It also remained chilly, with a brisk wind. Back on U.S. 3, I continued along on the dark, dank, day through Sandy Creek, and Sandy Pond Inlet. I was attracted by a "Rail City Historical Museum," which the sign said was the "Site of the First Operating Steam Railroad Museum in U.S. Sandy Pond and Ontario Railroad."

It not only was closed, it was deserted. A sign on the highway beyond the museum warned that I had "Missed It," and implored me to Turn Back.

Postings on the property, though, ominously warned everyone to KEEP OUT!

I stopped at a rustic store featuring camping goods, fishing equipment, and other outdoors gear.

"Whew, that wind is bad," said the elderly attendant as I stepped out at the pumps.

"Yeah. It cuts right through you," was my clichéd reply.

"What brings you to these parts?" he asked, noting my Midwestern license tag.

"I'm writing a book about the old Theodore Roosevelt International Highway. Most people have never heard of it."

"Well, I sure have," he said, surprising me. "I've been on it—on several parts of it. A bit of it was on Highway 11, wasn't it?"

"Right you are," I said, "and then on Highway 3."

"I thought so. I wasn't sure just where, but I remember driving on it a number of times. What's your book gonna be called?"

"Moose Crossing. My wife came up with the name."

"That's great. I'll look for it."

With that conversation under my belt, a fresh cup of coffee in the cup holder, and two full tanks of gasoline, I drove on a short distance until I could turn right on State Highway 104B, which soon became 104. The next few miles were out of sight of water, and the day remained dark as I drove on through Oswego.

The city is small, and nicely situated on Lake Ontario at the mouth of the Oswego River—well, at least at one time it was nicely situated. Now, barely over five miles east of the river's mouth and the population center, Lake Ontario benefits from the presence on its shoreline of the "Energy Center," and Nine-Mile Point Unit One Nuclear-Power Plant, Nine-Mile Point Unit Two Nuclear Power Plant, and the James A. Fitzpatrick Nuclear-Power Plant. Even closer in is a paper mill, with its characteristic stench. The Clean Air Act has helped greatly, but paper mills remain vile neighbors.

On the shoreline to the west of the river is Niagara Mohawk steam station—Oswego should never lack power. To its west is the State University of New York at Oswego. Although the city maintains Fort Ontario and a park at the river's mouth, the overwhelming presence in Oswego along the shore of this great inland sea is industrial. The pollution took many forms, of which the visual was only the most obvious.

The Fort has an interesting history, displayed in a military museum open to the public. The governments of Canada and the United States cooperated to put down the motley group of farmers, soldiers of fortune, and others who caused trouble from Vermont to Michigan, seeking to drive the British from Canada in their "Patriots' War" of

1837. The United States built a new Fort Ontario in 1839 on the site of older installations to keep the unruly "patriots" in line. During the Second World War, the Fort became the only emergency refuge in North America for Europeans fleeing the Nazis.

The rural isolation of northeastern New York was far behind me. As I proceeded west of Oswego on State Highway 104 I found the settlements still to be small, but they were numerous and the area obviously was fairly heavily populated. For a few miles, 104A, the original route, continues to offer a more scenic alternative to 104, which now drops somewhat to the south, but the alternative doesn't last long. Roughly at Red Creek, 104A returns to 104, which continues on west generally following the original route of the TRIH.

Shortly before reaching the Village of Sodus, I passed a bird sanctuary on the right. It was not an isolated area, but the human activity didn't seem to bother the birds. Just beyond Sodus, I turned left on State Highway 88, and immediately turned west on Ridge Road. It was a tree-lined route, with a mixture of rural and residential atmosphere, closely paralleling 104. Apparently it was the original route. Ridge Road picks up State Highway 404 at Webster.

Webster has the appearance of the typical prosperous American small town. Architecture buffs would appreciate its many interesting buildings, including the "Harmony House." I stopped at the museum, and was in luck. Although it was closed, a group was scheduled to have a private meeting there in a few minutes, and I waited for the curator to arrive, and was graciously admitted.

In the museum was a large map of the area from early in the century. It showed the route that the TR Highway later followed. That route's first number was 104. It was re-numbered 404 when the current modern highway, slightly to the north, was built and became 104. Although the museum had nothing specifically referring to the TR Highway, it did provide some detailed information about New York roads.

Armed with my new knowledge, and happy to have my findings verified again, I continued on into Rochester, the largest city since Portland. Although the 2000 Census showed Rochester proper with a population of only 219,773, that is enough to make it New York's third largest city, ranking just behind Buffalo.

Because of the nature of its industrial heritage Rochester not only calls itself "The World's Image Centre," but has copyrighted the name. Perhaps other cities have copyrighted slogans, but I've never heard of it anywhere else.

The title fits. The city's emphasis on optics and imaging goes back to 1853, when two men opened a small optical shop. Earlier, Rochester had been the "flower city," and earlier still the "flour city." The men with the optical shop were John Jacob Bausch, and Henry Lomb; their tiny enterprise grew into the international giant Bausch and Lomb. A quarter century later, in 1888, George Eastman's experiments with film and dry plates in his mother's kitchen led to a camera, and ultimately to Eastman Kodak. In 1906, the Haloid Company began almost as modestly, in a loft above a shoe store. In 1961 it changed its name to the now familiar Xerox Corporation.

Much of Rochester's business community is related in some way to imaging science. Among its numerous institutions of higher education, the University of Rochester and Rochester Institute of Technology are well-known for quality in various fields, including optics and related subjects. Not known for imaging science, of course, but funded by a fortune that grew from the industry is the world-renowned Eastman School of Music.

With all the corporate money available in Rochester, it's no wonder that it has lovely restored areas, formal floral displays, and a thriving cultural scene. Still, the city impressed me more as basically a working class town. Its gritty, rawboned, ambiance isn't shabby. Rather, it suggests a tough, no-nonsense, American city. Something about it reminded me of Baltimore in the 1960s, Kansas City in its heyday, Chicago as filtered through the creative imagination of Carl Sandburg, or its rough-hewn neighbor to the north, Milwaukee.

Rochester may not look worn down, but from the route of the TRIH it does look old. Like other eastern cities, it is. Ebenezer "Indian" Allan built a grist mill in 1789 south of the High Falls on the Genesee River—that was the first year of the new American Republic, with the ink barely dry on the United States Constitution—and settlement followed quickly.

But it wasn't easy. Much of the area was swampy, and infested with rattlesnakes. Well into the next century it was still possible for "Rattlesnake Pete" to decorate his saloon on Mill Street with the skins of local rattlers. Indian Allan in 1803 sold out to Colonel Nathaniel Rochester and a couple of speculators from Maryland. By 1810 or 1811, Rochester was offering lots for sale.

It was the Erie Canal that in 1824 brought the city a booming economy. It also came to be known as the residence of two of America's most outstanding leaders for human rights, Frederick Douglass, and Susan B. Anthony. Douglass, the former slave, prominent abolitionist, outstanding orator, and later the first African-American diplomat (Minister to Haiti) published his powerful abolitionist newspaper, *The North Star* in a building on Main Street. His statue on South Avenue supposedly was the first such monument in America to honor a black citizen. Anthony, the tireless campaigner for woman suffrage, also lived in Rochester, on Madison Street. In fact, she was in Rochester when she was arrested for casting a ballot illegally. Both Anthony and Douglass are buried in Mt. Hope Cemetery.

Rochester benefits from its location on Irondequoit Bay, almost on Lake Ontario, and the Genesee River flows through the city into the Lake, along the way coursing through forests and cutting deep gorges. One of the most spectacular is High Falls, a 96-foot drop. In November of 1829, Sam Patch, a daredevil "falls jumper," announced that he would make his last jump of the season at High Falls. He did, and it was. It also was his absolute last. He died in the attempt.

One who wants water views while in Rochester can find them from many places, including hiking trails, restaurants, and hotel rooms. Cruises and water sports are plentiful. The Erie Canal now flows directly into the Genesee, but originally a stone aqueduct carried it over the river. Remnants of the old locks are accessible for history buffs.

Also available are more museums than most travelers would be able to visit. The George Eastman House with its "Enhancing the Illusion," a fascinating exhibition of film and the history of photography, is a mansion of some 50 rooms at 900 East Avenue. Eastman, the philanthropist and hugely successful industrialist lived there until his death in 1932, when he shot himself.

The Strong Museum, downtown at the corner of Chestnut and Woodbury, celebrates American life and popular culture since 1820, and includes an enormous collection of dolls and miniatures with special exhibits for children. The Rochester Museum and Science Center (657 East Avenue), including the Seneca Iroquois exhibit, the Susan B. Anthony National Historic Landmark (17 Madison Street), and the Xerox History Museum (Midtown Plaza) are only a few of the attractions.

Undeniably, Rochester is modern in another respect. One of its two morning newspapers, the *Democrat and Chronicle*, recently swallowed the other, the 79-year-old *Times-Union*. There's no doubt that the city now is a one-newspaper town, following a lamentable trend, but in a way it already was. The Huge Gannett Newspaper Group already owned them both.

The TR Highway, now NY 404, enters Rochester on Empire, which later changes to Clifford. It proceeds left on Portland, left on North Street, and becomes Chestnut. It then turns right on Woodbury to pick up New York 31. Although Rochester is an easy city to drive through, construction complicated matters. A road sign indicated that NY 31 turned right at Clinton. It doesn't.

I turned on Clinton, and before long found myself two or three miles off the route. I stopped at a station to fill the truck's tanks. It also was a convenience store, heavily barred on its door and all windows. The customers, outside and in, were all black, and appeared poor.

One tall, muscular, man, very dark and probably about thirty years old, sat with a huge boom box on a wall at the side of the station. He had the volume cranked up full force, and seemed completely engrossed in the music.

It was Tchaikovsky's "Waltz of the Flowers."

I retraced my route downtown to Woodbury, then took Woodbury to Exchange, turned right, and proceeded to Broad, where I turned left. At that point, signs for NY 31 began to appear. I turned right on Plymouth, crossed Main, went past the Kodak Building, and turned left on Lyell. I had followed the TR route through the city with only that one bit of confusion.

State Highway 31 continues west fairly directly. I found the traffic to be the heaviest yet outside of a city. I passed nearby Ogden, and continuing on 31, rather than taking the more modern 31A, I drove through Brockport. The lawns there were neat and trimmed. The streets were excellent, and well-maintained. Holley, immediately west, reminded me of an isolated village, despite the heavily-populated area just a few miles distant.

At Fancher, NY 31 turns sharply left, passing a stone monument on the right. Curious, I pulled well off the road, and walked back to read the plaque. The small stone tower—probably about seven feet tall—was in three sections, each almost cubic, narrowing from bottom to top. The plaque was in the middle section, and the top one held a large clock. The monument, set in a bright green lawn, commemorates the soldiers of World War Two.

Other signs of the times along the way were abandoned drive-in theaters. I was surprised at how many there were in a rather short distance. I didn't find out why they were concentrated in the area.

Medina appears to be a typical American small town. I stopped in an independent bookstore, where the proprietor told me that she thought there was still a Roosevelt

World War II Memorial, Fancher, New York

Highway in the area, but she didn't remember just where. She directed me to the Chamber of Commerce, just a few doors away.

Marsha Winters there not only knew about it, but gave me a current map of the county, Orleans County. The map still identified the TRIH. It showed the route not on Highway 31, but on Highway 18 to the north, following the shoreline of Lake Ontario. I had to see if there were still "Roosevelt Highway" markers along the way, but first I needed to follow the Highway 31 route, toward Niagara Falls. When I discovered alternate routes, I was determined to cover them both.

Beyond Medina, at Middleport, is a multi-screen drive in theater. It was still operating—the only one I saw that continued to show films.

For some time, NY 31 had been closely following, occasionally crossing, the Erie Canal. At Lockport, the Canal's locks were impressive, and I discovered a Roosevelt Drive at the junction with Akron Road. It is just off Route 31, and possibly related to the TRIH. I discovered also that I was on the historic Niagara Trail. Off to the side I noted some of the silhouette figures that I had first seen in Mooers.

I pushed on through Cambria ("Est. 1808"), past the Tuscarora Indian Nation with its huge "Smokin' Joe's" tobacco store, and on to Niagara Falls. NY 31 enters the Town of Niagara in an industrial section. One of the first sights is a sprawling complex of wires and towers, a reflection of the hydroelectric power that the Falls have been generating since the 1880s.

NY 31 ends at College and Lewiston, and the TR route turns left at Lewiston on its way to the Falls.

The traffic had become increasingly heavy. Trucks were everywhere, and many had wide loads. The weather, though, was cool, bright, and beautiful. I turned around, and didn't mind retracing my path to Rochester.

From Rochester, I drove northwest toward the Town of Irondequoit, then to Greece. Just beyond the Village of Hilton and the intersection of roads 18 and 8, was the line for the Town of Parma. The road suddenly became marked as the "Roosevelt Highway." The signs were modern green street signs, not resembling any of the original markers. At Hamlin, I went through the intersection with route 19, and saw another Roosevelt sign.

The signs continued, past the Orleans/Monroe County line, past 212, and at every intersection for miles. Finally, they gave way to the designation, "Seaway Trail," which lasted through Wilson to Roosevelt Beach. On the county map, the entire stretch appeared to be the Roosevelt Highway.

In Roosevelt Beach, Highway 18 is marked as Lake Road. The community appeared to be a tiny, old, resort community characterized by small cabins. It was entirely residential, and I returned to the business district of Wilson, only a mile or so distant, to see what I could find out about it.

I found nothing at the library about either Roosevelt Beach or the TRIH, but I fared better at the Town Clerk's office. Personnel there told me that Roosevelt Beach was not incorporated, and actually was a part of the Town of Wilson. They looked up a local history and duplicated a page titled "Wilson in the 20th Century," for me. This revealed that the area originally had been the Foote Farm, and at one time it had been connected to "Sunset Island," by a narrow peninsula used as a sheep path.

View from Roosevelt Highway, New York

"Harwood later bought the Foote Farm," it said, "and Roosevelt Beach was born when he developed the property into 20 foot lots for cottages. Since the lots were small, sewage was inadequate and later became a problem." It did not identify "Harwood" further, nor did it provide dates. It said that as Roosevelt Beach developed it provided a market for local "chickens, eggs, fruit, and other produce," and that "some of the gravel that was used to build local highways was dug by hand along the north shore of 'Sunset Island.'"

I could probably learn more, the office personnel told me, from the Town's historian, and gave me his telephone number. I called him, but he didn't know the source of the name, and could add nothing to the information I already had. The description from the local history was consistent with the early 1920s, and the location of Roosevelt Beach suggests that the name might well have resulted from its location on the TRIH.

It would have been nice to be certain, but I didn't mind the scarcity of information about Roosevelt Beach. Finding miles of the Roosevelt Highway still marked with the name was more than enough to make me happy.

I drove on toward Niagara Falls, and set up my tent for the night at a campground near Lewiston. I hadn't come very far west that day because of all the exploration and backtracking, but I felt as if I had made great progress, and was discovering remnants of the TRIH.

The next morning, I found what appeared to be another. I drove into Niagara Falls on route 18, which runs south into route 104 along the Robert Moses Parkway. I purchased a Niagara Falls map, and found a Roosevelt Street. It is near routes 18/104, 61, and 31. The street is short, and blocked off at one end. It seems to have been orphaned when the new highways were constructed, but it still proudly bears the sign, "Roosevelt Street."

I continued toward the Falls on Lewiston. On the way, I passed the campus of Niagara University, a Catholic liberal arts school located in a pleasant residential area. The city mixes scenic excitement, congestion, tourism, and power generation. Expect to be charged for everything: climbing the tower, walking over the bridge, and of course parking—but expect also to find it money well spent.

One of the world's most awesome attractions overshadows any shabbiness of the downtown. Niagara Falls retains all its famous grandeur. Viewing the Falls, regardless of any other considerations, reminds one that this is a special place. I could only imagine how it had been for the early TRIH travelers—before commercialization—who found inspiration from the mighty cataract. Even before the Roosevelt Trail, there were the daredevils who went over the Falls in barrels (some even survived), tightrope walkers who pranced across the Falls from above, and even one child who fell into the water and survived the nearly 200-foot plunge.

Don't make the mistake of hurrying on through and bypassing the Falls. Experience them on both sides, American and Canadian. Take the Maid of the Mist from either side. Try to dine at the revolving restaurant at the top of the Skylon Tower in Canada.

When John Steinbeck traveled with Charley, he took the TRIH without knowing it, entering New York from Vermont at Rouses Point. He stayed as close to Lake Ontario as possible all the way until he reached Niagara. As a matter of fact, he had intended to follow what was the TR route through Ontario from Niagara to Windsor, but changed

Roosevelt Highway, Southern Shore of Lake Ontario, New York

his plans because he had no vaccination certificate for Charley. On the way to Niagara Steinbeck somehow managed to get lost just off Highway 104. Wherever he was, he thought he was near Medina. He finally found his way to Niagara, and liked it.

For eastbound travelers, viewing Niagara Falls provides a dramatic introduction to a dramatic state. For travelers proceeding west across New York on the TRIH, the Falls themselves are a worthy culmination to a trip through a state that is among America's most interesting.

The Falls are the result of the sharp drop in altitude as the Niagara River tumbles its 35-mile length from Lake Erie to Lake Ontario. The difference in elevation between the two lakes is about 326 feet. About half of the drop occurs right at Niagara Falls, and much of the rest creates a nearby series of falls and rapids over a stretch of some eight miles.

The close-up view from the water that the Maid of the Mist provides cannot be duplicated in any other way. In addition to the bridge between the U.S. and Canada, walkways along the Niagara Gorge a couple of miles below the Falls go right along the edge of the River near the Whirlpool Rapids, which are hardly less furious than the Falls themselves. A "Spanish Aero Car" suspended from cables another mile downriver permits aerial views, including those of the Whirlpool and the Rapids, while tunnels make it possible to see the Falls literally from behind, with inside viewing points, and an outside platform so close that raincoats are necessary to avoid being soaked by the spray.

Despite the natural grandeur, the call of the TR Highway remained strong. Hesitating no longer, I proceeded to the International Border.

Chapter Six

Ontario: International Travel

The line at the border crossing wasn't long; nor was my wait. The guard at the checkpoint asked me a few questions. Then, smiling, she wished me a pleasant trip, and waved me on into Niagara Falls, Ontario.

I drove to the Skylon Tower. At a height of 775 feet, it affords a view matched only by aircraft. I took the elevator to the observation area, and then had an excellent lunch in the revolving restaurant. The exchange rate makes Canada's attractions a bargain.

Canada and the United States share Niagara Falls—Canada's Horseshoe Falls being the most spectacular—and each of the Great Lakes except Michigan. The sharing is one of many symbolic ties between the two countries. The natural beauty of the Falls is superb on both sides. Also notable is the commercialism. Some observers think even that the Canadian side outdoes the American in poor taste.

The region is rich in history. As a destination of the Underground Railroad, perhaps 40,000 slaves managed to escape from the American South and make the hazardous journey across the international boundary into Canada. Niagara's "Freedom Trail" keeps the memory alive.

The first European to view the Falls was probably Father Louis Hennepin of France, but there had been inhabitants nearby for at some two millennia, the Senecas and their ancestors. Once the French arrived, they established a military presence at the mouth of the river.

In 1759, during the French and Indian War, the British replaced the French by capturing their fort, and the British themselves in 1796 withdrew to Fort George, in Canada. By 1805, Americans had settled the area, but the War of 1812 and American advances attracted the British back for bloody conflict. The worst battle was fought to a draw, the Battle of Lundy's Lane on the 25th of July 1814. On Christmas Eve of that year, negotiators signed the Treaty of Ghent. When the Senate ratified it the following February, it ended the war, established the boundary between Niagara Falls, New York and Niagara Falls, Ontario, and set the scene for growth and development. Steamboats arrived in the 1820s, the Erie Canal in 1825, and the railroad in the 1840s. But the region was still remote for motorists when the TRIH encouraged automobile traffic in the 1920s. It is anything but remote today.

For hiking, cycling, and the like, the Lake Ontario Waterfront Trail extends from Niagara for over 200 miles. Nearby is "Carolinian Canada," a region that displays plants and animals characteristic of lands far to the south, and boasting more rare species of flora and fauna than anywhere else in the country. The Niagara Escarpment is one of two United Nations World Biosphere reserves in the area. It's a ridge of rocky outcroppings beginning at Queenston, just north of Niagara Falls, and providing a winding touch of wilderness for some 450 miles through Canada's most heavily populated area.

Heading along the TR Trail, the most obvious difference across the border is that Canada uses the metric system. Speed signs are in kilometers, causing trouble for unwary Americans who fail to pay attention, thinking that "60" means 60 miles per hour rather than about 36.

I found Canadian sources ready to provide information, often with enthusiasm. The Ontario Ministry of Culture, Tourism and Recreation was especially helpful. The Ministry's Photographic Records Archivist, Mary Ledwell, went out of her way to assist me in uncovering forgotten information about Ontario's early roads, including the TR Highway, and to provide me with photocopies of important documents. The Central Ontario branch of the Canadian Automobile Association was equally helpful. Its Secretary for Public Relations, Helen Papadimitriou, searched the Association's records and supplied me with photocopies of anything I requested. She also graciously tolerated my many phone calls.

I knew the route. The earliest TRIH map that I had found showed the Highway crossing Ontario from Niagara to Hamilton, and on what came to be King's Highway 2 from Hamilton, Brantford, Woodstock, Ingersoll, London, Chatham, Tilbury, and Windsor—with other settlements in between.

It was fortunate that I had found maps, because A. W. Tracy's weak grasp of geography could have been confusing. Writing of the "international feature of the Highway," the TR Highway Association's secretary said erroneously (in the Montana Guide) that the road traveled "along the north shore of Lake Ontario." That shore is far distant. The relatively short drive from Niagara to Hamilton does go along Lake Ontario, but on its southern shore. That brief jaunt is the only part of the TR Highway in Ontario that runs along a lakeshore, except for a short stretch along Lake St. Clair at the other end of the province. From Hamilton on west the route leaves Lake Ontario behind. Hamilton is at the Lake's western end.

Some other early descriptions had the route re-entering the United States in Michigan at Sault St. Marie, or at Port Huron. Possibly there actually were alternate routes for a short time before things settled down, but maps early became consistent, and traced the Highway across Ontario from Niagara to Detroit.

In Canada, as in the United States, road building began as primarily a provincial responsibility. Ontario completed its first major hard-surfaced road in 1915, not long after the Lincoln Highway got underway. Ontario's pioneer road went from Toronto to Hamilton. John Jakle in his excellent study of North American travel, *The Tourist*, pointed out that Ontario generally concentrated on linking its cities with those in the States.

This policy worked to the benefit of the TR Highway, but there were problems. Perhaps it was to be expected that a memorial to an American president would find smoother going in the U.S. than in another country, however friendly.

Apparently there had never been any regular TR marker posts along the Highway in Canada. A brief article in 1921 on page one of the *New York Times* (14 April) announced that Ontario's Minister of Public Works, "F. C. Biggs" (identified in Canadian sources as S. C. Biggs) had refused the request of the Theodore Roosevelt International Highway Association to paint "TR" on posts along the route in the province. The *Times* said that the Canadian division of the Association would repeat its request, but I could find no follow-up article on the subject.

In 1922, the chairman of the International Joint Commission, Charles A. McGrath, received a letter from E. L. Turrell, of Duluth, field manager for the TR Highway Association, requesting him to intercede with the Ministry. The letter is in the Archives of Ontario's Ministry of Culture, Tourism, and Recreation. Turrell described the Highway as "extending from Portland, Maine to Portland, Oregon," and wrote that "it traverses lower Ontario from Niagara Falls over the main provincial Highway through St. Catharines, Hamilton, Brantford and London to Windsor, offering," he said, "a connecting link between eastern and western Canada."

Turrell mentioned that the previous August there had been a meeting "at the Royal Connaught, Hamilton, Ontario, at which representatives from every city along the Highway in Ontario were present. A provincial association was formed to become part of our International Association," he said, "and Russel T. Kelley of Hamilton was elected President and Col. F. M. Hasey, secretary. He noted that Minister Biggs had been present at the meeting, and "heard the full details of our program." The Minister "was in full accord with the exception of the marking of the Highway. In view of his objection we agreed to eliminate the 'TR' from our road signs and instead, post a large sign board at Niagara Falls and Windsor explaining the omission to the tourists."

He said that Biggs approved these signs, but "he was somewhat uncertain as to whether it would be advisable to integrate the marking of a red and white band on this part of the Highway inasmuch as his Department was working out a comprehensive system of marking of the entire Province." Later, Turrell said, his group was informed that Biggs had decided favorably, but that the Highway Association's own provincial president, Russel Kelley, was concerned about public opinion. Turrell thought Kelley's concerns were groundless. Based on the experience at the Hamilton meeting, he reported, the proponents expected enthusiastic cooperation from all the cities along the route, so he urged action.

On the 18th of December, McGrath did send Turrell's letter to Deputy Minister McLean, and asked what McLean might do to help. McGrath knew little about the issue, he said, but remarked that Theodore Roosevelt was "a pretty good name to conjure with." This letter remains in the Archives, but there is no record that there was any action, or even that McGrath received a reply.

Archival records do reveal that Tracy wrote on behalf of the TR Highway Association to the Ministry three times in 1922 to request information about the Highway in Ontario (March 14, April 6, and October 28). He asked how many miles of the TR Highway had been hard surfaced in 1921, how many had been graveled, and also how many had been graded; he asked the total mileage of work on the Highway completed that year, the cost of such work, the number of miles planned for 1922 with cost estimates for that work, and the number of miles yet to be built to complete Ontario's portion of the Highway. He apparently received no answer to any of the letters.

Regardless of what Biggs may have agreed to in the Hamilton meeting, there is no record that would indicate any cooperation from the provincial government with the TR Highway Association. The only remaining references are the requests to the government—without replies—and two reports, the *Times* article and Turrell's letter, mentioning that Biggs had refused to permit the TR markings. That's all. I could find no other information anywhere about markings in Ontario.

The initial stretch in Ontario is heavily traveled and appears primarily industrial. Little, if anything, remains from older, simpler times when the TR Trail went from Niagara to Queenston, St. David's, St. Catharines, Jordan, Vineland, Beamsville, Grimsby, Winona, Fruitland, and on to Hamilton. Even though I intended to avoid multi-lane throughways, the QEW freeway between Niagara and Hamilton now covers much of the original route. So for a time I was in heavy traffic. Monster trucks predominated— some had 36 wheels; some even had more than 40. I was driving through a rich fruit-growing area, but from my vantage point on the freeway I could see little of it. Even here there were compensations. After I passed St. Catharines, which is just a few miles from Niagara, the views of Lake Ontario were the best yet, and they remained so on to the Port of Hamilton.

At Hamilton, I connected with King's Highway 2, and turned west toward Ancaster. I was only on the freeway for a short time, but it felt too long. I found myself sympathizing with Steinbeck, who wrote that freeways were wonderful for rapid transportation of goods and people, but not for seeing the countryside. "You are bound to the wheel and your eyes to the car ahead and the rear-view mirror for the car behind and the side mirror for the car or truck about to pass, and at the same time you must read all the signs for fear you may miss some instruction or orders." Now that I was back on the real road, I was no longer part of a racing clump of vehicles. I was traveling, rather than just driving.

Ancaster is a pleasant suburb. On its outskirts, one of the black, silhouette figures such as I had seen in Mooers, New York stood prominently on a residential lawn. After Ancaster, I was beyond the congestion that stretches from Niagara around the end of Lake Ontario.

Of course I was outside the United States, but I noticed that I'd begun to *feel* being in another country. With the possible exception of Australia, Canada differs less from the United States than any other land. Anglophone Canada, at any rate, feels more like America than it does Europe, and yet it feels more European than anywhere in the U.S.

Just beyond Brantford, I found that a segment of King's Highway 2 had become Bryant Road 201. Shortly thereafter it changed to Route 5. A nearby expressway paralleled King's Highway 2 and its re-numbered sections. That expressway not only diverted traffic away from the road that had stretched from Michigan clear across Ontario since the 1920s, but had stolen its identity as well.

An article in *Canadian Motorist* for January 1919—the month before planning began in the States for the TR Highway—laid out the route for what was to become the King's Highway. "The route," is said, "as stated by Hon. Mr. Macdiarmid [Finlay Macdiarmid, Ontario Minister of Public Works and Highways], will run from Hamilton to Brantford, to Woodstock, to Ingersoll to London. This will establish a through provincial highway from Ottawa to London and from Niagara Falls to the connecting point at Hamilton." The article said "the only section needed to give Ontario a highway running from Quebec to the American boundary is the section from London to Windsor." That section was operational by 1921. All of this, the article said, was to be "a concrete fact after years of campaigning by the Ontario Motor League."

Until April of 1997, tracing the TR route from Hamilton across Ontario only meant following King's Highway 2. Since then, it requires keeping track of several changes where route 2 has become a county road. The changes became effective that year on April Fool's Day.

King's Highway 2 still exists, at least for now, but its identity as an uninterrupted cross-country road does not. Still, as with the TRIH itself, whatever it may be called the roadway remains. Canada maintains its roads very well, especially well in view of its harsh winters. Driving the course of the TRIH is as rewarding as ever. One of those rewards suddenly came into view in the form of Paris, Ontario.

The landscape had become progressively hilly, almost mountainous, by the time I reached Paris. I saw that it was a beautiful village nestled into the surrounding and especially picturesque hills. The streets were clean, and the houses a crisp white with bits of color. The architecture, the hills, the layout, and the pace—in short, the atmosphere—all gave the impression of some out-of-the way corner of Europe.

When I proceeded west, I was startled to see coming toward me a pickup truck decorated with a Confederate flag. The truck wasn't from the States; at least it had an Ontario tag. Was the driver a transplanted rebel, or a Canadian with a romantic attachment to a dramatic time in America's history? Was he a political extremist who was using the emblem as a racist statement? Did he merely find it aesthetically pleasing? I suppose such little mysteries are what help make of life a fascinating journey.

The road passed through a series of small communities: Falkland, Gobles, Creditville, and Eastwood, and the larger town of Woodstock. I followed the original TR route, which departed from what had again become Highway 2; it looped briefly south to Beachville and Ingersoll, and then on to Thamesford and returned once more to Highway 2. Before I arrived at London, the road again had changed numbers. It had become Bryant County 102, but entering London it again was King's Highway 2.

London was my resting place for the evening. Portland was about 800 miles behind me. Given road conditions in the 1920s, and the demands of early cars and tires for constant maintenance, not many of the early travelers could have kept pace with me. My guess, though, is that I was covering about the same distance as the fastest of my early predecessors—that is, of the tourists, not those attempting speed records.

I stopped at a Travelodge, and was amazed. For what I would have paid in the States for a budget motel—one, in fact, in less than the best location—I had a luxury suite.

It was large, clean, quiet, well-appointed, and had a superb view. There were two telephones and two televisions, one each in the sitting room and the bedroom. They received channels from both Canada and the States. The bathroom was large. There was a sink and mirror in an alcove outside it, and another sink and mirror inside. I had never seen a Travelodge so upscale, nor had I ever had such luxurious accommodations for a budget price. (Not every motel in London, of course, is like the Travelodge.)

I awoke early the next morning. It had turned very chilly. There were heavy clouds. A brisk, raw wind made it feel even colder than it was, but the weather did not diminish the city's charms.

London offers beautiful parks, monuments, and public buildings. It also has something else unusual, coal-black squirrels. Its architecture includes varied styles. Well-maintained and restored Victorian mansions are a treat. The city of 326,000 is compact, but it has ethnic neighborhoods with inviting groceries, cafes, and an array of deli foods. With some inevitable exceptions, there is an evident concern for visual appeal throughout.

One especially interesting sight is "People and the City," described as "a monument for the City of London." It is a two dimensional sculpture (cut from flat metal) in the center of the city, commemorating specific figures who were prominent in local development. In addition to early settlers, it contains some fifty representative men and women from the arts, religion, politics and law, research, education, sports and entertainment, business, labor, and other fields.

Sculpture, London, Ontario

The figures are small, except for that of John Graves Simcoe, who founded the city at a fork on the Thames River, now at the west end of the downtown core. The River long was the source of barge traffic that was the city's economic basis. Now it serves as scenery and for recreation. London itself has grown into a center for art and music, and along with museums it boasts an active theatre district in the midst of appealing restaurants. The city also is the site of the University of Western Ontario, and of the London Health Sciences Centre.

At the public library, Glen Curnoe, the London Room Librarian, helped in any way possible. He located many archival records, but found nothing that mentioned the TRIH. He pulled out copies of a 1946 map of Ontario that also showed portions of New York. It enabled me to check on possible relocations of roads, but it didn't show one with a TR designation. Mr. Curnoe photocopied the map for me—not easily done because of its size.

I paid him for the copies, and he accepted the payment with thanks and apologies. It seems that the provincial government had cut back so much on funding that resources for all public services, including the Library, were strained to the breaking point.

As much as I enjoyed London, it was time to be going. William Saroyan at one time had stayed in the same city. In *Short Drive, Sweet Chariot*, (1966), he brazenly recounted his departure from a London hotel. "Before leaving the room," he wrote, "I gathered together the usual souvenirs—stationery, ashtray, a small towel, and the *Don't Disturb* sign." Jackle said that in the early years of auto travel "such theft was epidemic. For example, in 1936, New York City's Hotel Pennsylvania reported 2,000 face towels and 300 bath towels stolen each month." I checked out, and was careful, as always, not to follow Saroyan's example.

King's Highway 2—the TRIH—enters London from the east on Dundas, and proceeds west on York. It jogs onto Horton, and turns left on Wharncliffe. The route is well-marked, and the signs are easy to follow. Driving in London is effortless. I carried with me good feelings about the city, as I drove away from it on Highway 2.

Unfortunately, not everyone has found Ontario as congenial as I did. Least Heat Moon groused about a two hundred fifty-mile haul across the province with rain all the way—he was driving east. He complained about getting lost (I don't know how) in London and even in Brantford.

Worse than mere ill humor was another experience in London, one causing legitimate outrage. The provincial government can act with a very heavy hand (its highly authoritarian measures in the 1930s after the birth of the Dionne Quintuplets being perhaps the most notorious example). On November 3, 1997, a few months after I stayed in what I found to be a charming city, *Newsweek* reported on a ruined honeymoon there.

Jeanette Little, a Canadian newlywed, stayed at London's Westin Hotel the same night as Ontario's Premier Mike Harris and his Tory caucus. Citing "security reasons," the Premier's forces routed her and her husband out of "their nuptial bed" at 3:00 in the morning. "People have asked if we ever consummated our marriage," she reported. "We were too damn mad to."

Occasionally, an early map of the TRIH showed its course between London and Windsor as dropping south and zigzagging between what came to be route 2 and the shore of Lake Erie. I tried that route and found it difficult to navigate. Except for an occasional view of Lake Erie, it was not worth the extra effort. I retraced my path to the old route 2, which in any case seems to have been the more authentic.

I drove by precise, well-kept farms, villages, and residences. The primary impression they gave was prosperity. The terrain was flat—flatter than the undulation of Kansas. There was no doubt that I was in prairie country. The traffic was light, but steady. I was definitely outside any urban area, but there was no feeling of isolation.

At a wooded area near the SKA-NAH-DOHT Iroquoian Village, a sign informed me that off to the right was the Longwoods Road Conservation Area. There were picnic facilities, but all was shabby, with an air of neglect that was especially jarring in contrast to the general air of prosperity in the province. Another sign explained why. It said: "Provincial funding to conservation areas has been eliminated. . . ." The damage from austerity budgets affects our northern neighbor also.

Turning back onto Highway 2, I turned on the radio. With timing that almost was eerie, I heard: "Our plan reduces the size of government, and permits Ontarians to keep more of their hard-earned money."

Continuing across the prairie, I drove through Melbourne and looked up to watch two tiny birds defending themselves, chasing a hawk. The hawk flapped its wings desperately, while its two tormentors continually dive-bombed it from above, pecking its head. Finally, it flew out of range and the tiny victors returned in courageous triumph.

This is a rather common sight. Size and power do not always prevail. One or more small birds frequently will chase a hawk, crow, or some other fearsome and much larger predator. No doubt the hawk would see it differently, but it seems rather reassuring.

Even well into rural areas the houses were frequent. Their design was traditional. In fact, I had rarely seen a contemporary house since setting out from Maine. The houses on this part of the Ontario Prairie are quite tall in relation to their length and width, as if an ordinary farm house had managed to grow taller, without adding girth. It looked as though they were reaching for the sky, seeking relief—giving relief—from the flatness that seemed to be everywhere, stretching from horizon to horizon.

Something up ahead on the left side of the highway came into view. It was a historical monument, but it didn't pertain to TR. Far from it; the subject of the monument predated his presidency by almost a century. It was the 1814 Battle of the Longwoods, during the War of 1812.

A plaque in English and French matter-of-factly remembered "Battle Hill," and the British dead. Consciousness of the War of 1812 appears to be at least as strong in southwestern Ontario as in the States around Lake Champlain and the St. Lawrence River.

I drove on into the center of Wardsville, probably the largest country town since London. The Wardsville Library on my left was a very small brick building with a peaked roof and a bit of gingerbread. The tall windows were arched. Except for the satellite dish above, it suggested a tiny church, or perhaps a doll house. A library of any size is always reassuring.

Next to it was Wardsville hardware—at least that's what the large sign across the front of the building above the windows and door said. Jutting out above that sign though, and across the sidewalk, was a different sign, "Wardsville café." Both signs were modern, and each appeared equally new.

I went inside to check it out, and if the place had ever been a hardware store, I couldn't tell it. I was in a cafe, and a good one.

After lunch, I found myself generally following the course of the Thames River. Just beyond Wardsville, I came upon another historical site, this one commemorating Old Fairfield Village.

At its center is a short gravel street. The stark white of the street's gravel rectangle in the middle of an expanse of bright green grass, when viewed from a distance gives it the appearance of a landing strip. It is the Avenue of Peace.

At one end of the Avenue is a monument. Its plaque, in French and English, memorializes the Village's destruction by invading American forces following the Battle of the Thames, 5 October 1813. Alongside the street is a directory a reddish wooden sign, describing the area, in English only. To its left are three flag poles, one each with the flags of Canada, the United States, and the United Kingdom. To its right is a cabin.

At the opposite end of the street from the monument is a sign, also solely in English:

AVENUE OF PEACE
COMMEMORATES THE LONG PERIOD OF PEACE BETWEEN CANADA &
THE UNITED STATES from 1814 to the present time.

Americans rarely think of American troops as being marauders. Except perhaps in connection with the Civil War, we tend to think of our forces as being defensive (we no longer have a Department of War, but rather a Department of the Army within a Department of *Defense*). Our monuments—again except for those relating to the Civil War—reflect this.

So this site should give an interesting bit of perspective to visitors from the States. I couldn't discuss it with anyone, let alone talk about my journey. There was no one in sight, and the highway was deserted in both directions.

I took my solitude with me, and continued southwest across Ontario to Thamesville. I found it to be a clean little community with a dignified town hall. The tall spire that adorns it holds a clock beneath a peaked bell tower. Below the clock on all sides of the square spire was what appeared to be a balcony. It reminded me of a crow's nest on a ship's mast.

The road took me next to Louisville, a tiny settlement. Beyond Louisville is Chatham. After so many places of just a few houses, it seemed almost to be a city. A sign said, "Number 2 to be removed April 1, 1997," but it was out-of-date—the first

Library, Wardsville, Ontario

of April had come and gone. There were people everywhere, and also construction with an unmarked detour. I found my way through with little difficulty, and crossed the Thames. The King's Highway 2 road signs had a 2 in the middle of a shield-like shape with a crown on top; newer signs reflecting the reduction in status have a different logo, with no crown. These signs, too, were changed on April 1.

Proceeding southwest, I came to Tilbury. At that point the road reverts to a due west direction, or even slightly to the north. On the outskirts of Windsor I drove for a brief time along the coast of Lake St. Clair, and saw again one of the black silhouette cutout figures that I had first seen in Mooers, New York.

Windsor is a true city with a population of some 290,000, and is the home of Windsor University. The French settled the city in 1749, but a great influx of American loyalists fled there after the American Revolution and gave it an English character. It is the only Canadian city south of an American city. At the American border, one looks south from Detroit into Windsor.

Detroit is America's automobile capital, and Windsor performs the same service for Canada. Many Detroit auto companies have built plants here across the border. Commercial relations between the two countries have made Windsor Canada's major crossing into the United States.

Windsor sits on the Detroit River, and is in the midst of a rich agricultural area. In fact, the city is full of flowering trees so lush that I thought more of the South than of Canada. Still, it is heavily industrialized. The TRIH enters the city on Cabana Road East, and turns right on Huron Church Road where it proceeds to the international border.

There were huge lines of trucks waiting, but fortunately separate lines for cars sped me along. Original travelers on the Roosevelt Highway would have taken a ferry across to Detroit, but by the early 1920s, the Ambassador Bridge was in place. I used the bridge to drive back into the United States.

Chapter Seven

The Varied Michigans

Detroit, the only true metropolis on the TR route, lay before me as I crossed over the Detroit River returning to the U.S. on the Ambassador Bridge. When the bridge first opened, on November 11, 1929 (Armistice Day), there was such enthusiasm that thousands of people refused to wait for the opening ceremony and broke through the barriers, stampeding across. The unruly crowd somehow managed to avoid killing anyone, amazing onlookers.

Previously, crossing the river required a trip by ferry, except for railroad passengers—trains had used a railroad tunnel since 1909. It took a half-century or so of planning, negotiating, and pleading before there could be a bridge. Strenuous opposition from the ferry companies was a major reason for the long delay, but eventually boats simply could not keep up with the volume of traffic.

Joseph Bower, one of the prime organizers of the bridge project, came up with the name. "I thought of the bridge as an ambassador between two countries, so that's what I called it," he explained, rejecting the suggestion from the bridge's board of directors that he name it the Bower Bridge. Bower said that he wanted it to "symbolize the visible expression of friendship of two peoples with like ideas and ideals."

The Ambassador Bridge is obviously old, but it still is impressive. Others have overshadowed it—the Niagara suspension bridge, the Mackinac or the Golden Gate Bridges—and it was never "considered the architectural marvel the Brooklyn Bridge was. Even so," writes Philip Mason, "it holds a significant place in the history of suspension bridges. For a few years, it held the distinction of being the longest suspension bridge in the world; and it has always been the longest suspension bridge over international waters." Mason considered it important enough to devote an entire book to the subject, *The Ambassador Bridge*, (Wayne State University, 1987).

Although it has only about half the population that it had fifty years ago, Detroit remains among the ten largest U.S. cities (just barely, however; in 2000 it ranked tenth). It is the premier city in a maritime state that sits on four of the five Great Lakes (every one except Ontario). Among the fifty states only Alaska has a shoreline greater than Michigan's 3,288 miles.

Crossing the bridge I was between two Great Lakes, but both were too far away to see. Lake St. Clair—a great lake, but not a Great Lake—was to my right, filled through the St. Clair River by water from one of the real Greats, Lake Huron, forty-one miles beyond it. Lake St. Clair drains through the Detroit River into Lake Erie, off to my left.

Re-entering the United States was even simpler than entering Canada had been. I was asked about citizenship and purchases—U.S. and none—and waived on through. Obviously, this was before 9/11.

Detroit is an old city. Control has passed back and forth among the French, British, and Americans. Although it was incorporated in 1815, it began as a fur-trading outpost over a century earlier, in 1701. The founder was French, Antoine de la Mothe Cadillac. The British seized control in 1760, and managed to hang on to it during Pontiac's Rebellion three years later. Following Jay's Treaty of 1796, control passed to Americans, but during the War of 1812 the territorial governor, William Hull, surrendered it back to Britain. When Admiral Oliver Hazard Perry became an American hero by winning the Battle of Lake Erie in 1813 ("We have met the enemy and they are ours!") American control of Detroit finally became permanent.

Despite its frenetic activity, the city continues to have an old feel about it—also an odd feel. I can't improve on the half-century-old comments in Henry Alsberg's *American Guide*. "In the absence of subway or elevated, traffic streams through congested streets." Detroit's population came from all parts of the world, it said, and was "predominantly serious," which "gives aspect of grim automation to city life," and contributes to the city's "tremendous, restless vitality."

There now are freeways, but traffic still does stream through congested streets, and the local vitality does remain tremendous and restless. "Grim automation" sounds somewhat dated, but continues to describe the city scene—and I would guess the city unseen as well.

The ethnic diversity also persists. Residents say that Detroit has the country's largest Arab population. Whatever the mix, it combines with the city's vitality to create an unmistakably American air. My jaunt through Ontario had been brief, but it was enough to make me especially sensitive to national character. The intangible quality that I found in New England and across New York, in coastal and inland areas, in cities and the countryside, I experienced also in this energetic and unforgiving metropolis with its links to Canada and to the sea. It is an atmosphere unique to—and everywhere in—this country, binding it together whatever its differences.

In common with any large city, Detroit has crime but also much to offer, including a rich cultural life. The Detroit symphony and the Cranbrook Academy of Art are renowned, and the Detroit Institute of Arts has enormous holdings, including one of the most extensive collections of American art in existence.

One of the most interesting attractions—certainly in relation to the history of ground transportation—is the Henry Ford Museum in Dearborn (Dearborn is just southwest of Detroit, still in the metropolitan area). The Museum is one of the world's greatest resources for automotive history, but it has nothing about the TRIH.

A huge fire in 1805 destroyed almost everything in Detroit. The city fought back to become—with all its troubles—one of America's great cities. It began anew on a pattern by Pierre L'Enfant, with intersecting streets similar to those he designed for Washington, D. C.

The architecture around Grand Circus Park and elsewhere is worth taking time to enjoy, and the Eastern Farmers' Market on Russell Street and the Detroit Historical Museum on Woodward both deserve a visit. Belle Isle is a thousand-acre island in the Detroit River. In 1879 the city purchased it to become a public park. It now has a children's zoo, the Whitcomb Conservatory, an aquarium, the Livingston Lighthouse, and the Dossin Great Lakes Museum.

Appropriately for the international motor capital, Detroit claims America's first mile of concrete highway, and most authorities agree. They point to a section of Woodward Avenue between Six Mile and Seven Mile Roads—completed on the fourth of July 1909—as the pioneer effort. Now and then someone asserts that one or another stretch of concrete elsewhere was earlier, but Woodward Avenue's status seems secure.

That mile became a part of the TRIH. TR travelers came back into the United States via Detroit at first on ferries, and later over the bridge. In either case, their route went along Woodward Avenue, which connects with the Detroit-Windsor Tunnel and is just east of the terminus of the Ambassador Bridge. The Highway proceeded out of Detroit along Woodward.

After U.S. highways became numbered, the TRIH through Detroit and northward to Flint and Saginaw became U.S. 10. That part of the route also was part of the "Dixie Highway," which included several alternative routes below Detroit heading into the Deep South.

The Interstate system caused many highways to be re-numbered and re-located, U.S. 10 among them; it no longer goes to Detroit. Not for many years has U.S. 10 come anywhere near the city, but I saw one of the old US 10 shield markers still in place somewhere downtown, not far from the border crossing. The Lodge Freeway is State (but not U.S.) Highway 10. What I saw was definitely a sign for the federal highway, a ghost from the past.

I must thank Dr. LeRoy Barnett, Archivist for the Michigan Historical Center in the Michigan Department of State. He supplied me with a map of Detroit city streets showing the location of U.S. 10 when it went through the city. That verified the location of the TR Trail.

On my way northwest through Detroit, I stopped at a service station to fill the truck's tanks. As I paid the attendant, I glanced outside and saw a couple of young men standing near the truck, looking it over, obviously noting the license tag. The truck was locked, and my computer was out-of-sight, but the gear in the back may have been tempting.

I hurriedly completed the transaction. The kids ambled toward the side of the building.

"Thanks," I said, and went out casually, but not wasting any time.

A beat-up old car sat around the side of the station. I could see only its hood peeking around the corner of the building. It was a large Detroit product. One of the kids had sat on the front bumper. The other was standing in front of it, lighting a cigarette.

The one with the cigarette fell in behind me as I walked briskly to the truck.

"Howya like Detroit?" he asked.

"Fine I guess," I said, "but I can't tell much, I'm just passing through."

I didn't stop as I answered, but quickly unlocked the door, jumped in, and slammed it behind me.

"Where're ya headed?" I heard as I closed the door. I waved, and drove off.

A half block back the old car was pulling out of the station, wheels spinning as it turned into the street. It came in my direction. As it drew nearer I could see the two kids from the station inside.

I was alert, but thought it was probably nothing. Traffic was heavy, so what could they do? Even if they wanted to, they couldn't force the truck off the road in that car. If somehow they managed it, they didn't seem especially formidable. I was prepared for a confrontation. Surprisingly (and irrationally) I almost looked forward to a bit of excitement to add to the experience. I was thinking (again, irrationally) that I needed to supplement my morning workouts, which were almost the only exercise I had been getting.

The sudden thought that they might have guns brought me back to earth rather quickly. It pays to be careful in today's gun-crazy society.

"I'm too old for this crap anyway," I decided, remembering loved ones and obligations. Instead of heading back to Woodward, I swerved onto the Lodge Freeway.

They pulled onto the Freeway behind me. I moved into the left lane. They followed. I let them draw nearer, then stomped on the gas. The truck leaped ahead, far faster than their wreck could accelerate.

But they tried, filling the lane behind them with black clouds as their racing engine poured out exhaust.

As I neared the next exit, I stayed in the left lane and slowed slightly.

The distance between us closed.

There was traffic in all lanes, but suddenly there was an opening and I saw my chance. I accelerated hard, cutting across the lanes to speed down into the off ramp.

I caused a wave of angry drivers. Horns blared. Fingers darted skyward.

I didn't blame them.

Still, I had plenty of space. No one even had to hit the brakes, so the maneuver was safe enough, even if it was highly annoying. Equally important: it worked.

No one followed. They couldn't change lanes fast enough to get over until they were well beyond the exit.

I was relieved to have no one—kids or cops—on my tail.

I retraced my steps back to Woodward, and continued on the old route of the TRIH, out of Detroit.

Good-bye, Motor City.

What had been the TRIH and later became U.S. 10, just beyond Detroit now becomes Interstate 75. The Interstate follows essentially the old route on toward Flint. Flint, on the Flint River, early in the century came to share a reputation with Detroit as an automotive center. Before that it was the "vehicle city," with firms producing carts and wagons.

Fur traders were established in the area before the 1820s, and a ferry service and tavern soon attracted settlers. Lumbering helped the village's economy. In 1903, the Flint Wagon Works merged with the Buick Motor Company, and established the city's automotive identity.

This was before there were any roads in Michigan that made automobiles practical. The state's constitution of 1850 had actually forbidden the state to spend any money on roads, leaving them entirely to local jurisdictions, often tiny ones. One popular road surface was sand, unsuitable for automobiles. Construction and maintenance usually meant local residents scraping and filling with hand tools. Since they could cut down trees to make way for roads, but couldn't remove the stumps, many roads were full of stumps, some quite high.

Thanks to diligent work by Horatio S. Earle, a turn-of-the-century advocate for good Michigan roads, the people in 1905 finally amended the Michigan Constitution to authorize state funding. Technological innovations in road building and pressure from motorists and the auto industry encouraged the Good Roads movement, and Earle became the state's first highway commissioner. The conditions were finally set for serious attention to roads, which meant that the new auto industry could blossom. That, in turn, meant that Flint, like Detroit, could thrive as never before—at least for a time.

It also meant that the way was clear in Michigan for the TRIH. The Detroit *News* on 25 March 1923 discussed the transcontinental route, and announced, that the "well-marked highway [stood] complete, with the exception of two short stretches, in Upper Michigan and Roosevelt Pass in Montana." It gave credit to Detroit backers for their efforts, especially to World War I hero Captain Eddie Rickenbacker, vice president of the TR International Highway Association. The article said that the TRIH was a "living memorial" to the late president, and that he would have approved of it, "heartily."

So that I could duplicate the early route as nearly as possible, I took Interstate 475 into Flint, and got off onto State Highway 54. On 54, I worked my way through town, and northwest back to I 75 and US 23. I found my way by comparing current routes through Flint with those on Michigan maps from the 1940s. The basic streets remain, although the numbers are different.

At Saginaw, I left I 75 and U.S. 23 to take State Highway 13 through Bay City. I was following the original route of U.S. 23, which was the TR Highway. The old U.S. 10 had veered off to the northwest at Saginaw. I didn't get any closer to Michigan's "thumb" than Bay City.

Sitting on the Saginaw River a few miles from Saginaw, Bay City is Michigan's second-largest port, after Detroit. It still is an industrial center, but I saw it as basically a quiet town, with some nice areas. Center Avenue, for example, boasts a number of mansions reflecting nineteenth-century lumber fortunes. The city is so situated that driving straight through offers no water views, but there is a three-mile trail along the river, and there are dockside businesses, including restaurants.

The Bay County Historical Museum is located in a former meeting hall where Bull-Moose Progressives met in connection with TR's presidential campaign in 1912. Some people locally believe that the Bull-Moose Party "originated" there, although in reality it sprang up almost spontaneously in many places when the Republicans denied Roosevelt the nomination. The mayor of Bay City, a dentist named Roy O. Woodruff, was a notable Bull-Moose success that year. He won election as a Bull Moose Progressive to the U.S. House of Representatives, and stayed in office for 34 years.

I followed Michigan 13 north around Saginaw Bay to Standish, where I turned right on U.S. 23, which had departed from the Interstate. Although traffic still was heavy, I had passed almost abruptly from a crowded and urbanized part of Michigan into a peaceful section of small towns.

Michigan is known for its three distinct areas. The southern half of the Lower Peninsula has the large cities, extensive farms, and huge factories that include more than one hundred automotive plants, and over half the state's population. The northern portion of that peninsula is sharply different, with forests and resort areas in addition to the small towns. The Upper Peninsula is another region entirely. Each of Michigan's three parts is supposed to have a distinct culture and geography. So far, the description had been absolutely accurate.

In just a few minutes I came to Omer, which proudly proclaims itself to be "Michigan's Smallest City." Almost before I knew it I had passed on through and come to Au Gres. Au Gres was not really on the TR Highway until the early 1930s, because the swampy terrain required the initial road to meander inland. It is another little rural town with a distinctively northern flavor. Forests surround the community, and the Au Gres River flows through it, but Au Gres is not quite on Lake Huron or on the Bay—not close enough for water views. I was sure there were campgrounds nearby but I was tired, so rather than hunt for one, I pulled in to a Best Western, the Pinewood Lodge.

After settling, I went out looking for local color and a good restaurant. A small sign I hadn't seen before drew my attention and directed me to the Point Au Gres Hotel. Following the sign's arrow, I started down a back road. Soon it became a dusty back road. For a couple of minutes, I wondered if I were on the right track. Then, really just a short distance from Au Gres, I saw something that reminded me of a rum-runner's hideaway. There it was, looking as if it were right out of the 1920s.

The Hotel was not opulent, but it provided a quiet and inviting seclusion. The restaurant offered panoramic views of the Lake and Bay. My fantasy of rum-running in the 1920s was somewhat off the mark, although there are some shady elements in its past. Legend has it that Leonard Booth, a wealthy bookie from Detroit who had turned state's evidence against Detroit's numbers racket, built it in 1938 as a gambling house and northern hideaway for his friends and associates. Unable to buy off the local law, he abandoned his original plans for a gambling den, and in 1939 opened it as a hotel and restaurant. In 1946 Ernie Lambert and Earl Gary bought the property.

In 1967, Lambert and Gary split up their partnership, and the property. Lambert operated the hotel for some years, selling it in 1975. By that time, there was little left but

View from Point Au Gres Hotel, Au Gres, Michigan

the building itself. It was run down. The new owner converted it to living quarters and no longer operated it as a hotel.

In 1980, Bob and Bib Jennings bought the property. Over the next decade they carefully restored it, and the hotel was re-born. The pier and a heated outdoor pool and spa were among their additions.

[Footnote: A few months later, I tried to make arrangements to return for a vacation to show off my discovery to my wife. When I telephoned the Hotel for reservations, giving a three-month lead time, I discovered to my regret that the Point Au Gres Hotel is no more. Once again, it has become a private residence.]

The next morning I was sitting in my motel's breakfast room talking with a retired couple, Jim and Marva Dorr of Lincoln, Michigan. The Dorrs are dedicated travelers, and had driven from Michigan to Seattle on old roads. Much of the distance they followed the TRIH, and even knew a bit about the Highway's history.

Traveling, they said, kept them young. Jim had a suggestion. He said the first thing he did when he went somewhere was to go to a barbershop. "You might try it," he recommended. "You get all kinds of information. I go there and always find the good fishing holes."

Some eight miles above Au Gres, I came upon a spectacular view of Lake Huron and the mouth of Saginaw Bay. It was the beginning of a rustic area of waterfront and woodland homes, tasteful subdivisions, beautiful forests, and even golf courses. A short distance before Tawas City (which is clustered with Tawas Bay and East Tawas) stood another of the silhouette figures.

In Tawas City, I called Neil Thornton, a local historian. I left a message on his machine. I assumed that would be futile, since as yet I had no cell phone and there was no way for him to return a call, and I would be in town only briefly. Just in case, I told him I would try again before I left.

Then I went to the Iosco County Historical Museum, which is located in an impressive house built in 1903 by the president of the Detroit and Mackinaw Railroad, James D. Hawks. It was closed, but a woman inside saw me and came to the door. When I explained my trip, she invited me in to speak with a group of women who were preparing a quilting exhibit.

As I left, I thought to ask about Neil Thornton, and told the woman escorting me out that I hadn't been able to reach him.

"Oh," she said, "he wouldn't be home now, he's at his bookstore downtown."

I readily found "The Booknook" on Newman Street. Neil and his wife Cathy greeted me warmly. They didn't recall the TR Highway—they think of the road as the Dixie Highway, another of Carl Fisher's named highways, a north-south road with several alternate routes—but Neil said he'd check his archives, which included a number of travel magazines from the 1920s. Nothing came of the search, but he did know that U.S. 23 had been Michigan 16, and before that was Michigan 10.

He is a prolific author of histories relating to the Tawas area, Iosco County, and the Lake Huron shoreline, and is the major authority for anyone studying the region. I purchased a couple of his titles—autographed.

No More Horses! is a 1990 history of automobile traffic through the county. It was here where I learned of the difficulties of road building in the marshy area before the 1930s. On page 99 Thornton includes a quotation from the Tawas *Herald*, in 1928. For my purposes, this alone would have been worth the modest price of the book. "A map of this road (old US-23) from Tawasville (at the intersection of Plank and Hemlock Roads) to Oscoda," it said, "looks as if an effort had been made to take the tourist in every direction on the compass and lose him if possible; and it is true that hundreds of tourists every year are hopelessly lost trying to follow the twists and turns of US-23 between these two points. Hardly a day passes during the summer that many cars are not turned back from the Huron Shore, the cemetery road, or Tawas Lake because the reasoning tourist refuses to go in the opposite direction from which he is traveling. This stretch of road is about 23 miles long and has 27 turns on which there are a number of fatal and expensive accidents every season."

Oscoda was the next town, beyond Tawas Point and Au Sable Point. Maps as late as 1948 showed a village of Au Sable just before Oscoda, but it is not on current maps. If it still exists, it must be so tiny that I missed it.

Between Oscoda and Harrisville, the road really opens up to dramatic seascapes. In this area I again saw black squirrels. They seemed to me to be the same as the ones I had seen in London. Beyond Harrisville, I took a little side trip, turning off the road a few miles to see the Sturgeon Point Lighthouse. It now is a museum.

Back on U.S. 23 I drove through the Mackinaw State Forest, through hilly country. For the first time I began to see references to Paul Bunyan, the legendary subject of

Sturgeon Point Lighthouse, Michigan

American folklore and tall tales. The northern timber country, especially from Michigan westward, celebrates the gargantuan lumberjack and his blue ox, Babe, whose horns measured "forty-two ax handles and a plug of tobacco" from tip to tip.

Another indication of the distinct regional variations in Michigan is language. New England has its own recognized speech. Upper New York, with its often French-tinged tones was different, and the standard American urban Midwest of Detroit was different still.

One mile south of Alpena, a sign designates the location of the 45th parallel, halfway between the equator and the North Pole. The road is built up above the marshy landscape—there was water with reeds on both sides. As I crossed the parallel, a white swan flew low overhead.

In Alpena, I met with Bill Speer, Editor and Publisher of the Alpena *News*. He agreed to run a piece seeking information about the Highway, but uncovered nothing about it in the newspaper's files. He referred me to Roger Mendel, Director of the Alpena Library, who in turn referred me to one of the librarians, Lori Grunet. Ms Grunet was very helpful, not only locating useful materials, but duplicating them free of charge. The most valuable of these was *Making Michigan Move* (1992), a history of the state's highways, and of its Department of Transportation (which published the booklet).

Before leaving Alpena, I admired some of its stately old houses, and then stopped at a diner. I asked the young waitress what she would recommend.

"Well," she said, "this area is known for potato pancakes."

I hadn't known that, but took her advice. If they were famous, I could see why. I recommend them.

I had known of another claim to fame, a claim that no one would recommend: shipping disasters. Alpena is situated on Lake Huron's Thunder Bay, which is full of islands and rocky shoals. The nearby Thunder Bay Underwater Preserve contains some eighty shipwrecks.

The road north of Alpena cuts across the point, away from Lake Huron, and the scenery shifts to impressive dunes, stately birches, and rugged quarries. The shoreline is to the left, rather than the right when it passes along Long Lake for a few miles. Somewhat off the route, around Grand Lake, is Presque Isle, with the Old Presque Isle Lighthouse and Museum. This road, though, reflects a change in routing. Until at least the 1940s, U.S. 23 went west from Alpena, turning north at Lachine where it continued, unpaved, to Rogers City, west from there—still unpaved—past Onaway, where, at Afton, it turned north (it now is Michigan 33). At that point, at least by 1939, it was paved on into Cheboygan, and from there to Mackinaw City.

Near Rogers City is "The World's Largest Limestone Quarry." A few miles beyond the town is the Forty-Mile Point and Lighthouse. This lighthouse is a white square tower, rather stubby and not especially high. At its top is an octagonal glassed portion in the middle of a square balcony atop the tower itself, which is attached to a large, brick, two-story house, with two brick chimneys.

On the lighthouse grounds is what appears to be a replica—complete with peeling paint—of the pilothouse of a Great Lakes steamer. It turned out to be a memorial commemorating the centennial (1886-1986) of the International Shipmasters' Association, the fraternal organization for the shipmasters. A large plaque explains that the Association traces its origin to the Port of Buffalo, where the death of the steamer "Boston's" first mate brought concern for his widow. The local masters and mates took up a collection for an endowment fund, and created a benevolent association, which spread throughout the Great Lakes in both Canada and the U.S.

The road between Rogers City and Cheboygan runs right along the water and offers especially beautiful views. Public authorities have made them easy to enjoy by providing many waterside rest stops. Beauty isn't something that springs readily to mind when you think of Cheboygan. It's an old port town, catering to hiking, camping and other outdoors activities. It has an interesting ambiance mixing rough seafaring traffic with (sometimes equally rough) devotees of hunting, fishing, and trapping.

From Cheboygan, the road hugs the water to the northern tip of the Lower Peninsula. Today it remains U.S. 23, and is easy to follow. In the very early years of the TRIH, though, it proceeded several miles inland because marshy terrain made road building along today's course, U.S. 23 following the coastline, too difficult. I drove both routes.

The inland path took me on Michigan 68 to Millersburg, a neat, beautiful, and very quiet village. Just beyond Onaway, I was startled to see a large metal head—it looked to be about half the size of a small car—placed in a field off to my left. I thought it might represent George Washington (in spite of a stark, modern, almost futuristic look) but I saw nothing to identify or explain it.

The next town was Tower. I stopped at a store and satisfied my curiosity. There was a sign, I was told—evidently I missed it. The Moran Iron Works cast the head and placed it there as part of a rotating exhibit. I was right—this one was George Washington.

Afton is slightly beyond the intersection with Michigan 33, and was on the original route. There is little remaining there, although it does still have a post office. Michigan 33 is the nearest road today to the original highway, so I proceeded north. On my right—certainly unexpected in this part of the country—was a bison ranch. I passed the ranch and Aloha State Park (that name seemed out of place too), and continued on through a woodsy, residential, area. I drove on into Cheboygan on Michigan 27, and reconnected with U.S. 23.

Beyond Cheboygan and right at the tip of the Lower Peninsula is Mackinaw City, a town heavily oriented toward tourism. Its atmosphere differs little from that existing wherever a local economy depends upon high-volume selling of overpriced but low-cost items to large numbers of people, who are merely passing through.

The motels are oriented to a wide variety of tastes and budgets. State historic parks, including Colonial Michilimackinac, Fort Mackinac, and Historic Mill Creek offer history lessons and replicas of 18th-century villages, arts, crafts, and military life. Each year a huge attraction is the lilac Festival.

The premier tourist attraction of the area undoubtedly is Mackinac Island, in Lake Huron just east of the straits, and between the two peninsulas. It is accessible by ferry from either Mackinaw City or St. Ignace. With several ferry companies, service is available most of the season nearly every half hour. Because of the crowds in Mackinaw City, those who opt for St. Ignace generally waste much less time standing in lines whether going or coming. The docks are attractive, with refreshments including espresso and cappuccino. At one time, visits during winter by sleigh over the frozen lake were common.

The first white visitors to the island probably were missionaries in the 17th century. From 1781 until Jay's Treaty in 1796 it was the site of a British military outpost, Fort Michilimackinac (presumably "Big Turtle" in an Indian language). During the War of 1812 they again seized possession.

Automobiles are banned from the island. Because of this, its has probably the only public intersections in the country where there have never been auto accidents. Its Main Street reflects a turn-of-the-century ambiance, with horse-drawn carriages, bicycles, bed-and-breakfasts, and stately hotels. One, the Grand Hotel, considers itself to be so stately that it charges the hoi polloi a hefty fee merely to enter the lobby.

The rest of the Island extends a warm welcome. There are hiking trails and unusual rock formations. My favorite activity there is to rent a bicycle and ride around the island, a distance of eight miles, all of which have unobstructed views of the water. The bicycles come in all variations, including the old single-speed, balloon-tired, models that you peddle backward for braking. Those are all that are needed, even for couch potatoes, because the road is flat and unchallenging.

Fort Mackinac is a State Historic Park that operates solely on admission fees, with no funds from the state. It operates quite well, with enthusiastic guides providing tours. Among the Fort's attractions is a huge and beautiful chestnut tree. I had thought all mature chestnuts were extinct in America because of a severe blight a half century or so ago, but there is at least one left on Mackinac Island. Perhaps the isolation from the mainland protected it.

The Straits of Mackinac separate the Upper and Lower Peninsulas by connecting Lake Huron with Lake Michigan. They were such a barrier that residents of the UP tended from the beginning to be culturally and politically more oriented to the neighboring Wisconsin, to which the UP was attached, than to Michigan, from which it was separated. During the formative years of the TR Trail, the state had two Theodore Roosevelt Highway Associations, one for each peninsula. Until 1923, those who wished to cross the Straits in either direction, in the words of *Making Michigan Move*, "were at the mercy of operators of railroad ferries, who cared little whether they got the business or not." This included the earliest travelers on the TRIH.

In 1923, the government stepped in. Michigan's highway department purchased a dock at St. Ignace, rented railroad facilities at Mackinaw City, and on July 31 established public ferry service on a regular basis at reasonable rates. From then until 1957, crossings were by public ferry—that included all TR travelers during the entire existence of the TRIH as an identifiable entity. On the first of November 1957, the Mackinac Bridge opened, tying the two parts of the state together, and the state-operated ferry service ceased. With speedy, high-volume crossing available, the Upper Peninsula gradually became more oriented to the rest of the state, but the residents of the UP, or the "Yoopers," continue to maintain a distinct cultural identity.

I couldn't duplicate the TR travelers' ferry crossings, but I tried to imagine it as I drove across the five-mile bridge, one of the world's longest, to St. Ignace on the Upper Peninsula. It had begun to rain heavily. The wind was fierce, bringing warnings to cars and a ban on trailers and RVs. The heavy chop far below might have offered more fun than the smooth bridge surface, but I can't imagine any ferry operator braving the wind and waves. An early traveler would have had to wait. Modern crossing not only is more comfortable, but it enabled me to go on without delay.

St. Ignace is much more to my taste than Mackinaw City. There is as at least as much for the tourist—including boat tours, gift shops, maritime museums, and the like—but it retains an atmosphere of community. It is laid out to take advantage of the splendid views, rather than constantly drawing one's eye inward to shops.

The road enters town down a steep hill and around a sweeping curve, providing ever-shifting vistas, despite the downpour. I drove the length of the business district and back, and stopped at an old, crisply-restored, small hotel, the Boardwalk Inn. The long, narrow, three-story brick building has an attractive lobby with an open staircase and high ceilings. Its two upper floors have a corridor down the middle, and a row of rooms on either side. The second floor has a "Fireside Gathering Room" for guests. From the front, bright green awnings stand out against the rust-colored brick, with gleaming white trim. The three awnings on the lower level are dome-shaped, large over the door in the middle, and smaller over each window to either side. Above the three windows on the second floor one awning with rounded ends stretches the width of the building. Two eyebrow-like awnings stand at the top. The hotel offered me both comfort and character.

Early the next morning I headed out across the Upper Peninsula. I was back on U.S. 2, which, after ending where Vermont, New York, and Quebec meet, begins again at St. Ignace. It continues westward across the continent to Everett, Washington. From St. Ignace to Spokane it follows the TRIH.

For a time there apparently was a northern spur of the TRIH across the U. P., proceeding westward from Sault St. Marie and re-joining the route at Iron Mountain. I found mention of it only in a few Michigan newspapers (The Detroit *News*, March 25, 1923, and several issues of the Newberry *News*, including May 2, 1919, October 6, 1922) and in some very early sources. Quickly, though, the U. P. route seems to have settled on what was to become U. S. 2.

Some people think of U.S. 2 as the "Great Northern Road," because from Minnesota westward it parallels the tracks of the old Great Northern Railroad. U.S. 2 in Michigan, as in most places, is a two-lane road, but a good one. Before the Good Roads movement, the U.P. was so isolated and the roads were so poor that during much of the year dog sleds were the only method of travel possible in many places. No one would ever think of this highway as a former dog-sled trail.

This road brings views at least as dramatic as those of Lake Huron on the Lower Peninsula, but here they are of Lake Michigan. I passed Straits State Park, and drove on through Gros Cap. The St. Helena Islands added an even more exotic touch to the atmosphere.

A sight less exotic, but to outsiders also unusual, is Paul Bunyan Pasties. "Pasty" rhymes with "nasty," not "tasty." Pasties may be thought of as the national dish of the Upper Peninsula. They are small pies of meat and vegetables—recipes may vary, but beef with finely-chopped potatoes, onions, and turnips is traditional—enclosed in dough and baked. Cornish miners in the mid-nineteenth century carried them into the mines each morning in their pockets, where body heat would keep them warm (some sources say the miners warmed them in shovels placed over candles), and ate them for lunch. It still was early, barely beyond sunrise, and I bypassed Paul Bunyan's—even though it is in the *Guiness Book of World Records* for baking, in 1994, the largest pasty ever: 233 pounds.

Manistique Lighthouse, Michigan

Presently, the countryside became marshy. As I drove through the marshes and crossed a river, I remembered that the entire southeast corner of the Lower Peninsula had originally been so marshy that it discouraged settlement, and later made road building especially difficult. The UP not only was even more isolated, but it presented settlers with some of the same challenges they had faced in the lower part of the state.

There was very little traffic, but the many campgrounds and recreational areas were indications that the narrow road would be busy at the peak of the tourist season. At other times, though, travelers can do as I did, savoring the trip across the UP as though they were early adventurers on the TRIH.

For an extended distance high sand dunes rise near the highway. They are as dramatic as those on an ocean coast. Before pavement, travelers must have found the shifting sand to present a major obstacle. Even now, although human ingenuity can protect the roadway, the sand resists control. An especially eerie sight greeted me as I saw what at first seemed to be just another dune to the right of the road. Instead, it was a small motel—apparently abandoned, but actually only waiting for the beginning of the season to open—that was being consumed by the sand. The sand was swallowing it into a large dune, covering it up the sides and on to its roof.

You can't turn away for long and expect things to be the same when you look back. But that's always true.

After Brevort and Epoufette, tiny fishing villages, I came to the Blue Haven Restaurant, and stopped for breakfast. The building has an especially attractive interior of light wood, with high ceiling had exposed beams. I was seated by a huge window, and could look almost straight down. The restaurant sits on the edge of a bluff above Lake Michigan.

Just on the other side of the window was a bird feeder that was attracting many small, brilliant birds. I especially enjoyed the goldfinches, and the many small bright blue birds that I thought at first might be bluebirds. I was told when I asked that they were indigo buntings.

Resuming my journey well fed, I passed Hog Island Creek and watched geese feeding at Black River, I stopped at a historical marker at the northernmost point of Lake Michigan, the only one of the Great Lakes completely within the United States. The significance of the location dated to 1805 when Congress created the Territory of Michigan. The western boundary of the new territory would be the middle of "Lake Michigan to its northern extremity, and thence due north to the northern boundary of the United States." The Upper Peninsula west of that line was then Indiana Territory, but in 1818 Congress revised the borders, extending Michigan's boundary west to the Mississippi. Michigan then included all of the U.P., Wisconsin, and part of Minnesota.

U. S. 2 had evidently been straightened from its original course, because I came to "Old U.S. 2," a gravel road. I drove down it for a half mile where it crossed the new highway. It then continued on for another half mile at which point it joined the new route. Soon there was another Old U.S. 2, which I also followed. It was paved, and snaked along the current road for several miles.

Old US 2, Original TR Highway, Wisconsin

Manistique is the largest city between St. Ignace and Escanaba. It is near Indian Lake State Park, with lovely lakeside campsites, and Palms Book State Park, which is on the far side of Indian Lake. Palms Book has no camping, but it does have Kitch-iti-kipi—also called Big Springs—the largest spring in Michigan.

The weather was perfect: bright and cool. The parking area is well maintained with a park store, and the rangers are polite and helpful. A short walk through the forest brought me to a small glade. The spring is at the bottom of a lake, 200 feet across and forty feet deep. The surface of the water was uncommonly smooth.

I was the only person on the path at the side of the lake, but some half dozen others were standing on what appeared to be a dock on its other side. When I walked to the end of the path, I recognized that it wasn't a dock at all. Rather it was a massive, square, wooden raft with wooden railings. It was attached to a cable stretched across the water a few feet above the surface. The cable passed through a hole in a long, thick, wooden handle not attached to the raft. By moving the handle along the cable, then putting it at an angle so that it jammed against the cable, and pushing against it, the raft moved. Several people were on board. Two of the men were operating the handle and bringing the raft back to where I was standing.

Their progress was slow, but in perhaps five minutes it had arrived. The people getting off were chattering enthusiastically about the spring's beauty. As they left, I headed across the water alone.

The raft had two large square segments at its center that were open for viewing. The scene below me as I looked down through an opening at the depths is hard to describe. The color was a deep green, but it was absolutely clear. "Crystal" sprang to mind. It was appropriate, if a cliché. More descriptive, though, was "emerald." It was as though I were viewing an active, dynamic, world inside a liquid emerald.

Water was coursing up from the bottom at more than 10,000 gallons a minute, but the sand that it kept in motion looked like cloud formations—far down rather than far up—with movement as rapid as the most violent storm, but with no suggestion of violence. Fish passed by as if floating above the lighter green in darker green air. Sunken trees encrusted with lime cooperated with rocky outcroppings to create shapes that were grist for the mill of fantasy.

I had reached the far side of the lake, slowly. I decided that I had spent enough time away from the TR Trail, so I reversed the handle to return. To attain any speed required force. Vigorously pulling the handle, pushing it, and walking the length of the raft felt especially good after so much time on the road. I quickly returned to the beginning. I think that if others had not arrived to embark by the time I returned, I would have made another round trip. The experience at any rate had been well-rounded, both physically and mentally.

Back in Manistique I looked for anything that might be a remnant of the TRIH. There was a landmark that would be impossible to miss, a thick, quite phallic, tower. Next to the tower was a log cabin. Signs proclaimed the Schoolcraft County Historical Museum and Watertower. It sounded promising, but upon close inspection the promise was an illusion. Not only was everything padlocked, it was all boarded up and appeared to be abandoned. I found two other interesting sights: a fish house with gulls packed solidly all over the roof, and the Manistique Lighthouse. But there was nothing about the TR Highway.

Heading toward Escanaba, I saw a dead deer by the side of the road. I had seen a disturbing number of them, more than ever before, since I began the trip. There was a short strip of four-lane highway, and small towns had become somewhat more frequent. Often they displayed signs boasting of their high school athletic teams.

Urban America tends not to recognize how important public schools are to rural areas and small towns. They not only educate the children, but they also serve as focal points for much of the community's activity. In many ways, they actually define the community. Escanaba, for example, maintained signs proclaiming the town team to have been the 1991 state champions in pee wee hockey B, and—more than a decade and a half after the fact—announcing to the world (or at least to the traveler) that it was the home *in 1981* of the state class A football champions!

I am not being facetious, or criticizing Escanaba. Town after town across the country makes clear its devotion to the sports of their children. High school athletic programs concentrate local energies no less than professional teams do for cities—probably more so. Cities survive when they loose their teams, even if civic boosters cry loudly that they cannot. Small towns, on the other hand, often do fade into nothingness when they no longer have a high school, and its teams, with which to identify.

Between Escanaba and Iron Mountain logging trucks became frequent sights. Fortunately, the old days of underpowered trucks impeding traffic for miles behind while they creep up hills only to race down them, are generally gone. Trucks now tend to race up hills as well.

At Harris, just a few miles west of Escanaba, I entered the central time zone. I had come some 1,500 miles from Longfellow Square. Down the road lay the Vulcan Iron Mine offering tours. Then came Norway, with its Norway Spring spouting through a stone marker. Beyond that was a picturesque waterfall, and then Iron Mountain.

Iron Mountain's population of nearly 9,000 made it seem almost huge, considering where I had been. It has a daily newspaper, some good restaurants, a public library, and the Cornish Pump and Mining Museum, displaying the "World's Largest Steam-Driven Pumping Engine." Edwin C. Reynolds designed the huge pump, and the E. P. Allis Company of Milwaukee built it in 1890/91. It lifts "200 tons of water per minute," and its flywheel is 40 feet in diameter.

Another, eye-catcher is a rough stone, dark brown, two story building. It is Gleason's 1891 Club, a restaurant. The manager on duty, Steve Corey, welcomed me. He turned out to be a history buff, and said that the building was an old firehouse. He thought that his grandfather might have had some old maps that designated the TRIH in the area, but he was unable to locate them.

As Steve and I were talking, a customer at the bar overheard us mention a book about the Highway, and joined in. His name, he said, was Aaron Krantz.

"Ya' know somethin'?," he said. "That's *one* book I'm gonna have to read!"

Hardly had I left Iron Mountain, when U. S. 2 dipped briefly into Wisconsin. The woods were thick, the ground was marshy, and the pavement was especially smooth.

The Wisconsin incursion lasted for only a few miles, and the road turned north to head back into Michigan, and on to Crystal Falls.

Crystal Falls is a surprise. It is a beautiful, hilly town with a stunning court house that suggests a medieval castle. U. S. 2 turns west again in the middle of town, and heads across the state toward Iron River.

For most of the distance across the U.P., I had been in the Hiawatha National Forest. This western area was in the Ottawa National Forest, and the woods had become even more dense. It had begun to rain heavily, and fog was becoming heavy. I stopped in Iron River and bought some fruit, and some bread and cheese for sandwiches.

I pulled into a campground, and stretched the mattress and sleeping bag out in the back of the truck. I opened the screened windows for ventilation, and to discourage condensation. It had become cold, but the sleeping bag would ward off any chill.

The next morning, the rain continued, and the fog remained thick. The damp country was, to my surprise, mountainous. I had some food from the night before, but I was ready for some coffee. I didn't want to stand in the rain to heat the water, though, and I certainly wasn't going to light the camp stove inside the truck.

I went miles with no settlement. A stretch of Old U. S. 2 appeared off to my right, which I took. Although it was late spring, there was snow beside the road. I had passed some run down residences, but very few. There was no traffic. The road was paved, but very rough, with breaks everywhere. A deer ran across in front of me. The surroundings were even more marshy than before. Moss grew on the pavement, and grass stuck up through its breaks.

Head of George Washington, Field near Onaway, Michigan

The country was so isolated, that I was surprised to find "Rogers Bar." I pulled in, hoping to find some coffee, but it was closed. The road rejoined the current U. S. 2., but quickly jogged left onto "Old U. S. 2" again. The pavement had narrowed so greatly that it was barely wide enough for the truck, and it continued to be very rough. Another deer darted across, and yet another, as did rabbits, and even a mink.

Finally, it rejoined U. S. 2—at least I hoped it was U. S. 2. Miles passed with no road signs. The pavement was narrow and rough, but far better than Old U. S. 2. At last, after crossing Presque Isle River, I saw a U.S. 2 shield. At the same time, the pavement widened out and became smooth. The remaining miles through mountains in Michigan were uneventful, if beautiful, until I came to Ironwood, right on the border with Wisconsin. There I was to find coffee, excellent pastries, and reminiscences about local history. Ironwood was to prove to be a fine place to conclude my varied experiences in the varied Michigans—and it brought me a nice surprise.

Chapter Eight

Across Wisconsin

Ironwood is still in Michigan, but just barely. As I drove into town I watched for signs of Wisconsin. I assumed I would be spending little time there, because U. S. 2 darts across the northernmost part where the state is narrow. Of all the states on the TRIH, Wisconsin contains the shortest stretch except for Idaho's.

I forgot all about distances and state boundaries when a huge, blue, coffeepot attracted my attention. The big pot was a sign with yellow and red letters identifying "Bakes Coffee Cabin." Should it have been "Bake's," or was it possibly a local usage meaning bakery goods? Regardless, it sounded promising.

The small shop was immaculate, and the scents bore out the coffeepot sign's promise. I ordered coffee and a pastry, and introduced myself to the attendant, Paula Vermetti.

I explained what I was doing, and she telephoned her father. "He's lived here forever," she said, "and knows all about the old highways."

He arrived within five minutes, a lean man, vigorous in appearance, and introduced himself as Roy Puisto. Roy's eyes twinkled behind lightly-tinted glasses. He had been born in the area more than 70 years earlier.

There were still suggestions of the toughness that he had carried through varied careers. He hadn't stopped his education at high school. For a year and a half he had attended Ironwood's community college. He had been with Michigan's liquor control agency, had been a copper miner, and had worked on a Great Lakes ore boat.

He had watched the community change sharply along with his employment. The Highway changed as well.

"U. S. Steel back in 1947, '48, and '49 had a fleet of forty boats on the Great Lakes," he told me.

"Their own navy."

"That's right. Or maybe merchant marine."

He remembered U. S. 2 as an unpaved road, so his memory went back before 1940—my 1940 road map shows that the road was paved from Watersmeet, over 50 miles east of Ironwood to Ashland, nearly 40 miles west. The only unpaved stretches in the U.P. at that time were between Brevort and Engadine, and a 27-mile portion

Sign, Ironwood, Michigan

ending on the west with Watersmeet. In Wisconsin, the map shows the entire TRIH as paved except for some 31 miles between Ashland and Iron River.

Roy's memory was as keen as it was long. He told me of some of the old sections that, being unmarked, I had missed. The old route within Ironwood now is Business Route 2, which I had assumed—business routes today often follow the older routes that went directly through towns—but you can't be certain without checking. It went on to Ashland, Wisconsin, he said, running south of the current road.

"This area used to be completely devoted to mining," he told me. "There were so many tunnels under everything that it became dangerous, and they had to move houses. Right now there's a large crack in the high school building."

"Did they have to move many?"

"Half the town—but only the south side. The tunnels were all south of U. S. 2. They don't mine here anymore, though. You'd have to go down so deep these days to get it that it's cheaper to buy ore from Canada. This is ski country now."

I went back to Wakefield, as directed, and followed the old route of U. S. 2 by turning south at Wakefield's stoplight. The road went from Wakefield to Ramsay and Bessemer, close to the new route. I knew to go by the Post Office, and not to be confused when Mill Street changed to Ramsay Street. On U. S. 2 back into Ironwood, I discovered something I had overlooked on my way in.

Connecting with U.S. 2 is Roosevelt Street. A half block or so off to the right is a small shopping center, Roosevelt Plaza. I went into the first business, Angelo's Pizza.

Jim Cottier owned the shopping center as well as the pizza restaurant, and he was the one who had named it Roosevelt Plaza. He came up with the name, he told me, because it was on Roosevelt Street, and was on land where there had once been a Roosevelt School. The street took its name from the school—and the school had stood on the Roosevelt Highway.

A mining company originally owned the land, but ultimately had deeded it to the city. There was, however, a restriction. The deed contained a clause requiring the city forever to maintain a playground on the site. It provided that the land would revert to the company if the city failed to do so. For years after the school fell into disuse, a sliding board remained on the grounds to meet the letter of the provision.

Finally the city dismantled the old school and sold the land to the Cottier family for development. By that time, the old mining company had faded from existence. It had been consumed by a series of larger firms. To get a clear title, it was necessary to trace a path through a succession of mining companies.

Ultimately the search succeeded. The remaining company relieved the city of its playground responsibility, which freed the Cottiers to create Roosevelt Plaza. That meant that it freed them to preserve indirectly—and inadvertently—a remnant (or at least a hint of a memory) of the Theodore Roosevelt International Highway.

Ironwood itself is small, and many of its landmarks no longer exist. Fortunately, local preservationists have managed to save and maintain a few of its mansions and historically-important buildings, among them the 1893 Chicago and Northwestern railroad station—now the Old Depot Park—and the Ironwood Theater. The Carnegie Library dating from 1901 is still in use, and was the first Carnegie Library in Michigan.

The business route took me through town and across the Montreal River into Wisconsin. When I entered Wisconsin, I also entered Hurley, Ironwood's twin city. At one time some residents of Ironwood thought of it as the evil twin.

Hurley had been a wide-open town of bars and brothels that attracted miners, loggers, and the roughest of customers. A Wisconsin friend has said to me that when he was young the state had a saying about Hurley: it was "where highway 51 ends and the fun begins!" Much of the original rowdiness has been tamed and yuppiefied. It still has its taverns, but today vacationing travelers and cabin owners (in the summer), and skiers and snowmobilers (in winter), are more likely than miners and loggers to set the tone.

A historic walking tour still reveals mining implements at the Iron Nugget, railway history at the Iron Horse and Freddy's Old Time Saloon, and logging memorabilia at the Bank Club. The Mahogany Ridge, though, no longer fronts for bootleggers, and it has been years since sounds of raucous humor have delighted—and sights of raunchy burlesque dancers have titillated—patrons of the old Silver Dollar.

I drove on through Hurley toward Ashland, and saw the first dramatic welcome to Wisconsin's visitors. It was a truly eye-catching liquor store. To be accurate, the store itself is unremarkable, but not its sign, a huge twist-type corkscrew. The handle, or crosspiece, above the gigantic spiral, announces the store as the "CORKSCREW."

"Rough isolation" is a term often applied to this northern part of the state. It fits. The Gogebic Range is the narrow band of mountains or hills that extends from the U.P.

"The Corkscrew" West of Hurley, Wisconsin

here into Wisconsin. This part of the TRIH threaded its way through the old mining area, far from major population centers. Early miners often lived in caves or tunnels, giving Wisconsin its nickname, "The Badger State." The name came from the burrowing miners rather than from the burrowing animal. Still, even with the prominence of mining and manufacturing, timber and agriculture have been Wisconsin's most important economic activities.

The entire State is associated with water. The greater part of its boundaries are either rivers, or one of the Great Lakes—Michigan on the east and Superior on the north—and the state has more than 8,500 lakes of its own. They range in size downward from Lake Winnebago's 215 square miles. The state's name itself, according to a 1939 promotional booklet, *Your Vacation in Wisconsin,* "was evolved from an old Indian word meaning 'Gathering Waters'."

I had found that booklet in an antique store, and the Conservation Department did an unusually fine job in producing it. Someone, probably an unheralded civil servant, had a keen editorial eye. It is a small treasure chest of black-and-white photos, many of historical interest. Along with natural features such as hills and rock formations, forests, and waters they include views of roads, highways, and automobiles. To accompany these are pictures of monuments, and of the last remaining covered bridge in the state. There also are scenes of villages, homes, old cabins and stone cottages, and other interesting buildings. The photos came from many sources, including the Department's own Photographic Section and from the Wisconsin Department of Agriculture.

Jean Nicolet, who arrived in 1634, was probably the first European to see the area. He searched unsuccessfully for a northwest passage, and successfully for furs.

Other trappers and fur traders followed quickly, but Europeans weren't the only newcomers. Because of increasing pressure in the east from the colonists, Indian tribes such as the Ottawa and Huron invaded the area. They pushed the former residents, the Winnebago and the Kickapoo, farther west. The Ojibwe (older people and formal documents still tend to use the name Chippewa), a part of the Anishinaabe people, came in strength to displace their kindred Sioux. Only the Menominee remained in the area with relatively little disturbance.

In 1686, Nicholas Perrot claimed the region for France, but in 1763, the British took control. In 1783, Britain ceded the land to the United States, but retained strongholds. In 1787 the new American government acting under the Articles of Confederation passed the Northwest Ordinance, creating the Northwest Territory. Jay's Treaty, ratified in 1795, officially brought American control over British outposts as of 1796. The British nevertheless continued to dominate the fur trade, and seized control again for a time during the War of 1812. After the war, European countries no longer were a power in the area.

The Indians, though, were another matter. They remained powerful, and resentful of white intrusion. In 1818, the Wisconsin area was transferred administratively from the Illinois to the Michigan Territory. By the 1820s, the discovery of lead brought an influx of miners, and the tribal peoples continued their fierce resistance to new settlement. Not until the Blackhawk War of 1832 were they overwhelmed and eliminated as claimants. In 1836, Wisconsin was severed from Michigan, and made into a separate territory.

At first, there was little in the way of flag-waving patriotism. In fact, for some time there was strong sentiment against statehood. Residents, fearing strong government and taxes, on four separate occasions voted against statehood. Eventually, in 1848, Wisconsin did enter the Union as its 30th member. That also was the year the discovery of iron attracted another wave of miners.

Among those flocking to the new state were many German immigrants fleeing European unrest. They brought with them something quite rare in America—socialist traditions. These have remained a factor in Wisconsin politics ever since. The Germans also brought good beer and skill in brewing. Wisconsin would become known both for beer and for socialism—the one renowned, and the other (in the hope that it might go away) often not mentioned in polite company.

Evidence of German culture is obvious, and beer is only one factor. I saw nothing suggesting socialism, but I was there only briefly. In any case, Wisconsin socialism always stressed reform and democracy rather than the more dramatic and disruptive class struggle and revolution.

At the beginning of the twentieth century, Wisconsin was a spearhead of the Progressive movement. The "Wisconsin Idea" involved close cooperation between the University of Wisconsin, and the state's government. It led to pioneering social programs that were to become part of the fabric of American life, including old-age pensions, unemployment insurance, and the graduated income tax.

At mid-century, Wisconsin's progressive image became tarnished. The state's junior senator was Joseph McCarthy, whose reckless and unsupported charges of communism ruined many lives and inspired a new word: "McCarthyism." But Wisconsin politics should not be stereotyped. Milwaukee elected a socialist mayor at the same time that the state was electing McCarthy to the Senate. Also, the state's German population rebuffed McCarthy's early attempt to curry favor by criticizing American treatment of captured German war criminals following World War II. Wisconsin's citizens of German descent preferred to stay with the American mainstream.

Local culture reflects a strong Indian presence. The largest tribe in the area, the Ojibwe or Chippewa, has several bands and is among the largest in the country. In 1995, tribal members decided officially that they would continue to describe themselves as "American Indian" instead of the increasingly-common term "Native American." Many other tribal peoples in the region reportedly also prefer to be known as "Indian."

Not long after I entered the state, I became aware of cars bearing tribal, not state-issued, license tags. Such tags as "Menominee Nation," and "Fond du Lac Band of Lake Superior Chippewa," no longer are oddities there. In 1974, Minnesota's Red Lake Ojibwe became the first tribe to issue its own plates. After a court ruling upheld the tribal government's authority and prevented states from interfering, many Wisconsin tribes began to issue their own. The resulting diversity is evident on Wisconsin roads.

In 1998 a special commemorative stamp celebrated a century and a half of Wisconsin. The stamp reflects a calm country landscape and a barn, but the reaction greeting it was anything but calm. As the Washington *Post* reported on May 29, "Poor Wisconsin. It lobbies hard and gets an attractive stamp with a pastoral scene to celebrate its 150th year of statehood. But then the U. S. Postal Service prints a paltry 16 million of the stamps, enough to be sold only in Wisconsin and at the agency's 400 philatelic sales counters. It is the smallest printing run for a statehood stamp since the first statehood stamp was issued in 1935."

The *Post* said that Rep. F. James Sensenbrenner, Jr., a Wisconsin Republican and a long-time stamp collector, was "furious." It quoted him as saying the tiny issue was a "slap at the people of Wisconsin." He was "stunned," it said, when postal officials tried to convince him that a run of 102 million stamps for Utah's centennial the year before had been a money loser. Utah's stamp, and all other statehood stamps, had been sold nationally. Sensenbrenner said in a news release, "Even Bugs Bunny's commemorative stamp enjoyed a larger distribution [378 million] than Wisconsin's is set to receive." Whether in outrage or exasperation, he argued, "Wisconsin is more important to our nation's history and culture than a cartoon rabbit."

"Roosevelt Plaza" Ironwood, Michigan

Much of the morning had gone by while I had been exploring and retracing some of my path. At Saxon, the temperature dropped suddenly, and the sky became heavily overcast. Thick fog curled indolently on the land. When I entered the Bad River Indian Reservation, I had the obvious thought: it was aptly named.

NPR stations generally are clustered at the left end of the dial, so I hunted in the low numbers. I found public radio with a difference: WOJB, an Ojibwe station. It not only broadcast NPR news and other features, but an interesting mix of music, and Native American programming. All the way across Wisconsin—and in fact for some distance into Minnesota—I had my choice of several public radio stations. Wisconsin Public Radio has some of the most valuable offerings to be found on radio today.

I noted that the area was forested rather heavily, but generally not with the tall, majestic, trees that I tend to associate with the north woods. The active lumber industry had eliminated most of those.

I knew I was near Lake Superior, but had not seen the water. Then I arrived at Ashland, and before me was a splendid view of the largest of the Great Lakes—or actually of Chequamegon Bay. At that point the scene was not open water clear to the horizon as I expected. I should have checked the map—islands studded the deep blue. I was looking out toward the Apostle Islands National Lakeshore. The fog had lifted, and the overcast had lessened. An occasional ray of sunshine added to the beauty. I understood how even a state agency could draw on the poetic, as the unknown writer for the Conservation Department did in 1939 when its booklet said—in words that I would not try to improve—that "Lake Superior, a magnificent cool blue sea, swells and breaks against a bold and rockbound shore."

Ashland itself is a pretty town, seemingly rather slow-paced, with interesting architecture. A six-block section of Main Street is on the National Register of Historic Districts, and Chapple Avenue from U. S. 2 to 11th Street is full of Victorian mansions, many of which reflect loving restoration. One of the more interesting, the Wilmarth mansion, now houses the Ashland Historical Society Museum which reflects more than a century of local history.

The original integrity of design remains for all to see, and the sense of community that so many places have lost remains strong. The thriving downtown offers within easy walking distance various shops, a craft center, restaurants, bars, clothing stores, a classic old movie theater, florists, and a bakery. In short, the diverse mix of commerce, entertainment, and social connection cements diverse human elements into a coherent wholeness. It is America as America was—in the best of senses. The concessions to modernity, such as an excellent lakeshore drive, are tasteful and worthwhile additions.

I stopped for lunch at "The Depot," the city's 1889 Soo Line railroad station that now is restored and is on the Historical Register. It houses an upscale restaurant and the Railyard Pub. Because it was noon, I opted for the brewpub. It had the best food I had eaten thus far on my journey; pub food gets no better.

While I enjoyed my lunch, I also enjoyed reading about the legend of the Depot's ghost. As the tale had it, twenty-one year old Tommy O'Brien sold tickets and provided maintenance to the depot in the 1890s, when there were hundreds of trains arriving and departing daily. He and Katherine Sullivan, the blacksmith's daughter, fell in love. Her furious father sent Katherine away to keep her from this lowly young

"The Depot" Ashland, Wisconsin

man, whose mother worked as a cook in one of the local "resorts" (actually brothels). She sent a message to Tommy that she would return and they could elope, but the meddlesome stationmaster intercepted the note and informed the blacksmith. In a fury, he charged into the station and shot Tommy. As a doctor bent over the dying young man, the telegraph key clicked the somber message of a great train wreck—one in which Katherine also had been killed.

As legend has it, Tommy remains a presence. His ghost still cleans the station, waiting for a train that will never arrive.

From Ashland to Superior, U. S. 2 today is the same as the TRIH, generally straight and almost due west. There is a more scenic route, which heads north on state highway 13 along the shore of Lake Superior. It goes through Bayfield and skirts the Red Cliff Indian Reservation, then proceeds west through Cornucopia and Port Wing before rejoining U. S. 2. This is a digression from the TRIH, but much of the scenery—including six varied lighthouses—is worth the extra miles.

But the TRIH didn't veer north, and the more scenic route would have been impracticable in the 1920s. Only in the very best of weather would it have been passable. Various maps from different years in that decade show the T. R. Trail as having a surface of gravel, stone, shell, or sand-clay. The drive around the coast had a surface much less inviting than its scenery—only dirt or sand.

Proceeding west from Ashland along the old TRIH route, I passed Fish Creek, and ran into more fog. I took a stretch of "Old Highway 2" off to the left. It was a dirt road, which continued for a short distance not far from the current highway and then reconnected with it. I passed through another Iron River—the other was in Michigan—and continued on into Brule River State Forest.

The Brule River is a popular kayaking and trout-fishing stream, where Presidents Grant, Cleveland, Coolidge, Hoover, and Eisenhower came to fish. Local promoters seized on the obvious slogan, and it became the "River of Presidents." Calvin Coolidge actually located his summer White House in the area.

Within a few minutes I was in Superior. I had been in nearby Duluth many times, but never before in Superior. An observation area provides a view of Hog Island, beyond it of a barrier island, and then a panorama of the deep blue of Lake Superior. I felt a tinge of regret that I soon would be leaving the Great Lakes.

Superior is the county seat of Douglas County, named for the "Little Giant," Stephen A. Douglas, Abraham Lincoln's opponent in the Lincoln-Douglas debates. Douglas is best known today for his support of "popular sovereignty," a doctrine that the moral issues surrounding slavery didn't matter much; that it should be left to the voters of an area to decide whether to permit the "peculiar institution" or not.

In fairness, Douglas did personally oppose slavery. Still, even if it was expedience and not conviction that caused him to place majority rule over human rights, it now seems clear that the "little" was more appropriate than the "giant," at least regarding moral sensitivity. This was not so clear though, during the 1858 debates. Douglas won. The Illinois State Legislature (before there was a popular vote for U. S. senators) sent Douglas rather than Lincoln to the Senate, and Wisconsin named this county for him.

The Superior area is old in terms of human activity. Pierre Esprit Radisson and his brother-in-law, Médard Chouart Grossielliers, visited in 1661. Sioux and Ojibwe contested for supremacy throughout the region, and a thriving fur trade developed between native peoples and the incoming whites. But it was not until 1853 that the building of the first log cabin signaled the beginning of an American city. Superior was incorporated in 1883.

The city's geography enabled it to thrive. Located at the mouth of the St. Louis River on St. Louis Bay, Superior Bay, and Lake Superior itself, Superior was a natural point for both maritime and rail traffic. In contrast to Duluth across the Bay, it is flat. Three railroad stations remain, all from the early twentieth century: the Union Depot (now an antiques mall), The Northern Pacific Depot (now a senior citizens' center), and the Soo Line Depot.

Superior shares with Duluth the largest international harbor on the Great Lakes, the Twin Ports. According to the Army Corps of Engineers, the Twin Ports—at 2342 miles from the Atlantic Ocean—are the farthest inland seaports in the world. Despite the heartland location the Twin Ports serve about 200 foreign-flag vessels annually.

There are many boat tours and other tourist activities. The Fairlawn Mansion and Museum suggests how the Harbor View Parkway East—which is to say U. S. 2 and the TRIH—once looked. Now, all along the way instead of the imposing castles of lumber barons, there are ranch houses that have the look of the 1950s. The stately 1890 Victorian mansion is a remnant of a more gracious time (more gracious at least

Harbor, Superior, Wisconsin

for those who could afford it). Its builders, Martin and his wife Grace Emma Pattison, of course had money—lumber money, and a fortune from mining as well.

The house faces the waterfront, and houses the Douglas County Historical Society's museum. The Museum has no material on the TRIH, but it does have excellent permanent collections and temporary exhibits. Among its resources are a splendid collection of David W. Barry photographs of Plains Indians—especially early 1900s Dakotas, and a collection of portraits and biographies of local Ojibwe people, "The Ojibwe of Lake Superior."

Across the road toward the water is an especially attractive waterfront walk and drive. Right beside U. S. 2 there is a statue and monument to James Hill, of Great Northern Railroad fame. I took this as symbolic. From here on almost for the rest of its journey across the continent, the TRIH would parallel this great railway. Long before good western roads, the Great Northern cut, and then puffed, its way west, even across the Continental Divide, to the Pacific.

There now are two bridges across the Bay. The newer of the two, the Richard I. Bong Memorial Bridge, named for a World War Two flying ace, looms high over land and water. U.S. 2 now follows Belknap Street, and then turns right onto this Bridge, but this is not the original TRIH route.

The drive across the Bong Bridge is exhilarating. Even though much of the vista is industrial, the height, the varied bodies of water, and the two cities combine to produce some of the most striking views anywhere. The 1984 bridge itself is especially beautiful because of its graceful and flowing curves.

The older bridge, the Blatnik Interstate Bridge, was named for a U.S. Representative from Minnesota, and is closer to the route of the TRIH. It enters directly into downtown Duluth. In the 1950s, it became the first free bridge across the Bay, replacing the toll bridge that originally carried passengers on the TRIH, and then on U.S. 2, into Minnesota.

There had been a bridge across the Bay since 1897. On July 13th that year, 4,000 people gathered to celebrate its opening. At the time, according to Pat Maus of the Northeast Minnesota Historical Center, there were only ninety automobiles in the entire United States and the bridge collected a daily average in tolls of $12. So, although they had to pay a toll, TRIH travelers never were faced with a ferry crossing to go from Wisconsin to Minnesota.

My time in Wisconsin was brief, but enjoyable. As I entered another state, I continued to be impressed by the distinct character of each; also by the common features that tie them together into a whole. I had arrived in Duluth, the birthplace of the Theodore Roosevelt International Highway.

Chapter Nine

Duluth Through Minnesota

The Bong Bridge carries U.S. 2 into Duluth past what must be one of the most beautiful visitors' centers anywhere. The Thompson Hill Travel Information Center is a polished building that sits on a high ridge. It offers panoramic views of cities, hills, and water.

But travelers on the TRIH entered Duluth in the downtown area, rather than at the city's southwestern edge where U.S. 2 now goes. The bridge that carried the TRIH no longer is standing, and it had led a hard life. The steamer "Troy" hit and damaged it in 1906, a huge forest fire in 1918 burned its Duluth approach, and it suffered damage from shipping in 1924 and again in 1956.

Each time, though, it re-opened quickly. It continued to hold firm until its well-earned retirement on the 3rd of December 1961. The Blatnik Bridge had opened the day before as the first toll-free passage from Superior into Minnesota. The new free bridge triumphantly carried U.S. 2—also the route of the TRIH—until the highway was relocated to cross the water on the Bong Bridge so that it could bypass downtown Duluth. The new bridge, dedicated in 1984, also provides free passage.

Today the closest I could come to the original course was to depart Superior on the Blatnik Bridge, enter Duluth near the Seaway Port Terminal, continue on Garfield Avenue, take Michigan Avenue to the right, and veer off to the left on Mesaba Avenue, up the ridge to Skyline Parkway and Central Entrance (which becomes Minnesota Highway 53). A short distance later it was marked Industrial Road. At what remains of a village called Twig, I turned left on road 7, which is paved, but quite rough. Past the intersection of Minnesota 33, it became smoother. I Proceeded on to Culver (there no longer is a sign, merely a crossroad), turned left at Culver on road 8, and continued due west to Floodwood, where the route re-joins U.S. 2.

That original course of the TRIH, for some twenty or thirty miles out of Duluth, is several miles to the north of today's route. It not only connected Twig and Culver, but also the village of Alberg (no longer on the map), before going west to Floodwood.

Early in the life of the TRIH, and after the designation of U.S. 2, there was a change in the local route. U.S. 2 was relocated to proceed southwest through the city along Michigan Avenue, turning northwest at the city's outskirts to go through the town of Proctor. The newer route appeared on roadmaps in the 1930s and 1940s, and is similar to the path that U.S. 2 traces today. The primary difference is that today's highway bypasses Duluth's downtown.

Either route is authentic. Staying on the current U.S. 2 is certainly quicker. It is almost as colorful as the original path, although it bypasses some truly out-of-the-way countryside.

More important than the choice of a way west, though, is Duluth, itself. Any traveler who fails to experience a bit of this fine little city misses something wonderful

Almost any entry into Duluth is spectacular. Think of a thin sliver of a city spread for miles along a river bank, the edge of a bay, and the coast line of a great freshwater ocean. Then, imagine that city sweeping away from the water up the side of a high ridge—at the top of which is Skyline Parkway that extends 400 to 600 feet above the city for some thirty miles giving unparalleled views—and you have Duluth.

The city has a third bridge prominent in its skyline, one that boasts a reputation. The noted Aerial Lift Bridge is in Canal Park, which also includes the marine Museum, lighthouses, and a Lake Walk. Unlike the other bridges and contrary to some descriptions, the lift bridge does not go to Wisconsin. Instead it connects the mainland with Minnesota Point, a thin slice of an island or sand spit over six miles long, similar to a barrier island.

Built in 1905 as a tall structure, nearly 140 feet over the water to permit ship passage, it originally was a "transfer bridge." Passengers entered a gondola, suspended from the high cross beams, that moved from one bank to the other much like a horizontal elevator. In 1929 remodeling created the current "lift bridge." Traffic now drives across as with any bridge, and its roadway surface can be lifted to open the way for ships. It provides access to Minnesota Point for hiking, swimming, and picnicking and has made residential development practical on the island.

Throughout the city there are quite modest homes with views that rival those of the most exclusive estates that sell for fortunes in other parts of the U.S. It almost seems as though in Duluth the average house is on an elevated lot with an open view of Lake Superior. This splendid little city invites exaggerated praise—but I could never go so far as to say, as the *Theodore Roosevelt International Highway Magazine* did in April 1921, that Duluth has "the most wonderful climate in the world. Lake Superior serves as an effectual barrier against the cold blasts of winter and the hot winds of the west and south in the summer." The Lake does moderate Duluth's climate, but even so its winters can be fierce.

One thing that Duluth fails to offer, in addition to "the most wonderful climate in the world," is an abundance of hotel and motel accommodations. Finding a room can be frustrating. I wanted to spend a couple of nights to give me time to go over archival materials in the Public Library.

My preference was to stay at Fitger's, a marvelous hotel amidst a complex of shops and restaurants in a remodeled building that from the outside looks as if it still could be the brewery that it once was. The rooms are as comfortable as hotel rooms get. Even the smallest are spacious, and half of them look directly out over Lake Superior—the hotel is right on the Lake. Many have a wall of stone, part of the heavy old beautiful

Hillside Residential Area, Duluth, Minnesota

brewery walls, and they all provide a quiet luxury that in an unpretentious way equals almost anything I have found at home or abroad. The rates at Fitger's are above the general run of rates in smaller cities in the Midwest, but in New York, Washington, or San Francisco they would be less than budget class. I have stayed in a huge, suite-like, lakeside room at Fitger's for less than half the rate of a suite even in Duluth's own Holiday Inn (which admittedly is not underpriced).

Unfortunately, Fitger's was booked solid that evening, but I was not entirely out of luck. There was an opening for the following night, so I made a reservation.

Finally I located a vacancy for the night. It turned out to be a shabby room in a shabby motel, but I was glad to get it. It didn't cross my mind to check out local bed and breakfasts. Duluth has several superb ones, in old mansions, but they, too, probably were unavailable.

As for old mansions, Duluth has plenty to offer. Tycoons in lumber, shipping, and mining saw to that around the turn of the century. Notable among them was Chester Congdon. He arrived in 1891 and apparently had a so-so law practice, but was a wizard as a speculator. Within fifteen years he was second in wealth in Minnesota only to railroad magnate James J. Hill. Duluth has him to thank for Glensheen, the most grand residence, and the largest, in the city. The University of Minnesota now operates it as a historical estate.

Charles Duncan (the lumber baron who brought modern utilities to Duluth), the grain shipper George Barnum, Harry Dudley (a mining engineer), Charles Weiss (publisher of the Duluth *Herald*), department store owner Mathew Burrows, and Ellery Holliday (who made a fortune in real estate), were among those who left opulent mansions. Many of these deteriorated. Some became institutions, while others were chopped up into apartments.

The rest of the evening I explored Duluth and took special note of Leif Erickson Park, north of Fitger's. The great Viking's statue is there, courtesy of the Norwegian-American League which had it erected it in 1956. A plaque proudly proclaims Erickson to be "Discoverer of America, 1000 A.D."

In the other direction, at the westernmost end of the city close to the St. Louis River and Jay Cooke State Park, is the neighborhood of Fond du Lac. This oldest part of Duluth was originally an Ojibwe village. Then it became the site where John Jacob Astor opened his fur-trading post in 1817. Also in western Duluth is Morgan Park, originally a company town that U.S. Steel built in 1913. The steel plant is gone, the town became part of Duluth in 1942, and residents long ago bought the houses.

After my brief excursion, I picked up a copy of the Minneapolis *Star-Tribune* (the "*Strib*"), and retired to the motel to type up my notes. When I turned to *The Strib*, I discovered something unexpected: an extensive review of John Davidson's "Bully," a one-man show portraying Theodore Roosevelt. Mike Steele, identified as a "*Star Tribune* Staff Writer," wrote the review of Davidson's show, premiering then in St. Paul. Steele was taken with Davidson. I have since seen the show, and agree with Steele that Davidson "is obviously committed to this show," and that he "turns in nothing less than a virtuoso performance."

Steele came down hard on the script, though. Davidson revised it somewhat before I had the opportunity to see the show, so that first performance may have had some wrinkles later ironed out. They could hardly have been as pervasive as the review made them sound.

Steele's trouble seemed based in distaste for—and a misunderstanding of—TR. The review surely would have been less annoying if he had gone to the trouble of conducting a bit of research beyond the show's program notes. Steele wrote of Roosevelt as "promoting the era of the 'fair deal'." That would have made TR even more prescient than he was. Roosevelt did call his program the "*Square* Deal," but the "*Fair* Deal" was Harry Truman's program, decades later.

Steele's discomfort with Roosevelt's enthusiasm for hunting and for war is understandable, but the situation is not so simple, nor so heartless, as he portrayed it. However much TR relished hunting, as Davidson pointed out he did argue that it should be for food or for scientific purposes. He recognized that the weapon of choice ultimately would have to be the camera.

No one who knows the facts can question TR's commitment to conservation, or think of him as a "self-styled conservationist," as Steele did. TR outraged the leaders of his own Republican Party when he defied them to protect wildlife or to withdraw millions of acres of public land from development. President Clinton nearly a century later received bleats of protest from Utah when he moved to preserve an area that is large, but tiny by comparison.

Steele wrote of TR that "the fact that three of his four sons were killed in war makes him more proud than sad. Is there a problem here?"

Well, yes there is, but it is with Steele, who apparently relied upon the program notes for information rather than taking the trouble to read even one good biography.

The notes did provide a "Timeline of Theodore Roosevelt's Life (1858-1919)." Steele actually complained about this as being too much of a "history lesson," which may explain why he seems to have been disinclined to look further. The notes did say, "all four served in World War I. One son was killed, and two were wounded. The three surviving sons served in World War II. Two died while on active duty."

They did not, however, say that the latter two were killed (and Steele should have recognized that when the US entered the Second World War more than two decades had passed since TR's death). Of the four sons, Kermit committed suicide in 1943 (albeit while on active duty), Theodore, Jr., died of a heart attack in 1944 (also on active duty), and Archie died in 1979 of a stroke at the age of 85. Only one son, Quentin the youngest, died in action.

TR admitted that something in him "shut down" as a result—that he could not write about Quentin without breaking down. Acquaintances thereafter heard him mutter "poor Quenikins," as he stared vacantly into space. His favorite son's death devastated him, and there is strong reason to believe that it caused Roosevelt to question his own romantic view of war—a view that he well knew had been partly responsible for that death.

There was coldness here all right. It was, however, more in the review than in TR.

[Footnote—Audiences flocked to Davidson's performances and were highly enthusiastic. Booking agents were not; they doubted the show could possibly have an appeal. (Who was it again? FDR? Oh, another Roosevelt? Almost a century ago? You gotta be kidding me.) Instead of being another Hal Holbrook, with a "Mark Twain," that he played for decades, Davidson found it so difficult to get bookings that he soon had to retire this splendid show.]

In the morning, I continued my exploration. Fifth Street was inexcusably rough.

A milk truck was making home deliveries. I wondered if this might be the last place in the country where residents can pick up milk on their front steps.

There was ample evidence that Duluth was starving its public services. I should have expected it. The budget-cutting frenzy was sweeping this country, and had spilled over even into Ontario. In an austerity move, Duluth's Public Library had adopted restricted summer hours and was closed all weekend—the time when one would think a public library might be busiest. I have to say, though, that the building—long, low, modern, and resembling a Great Lakes ore boat—is very fine.

There were many vacant storefronts downtown, but any appearance of an economic downturn was deceiving. There was more going on than it seemed. Duluth's system of "skywalks"—covered walkways from building to building above the street to shield shoppers and employees from Duluth's harsh winters—hid a considerable amount of activity.

The downtown was very much alive, in contrast to the central areas of many American cities.

It's fashionable to scoff at revolving restaurants, but they usually give splendid views of a city. The round Marriott Hotel is perfectly shaped for the rotating restaurant on its top. In Duluth, with its remarkable scenery, it would have been a shame to miss it. I didn't. I enjoyed a splendid panorama of Lake Superior, and also of the high ridge on the other side of the city which gives Duluth its unique aspect. I can even recommend the food.

Back on the street level I found broken pavement again, probably a result of the severe winters, but the streets themselves were very well-laid out and most were wide. Many old Victorian mansions and red-stone gothic buildings remained. As a rule they seemed well-maintained. The air in general was of a stable, working-class town, with old, smaller, inexpensive houses predominating.

And yet there is an extensive cultural life and range of activities for a city of barely more than 85,000 residents. "The Depot," an 1892 railroad station, has become a national landmark that since 1977 has housed the St. Louis County Heritage and Arts Center. Among other cultural agencies, the complex includes the St. Louis County Historical Society, the Lake Superior Museum of Transportation (which operates a real streetcar and exhibits locomotives and rail cars), the Duluth Children's Museum, and the Duluth Art Institute.

The Institute offers an extensive Ojibwe exhibition, and has the largest collection of paintings and drawings of Indian life by the American genre painter Eastman Johnson. Patricia Condon Johnston has reproduced these in black and white and provided historical detail in her fine little volume, *Eastman Johnson's Lake Superior Indians*, available in the Museum Store.

The Performing Arts Wing houses the Depot Theater, where the Duluth Playhouse and the Minnesota Ballet perform. The Duluth-Superior Symphony Orchestra, also connected with The Depot, may be the only bi-state municipal orchestra in the country.

Duluth's newspaper is reasonably good, the range of television channels available on cable is far greater than in most cities, and the Public Library (despite its restricted

"Antiques" Rural Minnesota

hours) is excellent. There is some material relating to the TRIH, especially some contemporary newspaper items, but less than I had expected. I was able to find much more
in St. Paul at the Minnesota Historical Society, although Pat Maus of the Northeast
Minnesota Historical Center earlier had located some valuable items in Duluth for me.
Apparently, Edward J. Filiatrault, the primary originator of the Highway, left no papers. He was prominent enough to rate nearly five full pages in Walter Van Brunt's
standard 1921 history of Duluth and St. Louis County, but nothing in his biography
shed direct light on the TRIH.

It did, though, shed some light on Filiatrault. He obviously was a skillful organizer,
and he pointed his talents in many directions. One of those directions might now raise
some eyebrows—although those who find the Ashcroft-Gonzales-Cheney argument
persuasive would applaud it as being in keeping with the Patriot Act. According to Van
Brunt, Woodrow Wilson's Justice Department, early in World War One, secretly asked
Filiatrault to assist in "investigating pro-Germanism and all organizations or individ-
uals who were working against our Government." Within thirty days, Filiatrault had
organized a local arm of the American Protective League, which Van Brunt described
as "a secret service volunteer division of the Department of Justice."

The gushing biographer wrote that "the activities of the Duluth Division of the
American Protective League has [*sic*] gone down in history as being the premier organization as regards efficiency of any district in the United States." It cleared up
"more cases of pro-Germanism and sedition," caused the "greatest number of arrests,
and detentions," and the like. He wrote that the local unit of the APL had seven divisions, each of which had "a captain and lieutenant, and these were the only persons in
each division who knew the Chief's identity, he being known as C-1." Continuing the
clandestine pattern, division leaders also were kept uninformed as to the identities of
personnel and leaders of other divisions.

It seems to have worked, if Van Brunt was correct. He wrote in 1921 that "The Department of Justice today has a complete record of every person living in the Duluth
district who uttered words against the Government from April 1, 1917, until the Duluth division was disbanded under Federal instructions on February 1, 1919. This was
a contribution made by Mr. Filiatrault to the winning of the great war which has never
been made public."

It must have sounded better in those days of Woodrow Wilson and his attorney general, A. Mitchell Palmer. On the other hand, Palmer's and Wilson's successors in the
early twenty-first century—as they tap into the telephone and e-mail communications
of Americans—would be likely also to beam with pride at such a program.

Regardless, one must give Filiatrault his due. He undoubtedly made his mark in
many ways, especially in the good roads movement. His death at the age of 48
shocked the Theodore Roosevelt International Highway Association. His life ended in
November 1922 after a long illness.

Irving Grover, an attorney and accountant for the Association, eulogized Filiatrault
at its annual banquet on December 5, 1922. The Highway, Grover said, was among his
major achievements. "He was the first to recognize the great possibilities, the potential value of such a highway," Grover said. "Now that the missionaries have done their
work and the trail has been blazed, it is easy for us to see that this highway ranks

among the greatest transportation systems of the world." But, he said, it had not been so obvious when Filiatrault first conceived the idea.

I had uncovered street names in Maine, New York, and Michigan that were remnants of the TR Highway. I also had found current map indications in Vermont and New York of segments of the old route that still bore TR's name. I even had met many elderly people along the way who remembered the TRIH. Ironically, though, I could find no remnant of the Highway in Duluth—the city where the idea of a Theodore Roosevelt International Highway originated—nor could I locate anyone who remembered it. Nevertheless, Duluth itself, however small and overlooked it may be, is a gem.

To continue my journey, I departed Duluth and followed the current U.S. 2 through Proctor, which has a huge steam locomotive by the road to greet travelers. It displayed to them the kind of engine that would have powered their journeys before there was a TRIH. Beyond the tiny town of Munger, I found a section of the older highway, now St. Louis County 161. After a short distance on the dirt road I came to a barrier and had to return to the main highway. I went only a brief distance before I was able to take another short stretch of Old U.S. 2.

Soon I was driving through woods and (being in Minnesota) beside water. The state modestly proclaims itself the land of 10,000 lakes. Geographic descriptions say that actually they number around 12,000, or even more.

By this point in my journey, remnants of the relationship between the TRIH and the Great Northern Railroad from the Midwest across the continent had become clear. Railway tracks paralleled the highway, which sometimes crossed under them.

The St. Louis River makes a loop south of U.S. 2 and winds its way east toward Duluth and Lake Superior. Right at the edge of the Fond Du Lac Indian Reservation, shortly after a brief stretch of four-lane road, the highway crosses the river straight west on a substantial bridge. Before reaching the bridge, a sign indicates that off to the left is an access point to the river. The unpaved road looked as if it might have been the original highway, so I turned off onto it, and drove down to the water.

Two Minnesota Conservation Officers, Darrell Danielson and Shawn Johnson happened to be standing near the riverbank. Their truck was nearby. They were interested to learn about the TRIH, but neither had ever seen any sort of marker for it. They did say that the access road had been the old road which forded the river before there was a bridge, and they shared a detailed map of the county with me.

For some time as I proceeded on I encountered rough pavement. The old road snaked back and forth along the straight route that U.S. 2 now takes. Even the newer road seemed old because of the poor surface. According to the map I was driving through the Fond Du Lac Reservation, but I saw no indication of it. By the time I passed the village of Gowan, I had left the reservation behind.

The town of Floodwood sits on the Floodwood River. Its population, the sign said, was 534 and it had been founded in 1895. The TR Highway Association in its booklet for Minnesota described Floodwood around 1920 as being "a comparatively new town in

Mural on Bank, Mcintosh, Minnesota

a comparatively new community. The surrounding forest line," it said, "is slowly receding before the ax of the settler."

I often look for something rustic, and the Savannah Portage Restaurant and Bar immediately drew my attention. I like log buildings, and this was the genuine article. Inside, deer and wolf skins adorned the log walls, along with antlers and wildlife paintings. Elk, moose, and deer heads gazed at the patrons. Stuffed owls and ducks represented feathered creatures, while mounted fish made certain that water dwellers were included. A small black bear, mounted of course, stood to threaten the room. Rather than the clear air of the woods, though, the room was thick with tobacco smoke.

I sat in a booth reading the signs tacked on the walls while I ate lunch. Hand-lettered posters announced birthdays. One sign advertised "Genuine Moose Horn Etchings" from the Holly Tree Craftshop, on the premises. Another for the Holly tree Knife Shop promised personal service. "Have your hunting, fishing or household knives sharpened here," it said. "Drop them off before you dine and they will be ready for you when you're through."

The place was quiet. The patrons and my server were friendly and happy to chat, but that was all. As I had expected, no one there had heard of the TRIH.

I passed the towns of Swan River and Warba (population 100+), and continued westward, paralleling the railroad tracks, which at this point were to the right of the road. The area had been marshy for many miles.

The road surface of course no longer presents a challenge. It was far different for early travelers. As late as 1927, except for a few miles of pavement from Duluth west, maps listed the TRIH's road surface clear across Minnesota at best as "Gravel, stone, shell, or sand clay." For several miles around Bagley, it was simply dirt or sand.

Almost immediately after crossing the Prairie River and passing La Prairie (pop. 483), I came to Grand Rapids. All along the way I had noted that many towns in the Upper Midwest had murals on the sides of buildings. I enjoyed their variety, and often their ingenuity. Grand Rapids had them too. Scenes from the Wizard of Oz decorated the exterior walls of many of the city's shops. Then I remembered that Judy Garland—or Frances Gumm—came from Grand Rapids. There is a Judy Garland Museum alongside U.S. 2, complete with a miniature "yellow brick road."

One store immediately caught my eye. It was "Longrie's 'Old' Car Store (Next to Norwest Bank)."

This was no flea market. Everything was neatly displayed and catalogued. The store was immaculate, and its stock was extensive, and all original. It included magazines, artifacts, pictures, posters, maps, signs, accessories, auto and truck sales literature, toys, and more. I bought three road maps from the 1930s. One of Oregon, one of North Dakota, and another of several states along the western part of the route. What the store did not have was any item specifically pertaining to the TRIH.

As I crossed an old, picturesque bridge on the way through Grand Rapids, I turned on a Public Radio station. "Talk of the Nation" was on. The discussion was especially timely. It was with Tom Brosnahan, author of several of the Lonely Planet guidebooks.

I passed Ball Club—where the TR Highway Association's Minnesota booklet said around 1920 that "in a short while now it is expected that a graded and graveled highway will be ready." I then crossed the Mississippi River. It would be easy to miss. It may be the Mississippi, but it was closer to being a trickle than a river. You could ford it easily. Here in the far north, I was very near to its source, and there was nothing to suggest that it is one of the world's mightiest waterways.

Most of the forest lands I had driven through after reaching the Midwest were disappointing. Rather than the majestic old growth that I somehow had expected the trees were smaller and apparently relatively young. Extensive logging had made its mark. After all, the great trees that once carpeted the land, along with the abundance of iron ore, had probably been the greatest lure to settlers. As soon as I had passed the Mississippi, though, real forests began to replace the younger growth. It was satisfying to find woods that were more like what I imagined they would be, but they still were less lush than I had anticipated.

At the small settlement of Bena (population 147), at West Winnie Road I came upon one of the unique sights that America offers its travelers, sights especially that dot the landscape across the country on the TRIH. It was the Big Fish Supper Club. Extending some fifty feet or so out from the right side of the building as you face it is the shape of a huge fish complete with eyes and a large open mouth with fearsome teeth. You walk into the mouth, around and below the long teeth, to reach an entrance. Is this Kitsch? Of course, but it also is amusing, interesting, and clearly Americana.

More Americana sat across the road. It was a small house that looked as if it might have someone living in it. Covering an entire side of the building was a painting of a forest scene with a close-up view of a bird on a tree limb. Large letters proclaimed it to be "PARTRIDGE IN A PINE TREE."

I stopped only to take pictures on both sides of the TR Trail, and drove on west. I was in the Chippewa National Forest, and passed a lake on the left, and a rest area—the first on the TRIH in Minnesota. I went on through Cass Lake, where the Forest Service has an office and an Ojibwe powwow takes place each summer. Birdwatchers especially would enjoy the nesting site there for bald eagles.

The marshy land continued. The area seemed sparsely populated and rather wild. Before I reached Bemidji, the forest at last had become more lush, with a beautiful and exotic pattern of light and dark greens.

Bemidji dates from 1896, and is the home of Bemidji State University. The city's early years were noted more for hell-raising, though, than for education. As a lumber town, it was full not only of rooming houses and sawmills, but also saloons and brothels. In typical Minnesota fashion, the city of somewhat over 11,000 population has lived down its raucous past.

It now boasts neat, broad streets and well-kept homes. Along with many other small cities across America, Bemidji also has a well-maintained Carnegie Library building on the one hand, and an abandoned railroad station on the other. A newer depot now houses a restaurant. An interesting and rather stately courthouse reflects the community's status as a county seat.

The Business Loop is the original course of US 2, essentially the TRIH. It crosses Lake Bemidji and the Mississippi, and goes past a park in the business area—overseen since 1937 by a huge statue of Paul Bunyan and his blue ox, Babe. Bemidji's Bunyan

Paul Bunyan and Babe, Bemidji, Minnesota

statue supposedly was the world's first, but in the nearly three quarters of a century since Paul and Babe first stood up in Bemidji, they have seen fit to grace many other towns in logging areas with their presence.

And to all those commentators who are "imaginatively challenged," let it be said that the stalwart citizens of Bemidji have accepted the legend whole-heartedly: Babe is blue, all blue, and bright blue—not merely "blue-eyed" as some sober writers have said of Bunyan's massive bovine companion.

Near where Paul and Babe stand is a visitors' center and a small museum. The museum houses some "Bunyan memorabilia" and stuffed wildlife. The center—appropriately in view of its location on what was the transcontinental TR Trail—has a fireplace made with stones from each of the 48 states (Alaska and Hawaii became members of the Union after the fireplace was built). This was another of the constant reminders along the way of America's unity as a country.

Departing Bemidji, I continued my journey. Back on U.S. 2, I passed the local airport and found myself on divided highway, coursing straight through the countryside. I crossed the Clearwater River, which was rather narrow, and at Shevlin passed a turnoff to Lake Itasca, where the Mississippi River originates some twenty miles to the south of the TR Trail. I proceeded through Bagley and Lengby, passed lakes, marshes, meadows, distant forests, occasional remains of log cabins, and another rest area.

At Fosston I admired a mural gracing the entire side of a building downtown. It was highly colorful, and detailed the town's founding and history. I took it as reflecting not only a concern for local history, but also a strong sense of community. The town of some 1500 residents has a public golf course, which also serves a golf team (the Greyhounds) from the high school. Several groups who appeared to be of high-school age were playing.

Fosston has something else quite rare along the TR route in this part of Minnesota: a traffic light. The town's motto, "Fosston, Where the Plains Meet the Pines," prepares the traveler who drives through on the green light for the prairie to come. The surroundings become flatter than before, the trees retreat to mere clumps, and farms become more frequent.

I turned on the radio, and the best station I found was from Manitoba. Although there still were some small woods, it was clear that I was proceeding onto prairie. But this was not dry prairie. Lakes, streams, and rivers were all around.

At McIntosh, another mural entertains the TR traveler. It covers half the side of the First National Bank. The style was similar to that of the mural in Fosston, and each was detailed and colorful. The same artist could well have painted them both. The bank mural represented the history of the community, and identified the founder as A. J. McIntosh.

The divided highway continued on through prairie landscape. I passed the villages of Erskine (pop. 422), Mentor (which held a centennial in 1992), and Marcoux. Along the way there were remnants, much of which was debris, of the older days of mining.

Changing the radio to an NPR station, I heard an announcement of a flood meeting in Crookston. Just then I found the photo opportunity that I couldn't resist. I stopped

Moose Crossing, Western Minnesota

and took pictures of the roadside warning, the silhouette of a moose, that this was a MOOSE CROSSING.

Coming into Crookston, I found it to be more of a city than was common in northwestern Minnesota. Its population was listed as 8119, but it seemed large. No doubt this was because since I had left Duluth, all the settlements had been tiny except for Bemidji and Grand Rapids. Also, the University of Minnesota has a branch campus there.

Crookston looks to be old but well kept. It has interesting small-town architecture. Its appearance benefits from the Red Lake River, which is big, and meanders through town requiring numerous bridges.

The Polk County Historical Society Museum is a local attraction. It houses some nineteenth-century exhibits, and maintains replicas of a prairie school, a smithy, pioneer houses and churches, and a caboose. A large and impressive church dominates the center of the city. Its three spires reach high above an already high building. The center spire is the tallest, and each has a cross at its top. In my line of sight there were two other crosses, on peaks on the roof. I was surprised to find, though, that it isn't a church at all. It has become the "Skyline Hope Center." That could be one of several things, but it isn't any longer a church.

West of Crookston I had left the forests behind, and was definitely on the plains. A prairie bird ran across in front of the truck, and was several feet on the other side of the road before it took to the air. It was not a roadrunner, but reminded me of one. It was similar in shape and gait, but was black and brown and smaller.

Before arriving at the very tiny town of Fisher, I saw some modern windmills harnessing the energy of the prairie's steady winds. A guidebook had mentioned the Fisher Cafe. It sits a couple of blocks off the highway, near some railroad tracks and the town's water tower. I planned to eat there, but it had closed at 4:00. There was nothing else along the way before reaching the border city of East Grand Forks except huge farm implements along the highway.

When I reached East Grand Forks, the twin city of Grand Forks, North Dakota, I was unprepared for the extent of the enormous damage of the disastrous flood that had occurred only a week or so previously. I could only admire the courage of the people in both communities as I drove across the invisible line that separated Minnesota from North Dakota.

Chapter Ten

North Dakota Surprise

I had turned onto Business Route 2 expecting to follow the original TRIH path through East Grand Forks and Grand Forks, the one leaving Minnesota and the other entering North Dakota. Counting on a business route generally to follow the path of the old highway laid down before there was a desire to rush past and avoid cities rarely disappointed me. It didn't in this case. This was the route of the TR Trail.

The Grand Forks experience was startling. I had arrived hardly a week after one of the greatest natural disasters the country had ever experienced. On 18 April 1997 a huge flood from the Red River of the North surged through the city. Great fires followed, gutting much of the downtown and destroying landmarks. It required the largest evacuation of a city in American history until the tragedy of Hurricane Katrina devastated New Orleans in 2005. Evacuating Grand Forks involved removing more than 55,000 people.

Huge piles of debris still lined the streets. Branches and pieces of timber hung on the side of a bridge considerably above the water. Downtown buildings, including the offices and plant for the Grand Forks *Press-Herald*, were vacant.

The paper's staff had re-located temporarily to quarters in the Manvel School. There, undaunted, they continued publishing. Their feat enabled them to provide uninterrupted coverage of the disaster, which later brought the *Press-Herald* a much-deserved Pulitzer Prize, its first. As the Albany (N.Y.) *Times Union* reported it on April 15, 1998: "North Dakota paper wins Pulitzer for pluck: Floods and fire couldn't keep "Grand Forks Herald" from publishing." The paper published through "floods and fire that devastated the North Dakota city and its own plant," and won the prize for public service.

I telephoned the editor, Mike Jacobs, and arranged to meet him at the school. Following his directions, I drove to Manvel, ten miles north of Grand Forks on US 81, just off I 29. It was easy to find.

The newspaper staff members, complete with computers and equipment, were occupying space in the school building while classes continued without disturbance. Mike received me graciously, in spite of the unusual pressures on him.

"I do know about the Theodore Roosevelt Highway," he told me. "We had an extensive file on it, but it was destroyed in the flood, but you should find some interesting material anyway. There's an intellectual tradition in North Dakota. People here are more likely to know of the TR Highway than people in other states are."

Just then his telephone rang—CBS News calling in connection with a special broadcast on the flood. Much of the conversation dealt with Whitey's Cafe, which the rushing waters had destroyed. Whitey's Bar and Cafe, downtown near the Red River Bridge, at one time had been a classic speakeasy. Through the years it had evolved into a celebrated local Institution—a restaurant actually known across the country for its excellent food (served to booths with individual jukeboxes) and its huge art deco stainless steel bar.

I had hoped to stop there, but all I could see of it was a devastated exterior. Mike indicated that there were plans to re-build. My guess is that it would be re-located out of the flood plain—we could only hope that the bar would be intact.

He assigned a reporter to me to do an article that would describe my project and ask readers to supply information. She conducted an efficient interview, after which she recommended that I try the Kite Cafe when I reached Petersburg. Before I left to return to Grand Forks, Mike suggested several sources that I could pursue for material. Finally, he said he thought he remembered seeing a Roosevelt Highway sign painted on the side of Lyons Automotive, downtown.

Back in Grand Forks, the residents were adjusting and carrying on many of their daily activities. Even with the destruction, it was easy to see that Grand Forks was a beautiful community. In 1921, the North Dakota Division of the Theodore Roosevelt International Highway Association published a booklet about the state's portion of the TRIH. It remarked that the Highway was fortunate to enter the state at Grand Forks, because "the tourist will find himself in the heart of the business district of this beautiful, thriving city." The booklet promised tourists a choice ranging from "excellent hotel accommodations" to a tourist camp in Riverside Park, which served thousands of travelers annually.

Grand Forks still thrives despite the setback, and still offers interesting architecture and stately trees. Its position at the confluence of the Red River of the North and the Red Lake River had obviously been a mixed blessing, but it made the city into a commercial center, and has ensured that it stays that way.

Steamboat traffic from Fargo to Winnipeg on the Red River began as far back as 1859. Alexander Griggs, a captain with experience in steamboats on the Mississippi, established the town site in 1870. He collaborated with railroad tycoon James J. Hill in the River Transportation Line of steamboats, but the steamboat era was brief. Hill's Great Northern Railroad came to Grand Forks in 1880, and river traffic quickly became non-competitive.

Cities tend to be small in the lightly-populated Great Plains. With fewer than 49,000 inhabitants inside its boundaries, Grand Forks is North Dakota's third largest city. Everything, though, is relative. Grand Forks is large enough to be a major presence in the area, and its promotional literature boasts that it "is perhaps the most cosmopolitan city in North Dakota."

Certainly the University of North Dakota is a strong institution and adds considerably to the city's culture, there is a substantial aerospace complex, and there are numerous special events, including the University's well-known Writers' Conference.

"The Kegs" Drive-in and flood debris, Grand Forks, North Dakota

Grand Forks has one unheralded but undeniable claim to fame: it was there that Frank Amidon, the chief miller of the city's Diamond Mills, in 1893 devised an invention that changed the lives of many Americans—Cream of Wheat.

The Kegs Drive-in remains as an intact reminder of earlier days. At each side of the building, reaching above its roof, is a giant replica of a root-beer keg. In spite of the piles of debris in front, it was open for business and serving customers. It still has car-hop service, reminiscent of my high-school days. The specialty at the Kegs is a good sloppy joe sandwich. There is no seating, though, so it's strictly carry-out or dine-in-the-car

Even Least Heat Moon, who tended to grouse about the northern Great Plains and its settlements, praised Grand Forks. "Who in America would guess that Grand Forks, North Dakota, was a good place to be stuck in with a bad water pump?" he asked; "Skyscrapers from the thirties, clean as a Norwegian kitchen, a state university with brick, big trees, and ivy." He had his van repaired speedily, and at reasonable cost. "I had expected to be taken for three times that figure," he marveled, "but I met only honest people."

I drove to Lyons Automotive, and found that there was a sign painted on the side of its building, but it had faded to outlines so faint that I could not be sure whether it had been a marker for the TR Trail. I thought I could detect evidence of the word "Roosevelt," but it could have been wishful thinking.

The next day I proceeded west into North Dakota. This was the part of the journey that I had looked forward to the least. The state is large, and I expected mile after mile of flat and uninteresting landscape.

Like Heat Moon though, I had been pleasantly surprised by Grand Forks. I soon found that—unlike Heat Moon—I did not find North Dakota boring. On the contrary, it was fascinating. The highway also was a surprise. U.S. 2 out of Grand Forks was divided, but traffic remained light.

The wind has little to hinder it as sweeps across hundreds of miles of prairie, often day after day, beneath skies that appear never to end. But the land, harsh though it can be, has always teemed with life. Wildlife is plentiful, and until they were exterminated around 1895 or so, it included vast herds of bison. Human life also has always maintained a foothold.

Thousands of years ago, paleo-Indian hunters gave way to mound builders, who began the area's tradition of agriculture. The Mandan and Hidatsa continued to raise corn, beans, and squash as their ancestors had, and supplemented their agriculture with bison hunts. They stand out prominently in the journals of Lewis and Clark, who set up winter camp in what came to be North Dakota. Others who have depicted North Dakota Native American life include Prince Maximilian, Karl Bodmer, George Catlin—and, yes, Theodore Roosevelt.

The Louisiana Purchase brought the northwestern half of the Dakotas under American control in 1803. The southeastern half came in 1818 as a result of agreement with Great Britain. The two countries then agreed that the dividing line between the U.S. and Canada would be along the 49th parallel.

Along with the Arikara, the Mandan and Hidatsa have come to be known as the Three Affiliated Tribes. All arrived long before whites, but the Arikara were relative latecomers to the area. The Three Tribes have a reservation surrounding the western end of a reservoir on the Missouri River, Lake Sakakawea. Other tribes have reservations in the area also. Lake Sakakawea is south of the TRIH, but it is worth a side trip. The campgrounds there are excellent—as is characteristic of campgrounds in North Dakota. Travelers interested in Native American culture will find much of interest in the region's museums.

Although whites rushed into the Dakota Territory in the late nineteenth century, the Indian presence has remained substantial. Much of the white immigration resulted from the railroads. James J. Hill, the St. Paul magnate, never did live in North Dakota, but when he transformed the old St. Paul, Minneapolis, and Manitoba Railroad into the Great Northern, the new railroad vigorously encouraged settlement—not only from the eastern U.S., but also from Europe. There was feverish railway activity in the 1870s and 1880s. The Great Northern cut its route from Grand Forks through Minot and on west into Montana and beyond. By 1893 it had connected the Midwest and the Pacific. The TRIH—and subsequently U.S. 2—followed its tracks across North Dakota.

Even as the railroad was becoming a ready conduit for settlers, millers in Minnesota had developed new techniques for processing hard spring wheat. Minneapolis became the largest center of milling activity in the world, and the North Dakota plains beckoned would-be growers to supply increasing needs of the Minneapolis mills. At first, the typical North Dakota farm was smaller than 300 acres, but the Great Dakota Boom brought about "bonanza farms," those of 3,000 acres and more; some as large as 20,000. The boom resulted partly from holders of railroad bonds who exchanged them for railroad land. Statehood came in 1889 for both Dakotas (along with Montana and Washington). North Dakota became the 39th state; South Dakota the 40th.

A combination of harsh weather, economic conditions, and the policies of the railroads and grain elevators brought hard times to the farmers. Struggles arose between agrarian and corporate interests, and they were tinged by the European cooperative traditions that many of the settlers had as their heritage. In 1892, the Farmers' Alliance joined with Democrats and Populists to elect a Populist Governor, Eli Shortridge. From 1906 to 1912, Progressives and Democrats cooperated to elect "Honest John" Burke for three terms. In 1915, former socialist Arthur C. Townley led the famous Non-Partisan League, which advocated state ownership of grain elevators and mills, state inspectors, subsidized housing for farmers, and rural credit banks that would lend money at cost.

The Non-Partisan League spread briefly throughout the upper Midwest, but failed to attract support from industrial workers. Its greatest strength was in North Dakota, where in 1919 it worked with Progressive Republicans to capture the legislature. The new legislature enacted virtually all the reforms, but the results fell short of the reformers' hopes. An Independent Voters' Association arose to represent Republican conservatives, creating a tension that to some extent continues to affect North Dakota politics.

Shortly after departing Grand Forks, I passed a large gray barn. Against a backdrop of trees, it presented its side to the highway—a side painted with a large white ghost, staring at passers by with two great black eyes, and with no explanation. Off

"Ghost Barn," North Dakota

to one side just a few yards away—again with no explanation—was an upside-down building.

The building literally was lying on its roof, which was peaked, causing the structure to jut upward from the ground at roughly a forty-five degree angle. There was no floor. The upside-down building was open to the sky from the bottom, much like a huge basket, as if some giant had kicked it over. "Another modest mystery," I thought contentedly.

I crossed a small river, and passed Turtle River State Park. Despite the ghost barn and the upside-down building, North Dakota impressed me as neat, clean, and well ordered. Farms appeared to be huge and prosperous. The land was mostly flat, but there were bluffs in the distance. I found myself agreeing with Howard Frank Mosher that, "like the deep North Woods of New England and the watery North Coast of the upper Midwest, the northern Great Plains" create their own distinct world.

U.S. 2 no longer goes through Larimore, as the TRIH did. Now, it goes a bit to the north of the small community. A pity. The town has a claim to fame. The author of the 1921 TRIH booklet wrote: "every time I think of Larimore, I think of baked potatoes, for it was this city that treated all the people at the San Francisco Fair in 1915 to baked potatoes and by so doing put their town on the map." Larimore still is on the map, but the renown of its 1915 potatoes was not enough to keep it on the highway.

It remains a community, though, which is more than can be said of McCanna, just a few miles distant. McCanna was also on the old Highway, but the relocated U.S. 2 now bypasses it to the south. Following the original TR route, I went from Larimore to McCanna by taking N.D. 18 north and turning left to proceed west on Grand Forks County 11, which at places is also marked 23rd Ave NE. Passing McCanna I saw prosperous farms and nothing else. I stayed on County 11 for no more than three or four minutes, and it connected once more with U.S. 2.

I had tended to picture North Dakota as dry, but I passed mile after mile of marsh, and flock after flock of ducks, geese, and other waterfowl. Driving through Petersburg, I looked, but if the Kite Café were there, I missed it.

By that time, I had learned that the chance of finding things where people had told me they would be at best was something less than even—and when relating to TRIH markers the chance would be approaching zero. I did remember Petersburg from the TR Highway Association's booklet. It said that there were fewer renters on the farms there than anywhere else in eastern North Dakota, reflecting the town's prosperity. I could only hope that the years had remained kind to Petersburg.

Past the town of Michigan, I saw snow by the side of the road. This was the small remains of a winter snowbank that must have been deep and substantial. I hadn't seen snow since New England. The TR Highway booklet said in 1921 that settlers from Michigan had named the town for their home state, and that "they have every reason to believe that their city is going to grow and considerable building is looked for." They may still be looking; the town remains tiny.

Lakota is a nice community with a comfortable feel about it. The 1921 booklet spoke of its beautiful homes, "and the citified appearance of the business district." I

Upside down building, North Dakota

could sense continued civic pride, some of which is displayed in the Lakota Museum in the City Library.

Before leaving, I filled my tanks. The service station attendant knew of the TRIH. When I mentioned it, he said that he remembered it well, but he knew of no markers. He volunteered that he knew also about the Lincoln Highway.

As I proceeded through the marshy country, off to my left was Devil's Lake, a substantial body of water. A few miles ahead I came to its namesake, the town of Devil's Lake, where I stopped at a store.

The clerk, "Edie," said "Sure I know about the Teddy Roosevelt Highway." When I told her most people didn't, she laughed and said, "most people don't? Well, I'm older than most!" If so, her appearance was deceiving. She certainly was not elderly. Mike Jacobs had been right. More people in North Dakota than elsewhere seemed to remember the TR Highway, and also to identify with Theodore Roosevelt.

I had no sooner pulled back onto the road, than I saw "Roosevelt Park" on my right. I stopped to take pictures, and drove on to the Park's northern entrance, where I took some more. Adjacent to the Park on the north, and too far to be seen from U.S. 2, I found another place to photograph: the "Rough Rider Mini Golf."

I explored Devil's Lake to see if it had a Roosevelt Street, and found that it has none. What it does have is impending trouble. For miles around Devil's Lake, the town, there is a threat from Devil's Lake, the lake. Along with Utah's Great Salt Lake and very few others, the lake has no outlet. Steadily, inch by inch it is growing, and swallowing roads, utility poles, farmland, trees, and homes.

In the late nineteenth century, Devil's Lake began dropping from its 30 to 40-foot depth, until in October of 1940 it reached a depth of 3 feet, its lowest recorded point. Over the next few decades, it rose and fell, but gradually regained much of its lost depth. In the late 1980s, it had reached 30 feet, but then dropped back to about 25.

In 1993, the trouble began with a prolonged wet cycle. The *New York Times* has reported that a steady rise since then has brought the lake's depth to 47 feet, and has tripled its size to nearly 200 square miles. People from 50 miles or so away come to Devil's Lake to shop. Until recently, that meant "a drive through fields of wheat and barley and sunflowers. Now those roads that have not disappeared entirely have become scary causeways with waves chewing at their edges."

The Army Corps of Engineers is considering creating an outlet so that some of the lake's water could drain into the Sheyenne River. That might bring its own troubles, though. The lake's high sulfate levels might contaminate water supplies, and the increased flow could create flooding elsewhere.

A clay and rock dike now protects the town, but residents are nervous. The seven-mile wall went up quickly, and without it most of Devil's Lake would be submerged up to two or three stories. The speed of construction, was necessary, but doesn't inspire confidence. As one resident remarked, it's holding back 30 miles of water, 25 feet deep—and it's only dirt.

Devil's Lake cannot grow forever. If it gains another 12 to 15 feet in depth, it will find a natural outlet, and will have reached its maximum. Unfortunately, that maximum would double the size of the already troublesome lake, and would leave a monster of some 400 square miles. That would be more than four-fifths as large as Vermont's Lake Champlain.

Roosevelt Park, Devil's Lake, North Dakota

Leaving Devil's Lake and its threat behind me, I was once again on U.S. 2. I soon stopped at the Cedar Restaurant for a bite to eat. There was nothing about TR there, but I found more Americana. Surrounding me was "saw art"—paintings on saw blades. The restaurant was a gallery of sorts. The hand-painted round blades covered the walls, providing unique décor. They also were available for purchase.

Back on the road, a bright red fox lay dead on the shoulder. NPR came back, faded out, then came back again. A brilliant yellow bird with black wings, like nothing I had ever seen before, flew across the road and fluttered onto a post. It looked at me quizzically as I drove by. I passed another dead antelope, but noted happily the proliferation of wildlife. Ducks, loons, and other aquatic animals filled the marshy land. A black bird of medium size with a bright orange head sat motionless and watched me pass.

Then came a reminder of road conditions on the original TRIH. For twelve miles, there was road work. It was bad, without pavement. There was mud, not enough to sink in to, but enough to be messy. A sign warned: Caution. 25 miles per hour. Watch for water." It was another reminder of Devil's Lake.

After the road construction, I took the smooth highway less for granted. I proceeded past towns named incongruously Leeds and York, and in the distance saw grain elevators marking the presence of Rugby. At the south edge of the town of some 3,000, on the south side of the road there is a large stone cairn, a monument shaped like a fat obelisk. Each of its four sides has a sign proclaiming "Geographical Center of North America Rugby, N.D." Rugby makes this claim, so the promotional material says, based on "a geological survey conducted by the U.S. Department of the Interior."

Nearby is the Pioneer Village Geographical Center Museum, which definitely is worth the modest entry fee—but because of the region's bitter winters, it is open only from the first of May through the first of October. The main view from the road is a cavernous set of buildings that house an extensive collection of early American prairie artifacts (Indian and Anglo), and an eclectic assortment of objects including old automobiles and antique farm machinery. There is even an Inuit, or "Eskimo" exhibit. I had hoped for some evidence of the TRIH, but could find nothing relevant.

Outside, behind the main area, is the Pioneer Village. It consists of nearly thirty restored buildings, with reproductions of shops, offices, a school, a jail, houses, a railroad depot, a telephone switchboard that a housewife operated from her home, and the like. Inside the two-story school is a life-sized figure of Clifford Thompson, who was born at nearby Silva.

Claiming him as a resident is a bit of a stretch, with no pun intended. Thompson moved with his parents to Wisconsin when he was young, was educated there and in Michigan, and practiced law in Iowa and then in Portland, Oregon until his death in 1955 at the age of 51. Still, he was born in the area, and did become a man of distinction. He was 8 feet 7 inches tall.

The school also contains an eye-catching mural. It is four feet high and eighty feet long. The eighty-year-old artist chose this unusual way to depict the county's century-long history.

According to the TR Highway Association's booklet, it was a Rugby florist who originated the slogan, "say it with flowers." He had attended a florists' convention in Chicago, and offered the slogan to the national association, which adopted it. His greenhouse shipped flowers as far west as Washington, and as far east as Pennsylvania. The town in 1921 welcomed TR Trail travelers not only with an invitation to visit Lindberg's Rugby Greenhouse, but also with the notice that: "The Park Commission of Rugby has not forgotten that they are located on the Roosevelt Highway and have set aside a place in their beautiful public park for a tourist camp."

Near Rugby, loping across a field not far from the highway, but away from any trees, was a moose. She wasn't a bull moose, but as the only one I had seen thus far, she definitely rates a mention in *Moose Crossing*.

The highway continued to be divided. I Passed the hamlet of Towner, about which the writer of the booklet for the TRIH in North Dakota said: "you might think I am exaggerating somewhat when I say that at Towner they ship hay by the train loads, but, never-the-less, this is a fact." He reported in 1921 that "excellent hotel facilities are to be had here and a tourists' camp was being prepared at the time we were there." He mentioned that "Towner would like to have a flour mill so that they could make their own flour." I saw no evidence of one. There was only a neat, well-kept community.

I crossed Mouse River, just beyond Towner. After some time a sign warned me of broken pavement. North Dakota was certainly courteous. The "broken pavement" was minimal—hardly a bump—but the state nevertheless believed it had a duty to warn drivers that it failed to meet North Dakota's standards.

About six miles beyond Towner was Denbigh. It would be easy to pass it by without notice, but it does have special relevance to the TRIH. In 1920 the TR Highway Association's North Dakota Division conducted a contest. The community that achieved the best improvement over a five-mile segment of the Highway was to receive a "large loving cup."

Denbigh was the clear winner. On the 4th of July that year, its citizens turned out enthusiastically for a "road building bee," and they "graveled a seven-mile stretch." The Association's booklet said, "considering the sandy condition of this territory this new road was a big improvement and the officers felt that they had well earned the cup which was presented to them."

The civic spirit, sadly, seems not to have helped Denbigh. I had hoped to find the "large loving cup" in a museum or possibly the town hall. There was no museum, no town hall. In fact, there was nothing except a handful of houses around a square block of streets, and some trailers. There was no one to ask, and there were no businesses, with one possible exception. An outbuilding had "saddlery" painted on it, but there was no one around.

The streets were unpaved. It struck me as odd, considering that it seemed almost to be a ghost town, that—gravel notwithstanding—each street was marked with a modern street sign.

Another oddity was one large building, right in the middle of town. It could have been a former academy or town hall, but there were no streets or walkways leading to it. It just sat there in the middle of a muddy field. It had curtains on the windows.

Isolated building, Denbigh, North Dakota

I left Denbigh, and hadn't traveled much farther—although I had driven through Granville, Norwich, and Surrey—when I saw Minot in the distance. Minot literally sprang into being overnight. In 1887 a tent settlement had grown up a few miles distant, but when news leaked out that the Great Northern Railway would be crossing the Souris River at Minot's current location, all the residents re-located immediately. Within a few months they had incorporated Minot, and there was a complete city government. Everything happened so quickly and Minot grew so rapidly that people began to refer to it as the Magic City, even though during the cowboy days it became one of a handful of places known as the roughest in the west.

Minot seeks travelers no less than it did in 1921 when the Minot Town Criers Club provided a "Motor Tourists' Night Camp" to service the TR Trail. The camp charged no fee, and supplied firewood, lights, and water along with the campsites. Accommodations no longer are free, but they are better equipped. The Leland Parker Hotel at $1.25 to $3.50 per night then had 175 rooms, of which 75 had baths. The Grand Hotel claimed to have the largest assortment of rooms with or without baths, but its rates ran as high as $6.00—which for the day was expensive. More reasonable was the Waverly Hotel, which offered the European plan at rates of $1.25 to $2.00, but only 25 of its 100 rooms had baths.

Today, the city has the standard range of hotels and motels found in all American settlements of any size, and camping facilities are good.

I had turned off on Business 2, and came into Minot on the Burdick Expressway. On my right were the fairgrounds. The North Dakota State Fair was in progress, so I turned into the parking area to the left of the road. Helping with the parking were Jill Colby and her group of Boy Scouts, Troop 433, from Minot.

The Fair's atmosphere was appropriately festive. Clowns dotted the crowd that I walked through on my way to the Pioneer Village. The restored buildings contained exhibits of North Dakota life around the period of statehood. I stopped to watch a rope maker, and then a wood carver who worked with a chain saw and a huge vertical chunk of tree trunk. With surprisingly few vigorous swipes, a grizzly bear began to take shape.

As I watched the creation, I struck up a conversation with another onlooker, a forestry teacher from Minot State. He had moved to North Dakota from Illinois. Not for a minute, he said, had he regretted the move.

"It may get cold in North Dakota, but I like the dry weather," he said, "it's great. By the way, I wish I'd seen you a few minutes ago. The governor was here. I could have introduced you. I'm sure he'd have been happy to discuss the Theodore Roosevelt Highway." He looked around hoping to find him again, but the governor apparently had left.

The governor likely would have been interested, considering TR's importance to North Dakota. With the concurrence of North Dakota's secretary of state and the superintendent of its State Historical Society, the governor selects recipients of the Theodore Roosevelt Rough Rider Award. Those chosen, all North Dakotans, receive the honorary rank of Colonel in the "North Dakota Theodore Roosevelt Rough Riders," a group dating from the 1961 Dakota Territory Centennial.

The Roosevelt Park and Zoo, in the middle of Minot, is one of the most tangible remnants of the TRIH, and boasts a larger-than-life statue of T.R. mounted on a horse and appearing to keep a wary vigil. Two articles in the Minot *Daily News* for the 11th and 12th of September 1924 establish the Park's connection with the TR Trail.

Dr. Henry Waldo Coe, a long-time friend of TR's, had commissioned the statue and donated it to the city. Coe lived in Portland, Oregon but originally came from Mandan, N.D. He was on hand in Minot on the 11th for the formal dedication. Businesses had closed for the parade and ceremony, and that day the paper's page-one banner headline read: "Coe Dedicates Statue of Theodore Roosevelt."

The accompanying article indicated that Coe had "presented a similar statue to his home city of Portland, and smaller casts to Mandan, N.D., and the Roosevelt Home Memorial association of New York." It said (apparently forgetting the statue in Portland):

> Dr. Coe told how requests for the statue had poured in from many other cities in the nation, and of why Minot should be chosen as the city where the only equestrian bronze of heroic size between the Great Lakes and the Pacific ocean should be situated, declaring that the pledge was given to James Johnson that the statue should come to Minot because the donor desired it should be given to a town in North Dakota—a state where a life long friendship had been formed with Theodore Roosevelt.

Johnson, a Ward County pioneer and friend of Coe's, presided over the dedication.

On the 12th, the *News* said that "F. R. Lambert, present member and former president of the park board," formally pronounced the "rechristening of Riverside park,

TR Statue, Roosevelt Park, Minot, North Dakota

henceforth to be known as Roosevelt park." The name change had been anticipated. "I am appearing before you in fulfillment of a sacred promise evidenced on the pages of the park board records," Lambert said. "Way back as far as 1919 when the 'Wonderland Trail' was changed to the 'Theodore Roosevelt Highway' a resolution was passed and a committee named to prepare for the enlargement and developing of this park under the new name of 'Roosevelt,' and as soon as we learned of the possibility of there being a Roosevelt statue to be had we got busy at once. This sentiment for a change in name was emphasized by both Doctor Coe and James Johnson after the dedication of the first statue in Portland. On the return of Mr. Johnson the board on December 5, 1922, passed the formal resolution."

Lambert then made the change in name official. "In fulfillment of this resolution and by virtue of the power invested in me by such action of the board," he proclaimed, "I hereby formally and solemnly in the name of the board of park commissioners of the city of Minot, North Dakota, publish and declare that this park in which we are now assembled be changed in name from 'Riverside park' to 'Roosevelt park,' and the same is hereby rechristened and rededicated 'Roosevelt park' in honor of him who has passed on before, he who stands in the front line of American presidents, he who was a winner of the Nobel peace prize, a fearless cavalry officer, a world statesman, a renowned hunter, a recognized naturalist, and a noble husband, father and friend—Theodore Roosevelt."

The sculptor was A. (Alexander) Phimister Proctor (1862-1950). The Smithsonian Institution records 107 of his sculptures, under such varied ownership as the Denver Art Museum, Brookgreen Gardens in South Carolina, the St. Louis Art Museum, the District of Columbia Department of Public Works, the San Diego Museum of Art, and the National Gallery of Canada in Ottawa. Proctor, who lived in Los Angeles, sent word that he regretted being unable to attend the ceremony, but hoped to visit Minot soon thereafter.

There is a slight discrepancy in the record regarding the statue. The foundry casting the heroic bronze was the Henry Bonnard Bronze Works at Mt. Vernon, N.Y. The Smithsonian records indicate that it was "the larger of two replicas of a Roosevelt statue in Portland, Oregon; the smaller version," they say, "is located in Mandan, North Dakota." According to a letter from C. L. Dill, Director of the Museum Division of the State Historical Society of North Dakota, however, the original is the artist's plaster model which "was donated to the State Historical Society for inclusion in the State's History collection in 1924."

Dill concluded that the plaster model "is of some intrinsic value as an art work, and historical value in its relation to the donor," Dr. Coe. "Two full scale bronze replicas were apparently made from this original," he wrote, "one each located in the cities of Minot, North Dakota, and Portland, Oregon." Additionally, "two miniature versions of the piece were made from the artist's working model, one located in Mandan, North Dakota, and the other scheduled (in 1923) for placement in the Roosevelt House in New York City. All were cast at a Mount Vernon, New York foundry." Dill's letter is in the records of the Minot Park District.

In common with Grand Forks and other cities on the far reaches of the prairies, Minot appears to be larger than its population—which is only about 35,000—would indicate,

Old Hotel on TR Highway, Outskirts of Stanley, North Dakota

and it is the home of Minot State University. Even so, no one would mistake it for a metropolis, but one urban amenity that Minot offers is a good newspaper.

I went to the offices of the *Daily News*, attempting to find information. There was nothing, but I found great interest in the Highway and especially in my project. I couldn't have known it at the time, but that interest ultimately brought me exactly what I wanted.

Eloise Ogden, a key reporter, interviewed me and wrote a substantial story on the entire project. As a result of her feature article, I was to receive invaluable information in the weeks to come from two sources. Each had both deep roots in North Dakota and connections with the TRIH.

Janet Waterman Gallagher now lives in Minnesota, but grew up in North Dakota. She still reads the *Daily News*. After seeing Ms Ogden's article about my journey along the TR Trail, she wrote me to tell of her connection with the roadway.

Ms Gallagher is the granddaughter of Albert F. Bacon, who died in 1941 at the age of 74. He had owned and operated a sign-painting company in Minot. According to his obituary in the *Daily News*, it was Bacon who blazed the "Teddy Roosevelt Trail"—which later became U.S. 2—in that part of North Dakota. He proceeded "southwest from Minot, in the early days," noted the obituary, "painting rocks and posts and setting up posts so that tourists could find their way across the rather precarious roads of those days."

Ms Gallagher has joined a growing group of writers who have made significant contributions through the personal narrative, often self-published. As the title indicates, hers takes the form of a tribute to her grandmother: *The Book I Wish Grand-*

mother Bacon had Written: An Ingredient Called Kate. The Minot Public Library has a copy; so does the library of North Dakota State University. It is a remarkable family book, presenting a compendium of several decades of North Dakota life and history, and it contains her grandfather's obituary.

Clifford Stubbs also read the piece in the *Daily News*, and began corresponding with me. He lived in North Dakota most of his life, although recently his health forced him to move to the Eastern Montana Veterans' Home in Glendive. In 1939, he began working for the Bacon firm. His story tells much about the TRIH and about conditions in depression-era North Dakota.

"I received a letter," he wrote, "informing me that I could work in the sign shop by J. Warren Bacon himself—for $15 a week as an apprentice in the business." At the time, he lived near a small town, Dore, N.D., which he says no longer exists.

His own words are the best way to tell his tale:

The winter before I had worked on a farm for $15 a month and since it was December, and I had no employment, I immediately answered the letter, borrowed $5 for train fare and came to Minot. Warren met me at the Minot Depot and took me to his parents' home where I could room, be fed and have my washing done for $8 a week. Warren's father: Albert F. Bacon was still living but quite feeble. Kate Bacon, his wife, was a good cook and even darned my socks and put patches on my overalls. Mr. Bacon liked to sit at a table in the kitchen and tell me stories about his work in the "good old days." The Sign Shop was in the Stearn's Building where Keating's Furniture World is today. The Sign Writer then was a red-headed man named Cecil Norris. Both Albert and Cecil told me about traveling across North Dakota in a Model T Ford Pickup to mark the TR Trail . . . .

I know the Pickup Truck they used was made from a passenger car with the back seat cut off and a wooden box made for it. Ford Motor Company never made Pickups until 1925.

I had been working but several months when I had to go "on-the-road" repairing neon signs and making deliveries of signs or taking orders for signs. Warren often went with me in the 1939 Ford Pickup the Company had but I soon had to travel alone. Number Two highway went through almost all small towns then and on my first time in many towns I would look for the TR signs on fences, on buildings—usually marking a corner, somehow, where one had to make a right or left turn. Many times it helped me to take the right street to the road out of town. Today Number Two Highway goes west from Williston to Bainville, Montana. Before that route it used to be by way of Trenton, Marley, Buford, Mondak, Snowden, Lakeside and then Bainville. Today much of the old route is changed and bypasses many small towns. Trenton still exists.

Bacon Signs today lays claim to beginning in 1901. That is so but the family business had two previous names: Minot Display Advertising Company under Albert Bacon, J. W. Bacon, Incorporated under Warren Bacon and later Arthur F. Bacon, then Bacon Signs as it is today under Bruce Bacon (Arthur's son). I retired (at 65) from Bacon Signs.

It is possible that there may be faint traces of the old TR Trail signs today as in the earlier days white lead paints were used—turpentine, linseed oil and oil colors were often added to gallon cans of white lead. Today that is considered illegal as white lead is poisonous and its use is prohibited. However, that paint really endured and even today on Main Street buildings in Minot there are faint signs painted by Minot Display Ad Co. and marked by that name on the brick side walls of some taller buildings. That paint was used for a while by J. W. Bacon, Inc. also, and some old signs have been marked at bottom center or bottom right of those signs. I haven't been well enough to travel for quite a few

Old TRIH, North Dakota

years but I would bet that in some small towns a person might yet find traces of the TR markers if one knew the original route.

That, of course, had been my thought too, but from Maine to Minot I had failed to find anything that definitely had been a marker.

If there were any doubt that this was TR country, finding the Rough Rider Campground would have laid it to rest. I had to stay there.

I set up camp next to a tent trailer. My neighbors were a Wisconsin couple who were on their way to the Idaho/Montana border to participate in the Chief Joseph Trail Ride. Each year, 300 to 350 people take to horseback to follow the route of Chief Joseph's journey. They ride 100 miles each summer, and the entire ride will take thirteen years; this was to be the fifth.

Heading west from Minot, I turned off U.S. 2 on 19th Ave NW—shortly it became County 10. I did some backtracking, so that I could follow both U.S. 2 and the original route, which is more or less parallel, but which goes through some towns that the modern highway bypasses. Des Lacs is right on the railroad tracks and was on the TRIH, but is a few miles off the new straightened road.

The Association's booklet said of Des Lacs in 1921 that "about two miles west of the city you will see the only oil well to be found along the North Dakota Division of the Theodore Roosevelt International Highway and while oil has not been found in any large quantities the people of Des Lacs have all the confidence in the world of bringing in a gusher in the very near future. I noticed no oil well, but where the old TRIH went through the town, the street signs now say "Roosevelt Street."

About ten miles west of Minot on U.S. 2 I passed a lake on the right, and then noted in the distance that I could detect signs of the Badlands—a rugged, heavily eroded, area spreading over parts of the Dakotas, Wyoming, Nebraska, and Montana. For modern travelers, they are primarily a region of wild beauty. For Theodore Roosevelt also, they were a place of beauty, but more important, a place that provided him with severe challenge. For the pioneers and the cowboys, the challenge was often all they could see. They described it as "Hell with the fires out."

The Badlands received their name for a reason. To Indians and whites alike, they represented toil and danger. Jagged bluffs, deep ravines, sudden weather changes, and other hazards obscured the vibrant colors, inky shadows, ever-changing patterns of light, and ruggedly-shaped rock formations that create an ever-evolving visual feast. It was just the place for Theodore Roosevelt. The Badlands defeated him financially, but physically and spiritually he met their challenges and triumphed. He remarked that if it had not been for his experiences in the Dakota Territory, he could never have become president.

But for the moment U.S 2 remained straight, smooth, and divided. The glimpse of the Badlands receded leaving the familiar prairie from horizon to horizon. U.S. 2 had been a divided highway since Grand Forks. This was far more divided highway than all the rest on the TRIH from Maine to North Dakota put together. About ten or fifteen miles from Minot, though, it ended; I was back on the customary TRIH two-lane.

Just as I passed a missile site, a jackrabbit jumped suddenly from brush at the right side of the road. He bounded directly toward the pavement, but turned 90 degrees as he landed, and charged along as though racing my truck. For twenty or thirty yards he

Roosevelt Street (Old TRIH) Des Lacs, North Dakota

kept pace just ahead of me, and then when I barely began to gain, he jumped back into the brush and was gone. I didn't think it was possible even for that short distance—I was going 65 miles per hour. Conspiracy buffs no doubt would think the missile site had something to do with it, but I assure them, he wasn't glowing. On the other hand, it WAS daylight. . . .

The sky was partly cloudy, and the wind was fierce. It swept across the plains, finding only my truck in the way as I fought it going westward. Both routes, U.S. 2 and the old road, go by town after town—all railroad towns. The new highway goes between Des Lacs, off to the left, and Burlington on the right.

Both were on the TRIH, and on U.S. 2 as well until it was re-located. A stretch of the old highway still follows the original route. It goes through Des Lacs to Berthold, crosses the current U.S. 2 to Tagus, and continues through Blaisdell and Palermo to Stanley. Burlington originally was a large coal-mining center.

On both the old and the new roads, came more isolation. From U.S. 2 there was a lake on the right, then a pond on the left, then lakes both right and left. The land became more marshy, with many lakes. There was even some sand. The only indication I saw of human habitation, other than a fence, was a protest sign off to the south, probably some twenty or thirty yards from the highway:

THIS HAY TAKEN BY US FISH AND WILDLIFE AND NDDOT WITH BROKEN
PROMISES NOT JUST COMPENSATION

There were grassy ponds and lakes; no trees; merely rolling grasslands. I passed a field with rocks piled into cairns, saw snow on the prairie, and experienced the beauty of the state that I feared would be dull.

Stanley loomed ahead. "Loom" is relative, and Stanley's population of close to 1,500 confers upon it the ability, here on the straight highway and the open prairie, to loom. The population in 1921 was only 700, "but one would think from the way they do things at Stanley that it was a city of at least twice that size," said the 1921 booklet. Now it actually is twice that size.

There's even a soda fountain in the Rexall Drug Store on Main Street. In a throwback to the early days of the Roosevelt Highway, the town still maintains a free campground for tourists.

I stopped in at the offices of the Montrail County *Promoter*, a weekly newspaper. The editor was interested in the TR Trail, and said that he would run an item about it. I asked him about Joyce's Cafe across the street, and he recommended it.

The coffee was good and the home-baked pastries were excellent, but the first thing that attracted my attention when I entered was a mural covering an entire interior wall. It was an interesting portrayal of a western ranch scene, with roads, a wagon, people and the like. I asked the server about the painting.

"A man came in here in 1977 and asked us if he could paint the wall," she explained. "We said 'sure.' That was twenty years ago. Look at it. It still looks like new."

Stanley is a convenient stopping place. The people were notably friendly, even on the street. The community is neat and clean, including downtown where the streets are wide and well-maintained. Even the derelict hotel that I drove by on the way back to U.S. 2 struck me not as an eyesore, but as a bit of nostalgia. It probably was in place as a comforting sight (and site) for early travelers on the TRIH, because it was on the old road, which went into and out of Stanley, not skirting it as the straightened U.S. 2 does today. The street must not have been considered significant enough to designate "Business U.S. 2," but it was the original route of the TR Trail.

From the tiny village of Ross, the old highway briefly runs alongside the railroad tracks. The badlands had become striking. Ahead was the turnoff to White Earth, which at one time was on the TRIH. Not only does the new US 2 bypass it, but the old route also was moved away from the town, which now sits on a spur about 5 miles off what is left of the original highway. The Association's booklet said that White Earth was the oldest town between Minot and Williston, and that it predated the railroad. It now has fewer than 100 residents.

Its setting, nestled among hills there in the badlands, is especially lovely. The village itself, though, is almost a ghost town. Although the badlands are not, strictly speaking, mountains, White Earth has the look of a tiny mountain community. Just outside the community is the White Earth Valley Wildlife Management Area.

A bit of the old highway goes to Tioga, which was on the original route, but now is just north of U.S. 2. The houses tended to be small and shabby, but on the west side there were some that were more upscale, including one in the form of a geodesic dome. There was an oil well—it must have been drilled since 1921—and the Norseman Museum in an old church building.

The town still offers something suggestive of services available to travelers on the Roosevelt Trail: one night of free camping. I departed on Williams County 10, and turned left on County 17. That was a mistake, so I went back to 10. 1921 sources do not mention Temple, but it appeared on my 1934 map with the road going through it. Today, the road goes around it, but it doesn't matter. Temple now is a ghost town, although current maps still show it. Finally, I encountered a detour on the old road around Ray, before it returned to US 2.

Ray itself seems to have been unusually progressive when the TRIH first went through the town, and in the previous decade. Its population of 800 has shrunk through the years to barely more than 600, but according to the booklet, the town as early as 1912 had installed along its Main Street a "white way." This was a modern street-lighting system heralded in the first third of the twentieth century. The booklet praised Ray as being the smallest community in the country with such a system. I wasn't there at night, but there seems nothing any longer to distinguish Ray from any Great Plains village of similar size.

To follow the real TR Trail—the one that U.S. 2 departed when engineers straightened the highway—I turned left just beyond Ray and headed south toward Wheelock, a few miles distant. The 1921 booklet lists Wheelock as 342 miles along the TRIH from its entry at Grand Forks. It describes the community as "a thriving village," which was the "trading, banking and church center for a vast territory." It had stores that carried "large stocks," and, said the booklet, "hotel and garage accommodations are to be found." No longer. Wheelock today with its fewer than two dozen inhabitants is but one step removed from a ghost town.

Temple, North Dakota

The road proceeds west from Wheelock to Epping. In 1921, Epping had streets that were "graded and graveled and are lined with concrete sidewalks." Today Main Street is dusty, and, having shrunk to fewer than 70 residents, the former railroad town has almost dwindled away. It does have two attractions, though. One is the Buffalo Inn Cafe with decent food and local color. At noon on Sundays, it becomes quite busy.

The other is the Buffalo Trails Museum, spread out over seven buildings, a former general store, pool hall, hardware store and the like. The Museum has a surprising array of artifacts and exhibits. There are immaculate antique autos, dioramas, Civil War era exhibits, and some quite astonishing objects. Its curator, Jeff Thompson, is doing his best with no funds and no training. His is a labor of love.

Beyond Epping is Spring Brook, the location of the Spring Brook Dam. Henry Alsberg's *American Guide* said as late as 1949 that it was the largest earth-filled dam in the state. The TR Highway passed through Spring Brook's Main Street, according to the 1921 booklet, but today, with only 29 residents, the dam is almost the only thing left. By 1934 U.S. 2 had bypassed the town, even before the modern highway had been straightened to snub so many villages that then quickly withered. The highway now goes directly west from Ray to U.S. 85, north of Williston.

Wheelock, Epping, and Spring Brook are relegated to back—and dirt or gravel—roads. My 1934 map shows U.S. 2 connecting Ray, Wheelock, and Epping but already missing Spring Brook; it went directly west from Epping to U.S. 85. The road west from Epping is blacktop. The locals in the cafe warned me that it is rough and broken, but I found it to present no trouble to the truck. The road from Spring Brook similarly is passable, and joins U.S. 85/U.S. 2 just north of Williston.

Wheelock, North Dakota (Old TRIH)

As I neared Williston, I pulled into a Conoco station, which also was Gramma Sharon's Cafe. I had eaten my fill at Epping, so I didn't eat at Gramma Sharon's, but I filled my tanks. While I was paying my bill, I struck up a conversation with another customer, Art Jensen, a trucker who had just climbed down from his big rig. He had come from the west coast and was heading all the way to the east.

"Ever heard of the Theodore Roosevelt Highway?" I asked. "Sure I know a lot about it. I learned about it in school here in North Dakota. This is where I grew up."

"I've been looking all the way from the East Coast for a Roosevelt sign or marker that might have survived, but I haven't found one yet. Have you ever seen anything like that?"

"There *is* one," he said. "Let's see, it's on the left side of the highway going west. It's a big sign on the side of a car company. You can still read 'Theodore Roosevelt Highway.' Look for Case Crow Motors. I'm not sure just where it is, but I've seen it. I think it's in Idaho."

"You've made my day," I told him. "Many thanks."

Williston's population, around 12,000, makes it a substantial presence in western North Dakota. I telephoned Bill Shemorry, a retired photojournalist who has written some 15 books on local history. He invited me out to his home.

He was familiar with the TR Highway in that part of the state, and traced its course from White Earth west to Tioga, Temple, Ray, Wheelock, Epping, and Spring Brook where it generally followed the railroad. This was the way I had come. From there, he said, it went a bit west of the tracks into Williston.

"It came into Williston on 5th Avenue East," he said, "which now is called University Avenue. It entered the city about where the agricultural station is located, and turned west for two blocks on 8th Street. From there, it went south to East Broadway (that would have been 3rd Street, if it had been numbered), and went straight west out of town. It followed the railroad, a bit north of the tracks. West of Williston it went to Trenton, Buford, then Mondak. Mondak doesn't exist anymore. It died when a bridge across the Missouri enabled farmers to take wheat by rail instead of wagons to the river and across to Mondak. Mondak also supplied drink to North Dakotans, this state was dry, and breweries had warehouses there."

He showed me examples of his photojournalism. It was impressive, and much of it had received national recognition. I looked through some of his books, and bought two.

"All the main roads in North Dakota are divided," he told me, "except for 2 and 854 in the west. We don't get our share. If I had my way, I'd divide the state. The western part could affiliate with Montana."

He was right about the divided highway. Shortly out of town, the road narrows into two lanes. There are clusters of electric lines, and then rolling, green prairie. Mountains enhance the horizon.

Just before the highway becomes two lanes, U.S. 85 turns off to proceed south. Fans of T.R. would do well to take the time to digress along that highway to the two units of the Theodore Roosevelt National Park. It's too bad that they are off the TR route, which had dwindled to insignificance before the Park was founded.

I drove on U.S. 2 straight west across the prairie to Bainville, Montana, to check out the new highway. Then, in order to follow the original route, I backtracked to North Dakota State Highway 1804, which connects with U.S. 2 just east of the point where it changes from four to two lanes, and just west of the intersection with U.S. 85. From there, I headed south toward Trenton and Buford.

Fort Buford now is a state historic site. A company of African-American cavalry — "Buffalo Soldiers" — once was stationed there, but there isn't much left today. The Fort, though, does have a sad history. Chief Joseph of the Nez Perce was brought there after the touching speech in which he said, "I will fight no more, forever." Despite promises to him, he was never again permitted to see his homeland. Beyond Buford is Fort Union, and what formerly was Mondak.

North Dakota became a state on November 2, 1889. The voters quickly ratified a constitution by a vote of more than three to one, but there was a companion measure prohibiting the sale and manufacture of liquor that they ratified by a bare majority. Shemorry has written that "during those first dry years of statehood, the ingenuity of the average drinking man was brought to focus on the problem and thus, in spite of the law and the authorities who attempted to enforce it, liquor of all description was readily available most anywhere in the state."

Mondak, a town straddling the state line, became a prime shipping point. Shemorry has said that distilling continued in the area during the years of national prohibition, but only on a small scale. It required innovation, because equipment was no longer available and ordering supplies could attract attention from the authorities.

Clifford Stubbs lived in Mondak for some five years, and remembers the TR "Trail going from Williston west to Montana. For some reason," he wrote, "the little town of Trenton still exists and is still about the same population as many years ago.

Stubbs says that his cousin, Ed Jack, "was one of the earliest homesteaders in the area and had the foresight to dam a coulee and create his own irrigation system on his farm (and sheep ranch)." He drove the TR Trail, which "ran between the dam and his irrigated land." Jack "had one child, a daughter who was the first white child born in Trenton. Esther Jack was the only girl in the class to take a Civil Engineering Course at the University of North Dakota. She graduated in 1913. She wanted to run for the position of City Engineer in Williston but people were against the idea of a woman holding such an office. Later it was reasoned that a woman would not be drafted for duty in World War I so she later got the position."

The TRIH, Stubbs said, "followed the Great Northern Railway west to Buford, a town just a short distance from Fort Buford, the early Indian Days Fort after Fort Union was closed. Fort Union's site was two miles west of Buford. Esther Jack's mother was a cook at the officers' quarters at Fort Buford before she married."

Mondak, he continued, near the Fort Union site, "was sometimes called a 'jumping-off place' as it had the Railway Station where many people came by train and then fanned out in all directions to places where they homesteaded." His father had done just that when he came from Ontario. Mondak was the trade center for a large area, straddled the state line (hence the name), and had a population variously estimated as 500-800.

Stubbs moved with his mother to Mondak in late 1923, when she became school principal there. "Prohibition," he said, "was supposedly in effect then but there was still much illegal liquor and beer sold by quite a few residents. There were three teachers for 8 grades and 2 years of High School—and a full time janitor. By 1928 the school was down to 8 grades for 1 teacher who was also janitor and she and her husband lived in one large room in the building."

As the school's decline indicates, Mondak's appeal had already begun to dwindle. The 1927 Lewis and Clark Bridge, according to Shemorry "the first permanent structure to span the river," was partly responsible. Then two other things settled the issue. First came a disastrous fire, and then came relocation of the TR Highway/U.S. 2 some ten miles or so north.

Stubbs explained much of what happened. "In 1928," he said, "a special train carrying John Phillips Sousa's Band on its way to a branch line to Glendive, Montana, set fire to the prairie in a high wind, because the smokestack on the steam engine had no screen or spark arrestor, and the fire burned almost all of the buildings in the town. Luckily," he noted, "our home was not burned and is still in Fairview, Montana, where it was moved to across the ice on the Missouri River when the ice was thick enough in the wintertime in the 1930s. I think there is no trace left of Mondak. My Father used to haul the wheat, flax, and other grains that he raised to Mondak from his homestead 5 miles west of a Post Office, School and Store at a place called Sioux Pass, Montana, about thirty miles cross country. With horses and wagon the trip took two long days and he had to cross the Missouri River on a ferry boat after staying all night in another village called 'Java' just across the river from Mondak. The grain elevator where he

TRIH—Former Main Street, Mondak, North Dakota/Montana

unloaded was on the edge of the TR Trail—all 3 elevators that I remember were in Montana."

Actually, there are remnants of Mondak, but grass obscures the foundations of what once were the town's buildings. I found them, across the road and the railroad tracks from the turnoff to the Fort Union National Historic Site, along what had been Mondak's Main Street. I left the truck for an inspection, and rapidly dived back in. The mosquitoes are fierce, and came in huge clouds.

When the National Park Service took over the Fort Union site in 1966, it was nothing but grassland. In spite of its name, it had never been part of the military, but was an old trading post. Rangers there told me that they had excavated many Mondak artifacts. The town's dump had been on the Fort's grounds. They even managed to dig out of the trash an intact Model T Ford. Mondak had such colorful past, they told me, that it would make it an ideal subject for a book.

It's hard to tell, but at Fort Union I had already crossed the state line, and was actually in Montana. I said goodbye to North Dakota and its attractions, obvious and subtle, but I must mention one of the state's more obscure virtues. No public road in North Dakota has parking meters. State law has banned them since 1940 when a state legislator grew furious over his parking tickets, and the legislature renewed the ban in 1999. My guess is that most Americans would cheer.

Chapter Eleven

Montana from Plains through Mountains

The original TRIH crossed into Montana at Mondak, a town split by the state line between Montana and North Dakota. Even though the town has vanished, the original road remains. It runs between Fort Union and Mondak's old location. The road becomes State Highway 327 in Montana, although there is no marker indicating the boundary.

Entering Montana, either by the original road or farther north on U.S. 2, brings the traveler also into Roosevelt County. Until 1919 it was Sheridan County. Then, Sheridan County was divided, with the southern part becoming Roosevelt.

Jon Axline, historian for the Montana Department of Transportation, indicates that the creation of Roosevelt County was "part of the county-splitting movement that took place in that portion of the state during the homestead boom. It had nothing to do with the Roosevelt Highway," he said, "but everything to do with TR."

The dynamic former president had just died. Because his ranch had been relatively nearby, many residents had known him personally and most knew him by local as well as national reputation. Ironically, Roosevelt County came into existence almost simultaneously with the February 1919 meeting in Duluth that proposed the TRIH—so, the county was there before the TR Trail.

The county-splitting movement is interesting in itself. As Spritzer's *Roadside History of Montana* describes it, the movement resulted from a 1911 Montana law that permitted citizens to petition their county governments to force elections to split counties. A Scottish immigrant, Dan McKay, established himself in Spritzer's words as "a professional county-buster." For a fee, he managed campaigns between 1912 and 1923 that led to the creation of seven new counties along the Hi-Line (originally the popular name for the railroad), and others south of the Missouri.

As for the homestead boom, local interests had joined with promoters, speculators, and the railroad to publicize the opportunities that awaited settlers on the Great Plains. To explain how homesteaders could prosper on 320-acre plots on the dry prairies, they promoted the myth that "rain follows the plow"—or the railroad.

For the first few years, the idea that plowing the prairie—or operating locomotives—generated rain seemed plausible. Unusually wet years brought good crops to the new immigrants. Inevitably, the normal dry years returned and drove countless farmers from their land.

The unrest generated by the tragic conditions encouraged reform movements and even radicalism among those who stayed. The Non-Partisan League from nearby North Dakota influenced the eastern Hi-Line counties to pursue reform, and the often-violent "Wobblies" (Industrial Workers of the World, or IWW) briefly established a "direct-actionist" presence. As is typically American, though, the radicalism could not sustain itself, and quickly dwindled.

The stretch from the state line to Bainville occasionally is passable by automobile—I have, in fact, driven it when it was—but it rarely is. At times it presents a challenge to a good pickup. At other times it's even worse. This is the one quarrel that I have with Spritzer's *Roadside History*. Some of its tidbits are priceless. In 1944, for example, the state made its license tags from a fiberboard material in an attempt to save scarce wartime metal. It didn't work. The material deteriorated. Worse, farm animals often ate the tags. But when Spritzer wrote that Fort Union "can be reached via a fourteen-mile good gravel road (Montana 327) running southeast from Bainville," he was dangerously mistaken. He must have driven it on an uncommonly good day—or else his definition of "good gravel road" is anything that won't stop a Humvee.

When I made a later trip across the length of the TRIH from west to east, I thought about attempting to take Montana 327 to Fort Union in an auto. I asked at the store in Bainville if anyone knew about the condition of the road.

"I just drove it and it beat my vehicle to death. I wish I hadn't come that way, and I'm sure not taking the same way back," a woman said. "If you're in a car, you'd never make it."

"What are you driving?" I asked her.

TRIH, Fort Union (Mondak) to Bainville, Montana

"A pickup," she told me. "Four-wheel drive."

The TR Highway Association's 1921 *Guide through Montana* described the road from Mondak to Bainville as "6 mi. graded and grav. Generally good." There appears to be little or no effort to keep it graveled today, however. The dirt surface deteriorates rapidly, even after maintenance. Rain and snow eat into it quickly. My guess is that it wouldn't stand up to much traffic even in decent weather. As Robert McColly, a life-long Montanan then in his eighties put it, "this country was all gumbo. When it was wet, you didn't go!" No place is good to be stranded, but many places would be better than that isolated part of the original TR Trail. Staying on U.S. 2 was the only reasonable course.

The road from Trenton, North Dakota to Fort Union has a modern hard surface, so the Fort is accessible even when the road beyond it into Montana is impassable. If they search, travelers can find the ruins of Mondak across the road from the Fort and the railroad tracks. But if they do, they will discover also that it's a good idea to have mosquito repellent handy.

On this trip if I had been driving my car instead of Alan's trusty truck, I would have had to turn back. The day was clear and beautiful, but there obviously had been bad weather. Some of the road had been washed away, and the ruts were too deep for an ordinary auto. As it was, I went that way for authenticity, and it could have been worse. I had no trouble because the truck gave me ample clearance, but I needed it. Four-wheel drive that time wasn't necessary—which was a good thing because the truck didn't have it.

The country is wild, with bluffs by the roadside and occasional broad vistas. The train tracks alongside at times are the only indication of human presence—except for the road itself, of course. I was surprised that there was so much activity on the rails.

The 1921 *Guide* listed Bainville's population as 500, noting that it also had "local and long distance telephones." That golden age is past. Today, its population has declined by more than two-thirds. The old road goes through the tiny village, and intersects with the new highway, U.S. 2.

Most motorists today would take U.S. 2 directly west from Williston toward Bainville. Since the road was relocated while the TRIH still was an identifiable route, that could still count as the "real" TR highway. The new road is smooth and modern, built several feet higher than the surrounding terrain. Just after it crosses into Montana, it passes a pond down on the left. The vista on the way to Bainville, which is fewer than ten miles past the state line, consists of bluffs, vast plains, and even vaster skies.

Once past the state line into Montana, the road is the "Hi-Line." The term predates even Theodore Roosevelt's presidency. In 1887 the old St. Paul, Manitoba and Pacific—the predecessor of James Hill's Great Northern—first brought white settlers to the territory. Although the altitude is not greatly elevated, the railroad became the "Hi-Line," and so did the surrounding country. The road came later, and because it paralleled the tracks, it took the same name. The name stuck even after the road became the TRIH, and then metamorphosed into U.S. 2.

Although the railroad shaped the entire area, the Highway superseded it as the major force. The railroad towns had been built as shipping points, and later became commercial centers. This change intensified with the creation of the TRIH and U.S. 2. As Carroll Van West put it in his 1986 study, *A Traveler's Companion to Montana History*, the coming of the automobile "made a handful of towns—Cut Bank, Shelby, Havre, Glasgow, and Wolf Point—into the region's major trade centers."

Still, the region continues to bear the indelible imprint of the railroad. The towns tend to be laid out in one of two ways. The strip design spread out along either side of the tracks, with the depot on one side and the business district on the other. The "T-style" design has a business street running perpendicular to the tracks, which form the top of the "T." Along the tracks are the depot, grain elevators, and the like. Sometimes towns designed along the "T-style" relocated their businesses along the TRIH when it came through, thus converting themselves into a strip arrangement.

Hardly more than twenty miles along the Hi-Line from Bainville lies Culbertson. Despite its small size, it boasts a Montana Visitors' Center, which houses the Culbertson Museum. The Museum is large and well laid out, and its collections thoughtfully displayed.

While there, I overheard a conversation between a guide and a young couple traveling through on bicycles. They had shipped their bikes to Minnesota, and began riding cross-country back home to the West Coast. He asked them how long it had taken them to get into condition.

They said they hadn't worked out at all—they simply assumed that they would manage without a problem. The trip was almost killing them, they said, and they despaired of ever making it home. They seemed like nice kids, and I felt for them. I had more confidence in them, though, than they had in themselves at that point.

I hadn't come very far that day, but I had done quite a bit of exploring and the sun was dropping. I stopped at the King's Inn Motel, walked past a row of electric plugs for guests' cars, and checked in. It was clean and comfortable, and the cost was only about double what I had often paid for a nice campsite.

Early the next morning I stretched and worked out. My regular before-dawn exercise routine was even more important than usual, because I was getting so little physical activity otherwise. During my workout I turned on television, hoping to find a useful weather report, even though in that part of the state the broadcast would be coming from across the state line behind me. My timing was interesting. The announcer way saying that North Dakota's governor had presented the Theodore Roosevelt Rough Rider Award—North Dakota's highest award—to aviation pioneer Carl Ben Eielson.

West of Culbertson the horizon seems to extend forever. Least Heat Moon found this part of his journey to be unsettling, disquieting. John Faris back in the glory days of the TRIH had a different reaction. There were "joys," in following "for one hundred miles the sometimes deeply eroded channels of the Missouri River, then . . . the Milk

River." He was openly excited by the "boundless sweep of the broad open spaces" of Montana. As for John Steinbeck, "I am in love with Montana," he wrote.

The Hi-Line crosses the Fort Peck Indian Reservation, but most of what I saw was highway and prairie. I drove on through Brockton, listening to Rod Stewart singing, "What Made Milwaukee Famous Made a Loser Out of Me." At about Brockton I was in Montana's Bad Lands.

Poplar came next. Although I didn't see it, Daniel Vichorek said that A & S Tribal Industries there is the largest manufacturing plant in Montana. The plant's owners are the Assiniboine and Sioux Tribes of the Fort Peck Reservation. Vichorek's *The Hi-Line* (1993), as its blurb says, "captures the spirit of this survivors-only area."

The 1921 *Guide* listed Poplar as the county seat of Roosevelt County, but the seat now is at Wolf Point, which came next. Least Heat Moon recounts the often-repeated story of how residents there over a century ago slaughtered a huge number of wolves. They left the carcasses to rot. No wolf, he said, has been seen in the area since, and there was some thought that the stench had driven them away. My thought is that it was a tall and unpleasant tale, but one that fit with Heat Moon's view of Wolf Point.

Next, came Nashua. There, I digressed to take State Highway 117 south to Fort Peck. The distance is only about ten miles; near enough to the TRIH to be considered a point of interest on the Highway.

Fort Peck attracts more than Hi-Line travelers. It is known throughout a wide region for its summer stock at the Fort Peck Theatre. The building is barnlike, large and gaudy but still appealing. Within it are live performances in a too-short season, mid-June to Mid-August, and the Fort Peck Hotel provides accommodations to theatergoers and others.

Fort Peck itself has a shopping center, but the entire town was very quiet. Few people were around. Not far distant were the Fort Peck Dam and Reservoir. Vichorek wrote that the reservoir is "one of the planetary features visible from earth orbit." I can believe it.

The Powerhouses are twin towers housing control valves for four water release tunnels 250 feet down. Two of the tunnels supply water to the towers for power generation. The other two are for emergency release. Each is a mile and a half long, and 24 feet 8 inches in diameter.

Inside the Museum the atmosphere is bright and cheerful. Outside the Powerhouse is another matter. The towers themselves impressed me as dark and foreboding. I remember them as black, even though in fact they are a rather light gray. They reminded me of some art deco version of "1984"—imposing structures towering over the lake and the prairies. This has nothing to do with their purpose or function, but their visual effect on me was eerie, suggesting some dehumanized, totalitarian, future. I had the same feeling even when I drove through the recreation area in the hills above them, looking down to see their dominance of the plains.

From Nashua, the Hi-Line and the Missouri part company. The river's course drops toward the south while the road's veers farther to the north.

Glasgow, the county seat of Valley County, is one of many railroad towns along the Hi-Line with names that Great Northern officials chose at random from a globe. This one is larger than the typical Hi-Line town, which consists of a small cluster of buildings and grain elevators. Glasgow may in fact be the largest along the eastern part of the Hi-Line—and it has the "Glasgow International Airport," and the potential of a former Air Force base—but "large" is always relative, especially on the Great Plains. The town has a population of about 3,600.

Unfortunately, Glasgow's Pioneer Museum was closed for the season. In December 1996, along with the Montana Historical Society and the Montana Department of Transportation, the Museum had sponsored the reprinting of the 1921 *Guide to Montana*. The Montana Division of the TR Highway Association originally published the *Guide* to assist travelers who were making the difficult journey along the TR Trail.

There were ridiculously few of the new booklets. The entire run, in fact, consisted of only 25 copies. But there is a saving grace: it is widely available. Recognizing its great historical value, the Department of Transportation put the entire publication on its web site.

A lifetime resident, Manson Bailey, Jr., told me that the Museum reproduced the booklet to honor 98-year-old Edward Gersgacher, who was the oldest person living who had been a construction worker on the TR Highway. Bailey is well-versed in regional history. His extensive involvement in public service includes three terms in the Montana House of Representatives, and an active role in helping to establish the Museum. He said that Gersgacher, who died later at the age of 99, had "taken 50 head of horses to Chinook, where they helped construct the road."

Bailey remembered the route of the Highway through Glasgow, south of 6th Avenue and across the bridge over the Milk River. He also recalled a local man engaged in real estate and insurance who painted, and planted, posts marking the TRIH. Bailey's father, Manson Bailey, Sr., some three-quarters of a century previously, had been elected county surveyor. In that office he worked on the TRIH in eastern Valley County.

My explorations had eaten up a good part of the day, so when I discovered a Roosevelt Hotel, I checked in. It still serves Burlington Northern personnel. Bailey said that it had been built during the construction of the Fort Peck Dam, a New Deal project. It therefore took its name from FDR, not TR.

Glasgow seems far from affluent. In an odd way, it reminded me of run-down communities in the semi-desert country of eastern New Mexico. There was little traffic, or movement.

After dinner, I sought local color in "Montana Bar, Stan's Saloon." I entered and found a bar on my left, along the wall. To my right was a raised platform with a large-screen television, and huge speakers. I then remembered the sign outside that said "karaoke." A man was near the television adjusting the equipment.

I sat on a barstool, and the bartender, a pleasant-faced but rather tired-looking woman, took my order. Three or four men were clustered at the other end of the bar. As the she was getting my beer, the bartender turned to yell to a middle-aged woman just walking in from the street.

"Here comes the stripper!" she said laughing.

No way. I wouldn't impose that on anyone—not even on these guys!" the woman retorted grinning as she joined the group at the bar. She sat, and a spirit of camaraderie was obvious from the easy-going banter.

The Hanger Bar, Montana

The bartender brought my beer. "Where you from?" she asked.

"Kansas City," I said as I laid down my money.

She gazed at me in puzzlement.

"Then what in the HELL are you doing in Glasgow?" she wanted to know.

I told her about the TRIH, and the more I talked, the more interested she seemed. Then I told her I was writing a book.

"No kidding!" she marveled. "Hey guys," she yelled to the group at the end of the bar, "this fellow's writing a book!"

Before they could reply, there was a sudden blast of sound from behind me. It almost knocked me from the stool.

"JEEsus **CHRIST**!!" she shouted as I jumped and turned to look.

The man on the stage behind me laughed, and said, "Just checking my sound system."

I turned back to the bar as a Beatles song began, followed by other pieces. The music was too loud for conversation. Then, as I emptied my glass, I noticed everyone had turned to face the stage. The bartender also was staring.

Twisting around on my stool to see what was going on, I saw something I hadn't expected to find along the Hi-Line: semi-nude soft-core porn videos. In true karaoke spirit, they had large and legible words to the music running along the bottom of the screen. The words were coordinated to the songs, but had nothing to do with the images.

I finished my drink, put a tip on the bar, and started for the door. Seeing me leave, the bartender called out to me. I couldn't hear over the music, so I walked back to see what she was saying.

"My name's Pat," she told me, "in case you want to put me in your book."

"I'll do that," I told her.

I left early the next morning. On a hill not far down the road were huge animal figures, including dinosaurs. The new Highway 2 goes to the north of the Milk River. Along the south bank of the river, the original road goes for a few miles from Glasgow through Tampico and Vandalia before crossing back to rejoin U.S. 2. This is the route that Manson Bailey remembered.

Passing Hinsdale, I drove until I stopped for a break in Saco. I parked at the curb, and walked past a shop. According to its sign it offered an interesting array of goods and services: Liquor store/Laundrymat/Library, and ANTIQUES. I stepped into Bob's Bar for a Coke. After the bright sun of the plains, it was dark inside. It was light enough, though, that I could read the small sign on the wall. "If assholes could fly, this place would be an airport." Bob probably knows his customers, but at that time of day there were only a few of them, all sitting quietly.

The country west of Glasgow to my surprise had become somewhat marshy. I kept expecting the plains to be much drier than I often found them. Along the way was a stream that probably was an irrigation ditch. On both sides of the road for some distance were mounds. They seemed to have been manmade. At Lake Bowdin I found a wildlife refuge, along with beautiful vistas.

Malta, another town with an international name (and another that was picked at random from a globe) was next, then Wagner. Between the two near mileage post 467 is one of Montana's signature highway signs. It marks the site of a famous train robbery. Attacking the train with Kid Curry's gang, tradition has it, were Butch Cassidy and the Sundance Kid. The lengthy sign concludes:

> Kid Curry's stomping ground in the 1880s was the Little Rockies country about forty miles southwest of here. July 3, 1901, he pulled off a premature Independence Day celebration by holding up the Great Northern No. 3 passenger train and blowing the express car safe near this point. His departure was plumb abrupt. The Great Northern would still probably like to know where he is holed up.

The Old West was notorious for producing outlaws, and the Hi-Line region was no exception. Havre historian Gary A. Wilson fed the hunger for details about Western desperadoes in his 1995 *Outlaw Tales of Montana*. He includes famous and lesser-known miscreants from throughout northern Montana, among whom in addition to Kid Curry were George "Big Nose" Parrott, George "Flat Nose" Currie, "Long" Henry Thomson, "Con" Murphy, and many others.

The sign, by the way, is one of scores of such whimsical roadside markers scattered throughout Montana. Their texts stem from the wit of Robert H. Fletcher, who founded Montana's historical markers program in the 1930s. He worked for the state as a traffic engineer, and also provided it with creative travel literature. Asa T. (or "Ace") Kendrick was responsible for the lettering, and Irvin H. "Shorty" Shope, for the artwork. The signs warranted a book of their own, so Glenda Clay Bradshaw compiled them for the Montana Historical Society. Her volume, *Montana's Historical Highway Markers* (1994), not only reproduces their texts and illustrations, but also identifies their locations and provides a bibliography of related materials.

Business District, Saco, Montana

Wagner is a run down place, almost a ghost town. I found a stretch of the old highway, and followed it for miles along the railroad, back in the direction of Malta. I settled in Malta in the middle of the afternoon, so that I could do my laundry, and checked into the Great Northern Hotel.

I found a coin laundry and also visited the Phillips County Museum. Although I found no TRIH information there, it had a very nice dinosaur exhibit, bones and all. Least Heat Moon wrote of the desolation and empty space along the Hi-Line, but beneath that there seems to be a historical consciousness within these small prairie communities, and a devotion to preservation.

Relaxing in my room after dinner, reading, I was startled by a loud siren. It sounded like a Midwestern tornado warning. I looked out the window at the city, the plains, and the sky. There was a large, dark black cloud, but nothing to indicate wind, and I didn't think the cloud looked especially threatening. I called the desk to ask if it were a tornado warning. "No," she laughed. "That signal goes off every night at nine thirty to warn young people to get off the streets."

The next morning I checked out and went to the truck. Parked in front of it was a sheriff's car. Deputy Greg Sandsness was sitting at the wheel, observing traffic. I introduced myself, and explained about the TRIH. The Highway was news to him, but he was interested, and said he would look around for some sign of it. I also asked him about the siren, and whether there was a problem with young people.

"No," he said. "We do have a curfew, but it's midnight. We don't have any real problems, especially with kids. I don't really know how it got started, but the 9:30 siren is a tradition. It just warns kids they shouldn't be out."

The day was bright and hot. I had a good view of Dodson as I drove through. The town is tiny and deteriorating, with a population not much over 100. The 1921 *Guide* said that it had a population of 400, and had "hotel and long distance telephone." Nowadays, except for a restaurant, the only business seemed to be the one requirement for a Hi-Line community: the "Cowboy Bar."

I crossed onto the Fort Belknap Indian Reservation. On my left was a small dam creating a pond. I stopped at the Fort Belknap Indian Reservation Visitors' Center, chatted with the attendants, and then visited Fort Belknap College.

The College's buildings were small and rudimentary, but when I heard about them, they became impressive. The College (Box 159, Harlem, Montana 59526) was a source of pride to the impoverished community. Eva English, its Library Director, told me that the students had been so determined to have a community college to serve the Reservation that they built the buildings themselves. The College library was small, but professionally arranged and administered with loving care.

Driving on, I passed out of Harlem, which in addition to Fort Belknap College boasts the tribal headquarters. The landscape remained somewhat bleak. I passed lazily through Zurich.

Down the road was a bridge. Its overhead structure had a large, orange sign. Between two large black arrows pointing downward was the information, also in black, "14 FT 6 IN."

On it was a large truck carrying a piece of heavy earth-moving equipment. The truck's displayed a yellow, "OVERSIZE LOAD" sign. I reduced speed. My first thought was that the truck was creeping slowly across, but as I drew nearer I recognized that it was stuck. The roof of the cab of the earth-mover on the truck was solidly against the bridge's superstructure. I had to wait until traffic cleared to go around the unintentional blockade.

The next town was Chinook, where I visited the Blaine County Museum. In addition to fossil exhibits and pioneer artifacts, there was a multi-media presentation on the story of Chief Joseph and his ultimate surrender, which occurred in 1877 near Chinook. A temporary employee told me that she didn't know anything about the TRIH, but she knew many of the old routes.

Holding her hands about three feet apart, she said, smiling, "I drove U.S. 2 when it was only this wide." Lowering her hands, she thought briefly, and asked rhetorically, "You know what would be the best thing for you to do? Go to the Chinook *Opinion* and talk to its editor, Mike Perry."

On the way to the *Opinion*, I saw the offices of the Blaine County *Journal*. I asked the woman behind the desk if she knew about the TR Highway, and she said, "Mother is 95. When I was very small, I remember my father speaking of the Theodore Roosevelt Highway coming through." That's all though.

At the *Opinion*, Mike and Mary Perry said they would look forward to my book, and asked me to send them copies of any articles I might write on the TRIH. The pa-

TR Monument, Marias Pass, Glacier National Park, Montana

per's files were incomplete, and there was nothing for the years 1921-1922. I was surprised that there was not even anything about the dedication of the monument at Marias Pass in 1931. Although it is in the same state, the Pass may be so far away that activities there weren't considered news in Chinook at that time.

I was able to find two articles about accidents on the TRIH. On the 11th of October, 1923, under the headline "Many Upsets and Injuries," the *Opinion* expressed concern about dangers on the road. On the 22nd of November, the paper reported that the TR Highway had claimed a fatality.

When I entered Chinook, I had passed the remains of the Utah-Idaho Sugar Company. Its smoke stack still reached high toward the sky. Spritzer wrote that the factory had moved to Chinook from Yakima, Washington in 1924 after insects had devastated Washington's sugar beet fields. He said it had "helped the town weather the lean decades of the 1920s and 1930s better than most neighboring communities," but by 1951, competition had caused it to shut down. Still, a legacy remains. Spritzer noted that "The local high school athletic teams proudly sport the nickname 'Sugarbeeters'."

It was in Havre (pronounced HAV-er) that I received a number of surprises. By Great Plains standards, Havre is a city. Its population of nearly 10,000 makes it substantial presence. Vichorek called it "a sort of capital of all that territory," the Hi-Line. "Located somewhere near the middle of it," he wrote, it had a modern hospital and a university. Demonstrating clearly that it rejected its isolation, it even had a mall!

Regardless of its size, Havre has something that many larger places lack: a book of its own history. Gary Wilson first described Havre's colorful past in 1985 in his *Honky-Tonk Town*. His book has gone through at least five printings, the fifth being in 1995.

Wilson demonstrated that a small town can have a background as interesting—and as corrupt—as that of a major city. Machine politics and urban corruption formed a well-known pattern during a portion of American history. What is much less well-known, is that corrupt boss politics in small-town, rural America has often equaled and sometimes exceeded its urban counterpart. The difference is that writers rush to produce urban exposés—they sell. Few publishers would risk bringing out a work about politics in a small town; none would dare to do so about a lightly-populated rural area, so we tend to think of machine politics as being exclusively urban. Wilson's work is exceptional, but the rule applied to him as well—he had to publish with a local firm, and it is doubtful that his multiple printings have translated into broad distribution.

Havre sits on a site originally called "Bull Hook Bottoms." Wilson called it the heart of Milk River country. Lewis and Clark, by the way, as their Journal notes gave the river its odd name; the water's color made them think of tea with milk. Almost a century later, James J. Hill's Great Northern Railroad puffed into the area in the early 1890s displacing earlier settlers.

Hill quickly selected a committee to devise a new name. He thought "Bull Hook Bottoms" lacked dignity. The largest Great Northern maintenance facility west of St. Paul, over 900 miles east, deserved better. The committee's choice of "Havre" reflected the French background of its members. Their first suggestion, "France," apparently impressed no one.

As for the town's background, Hill almost relocated his railroad from the area because it was so corrupt. He discovered that it was almost impossible to get good family men to agree to live there, and his single workers were likely to be lost to "corrupt influences." Those influences included gambling, prostitution, narcotics, bootlegging, the smuggling of Chinese laborers, murder, kidnapping, highjackings, and more. Local police, in fact, were known to have committed some of the highjackings. During prohibition, despite one crackdown after another, liquor flowed freely across the border from Canada, where it was legal. The Havre bootlegging ring boasted that it had supplied illegal liquor to every state in the Union except for Maine. The tiny, isolated, town apparently even served as the headquarters for an international ring of bank robbers.

Wilson cites a Chicago *Mail-Tribune* news release of January 1916 calling Havre "One wicked little city." A "Law and Order League" of Chicago had journeyed from there to the West Coast, and issued reports for each of the 28 "principle cities en route." Of all the places visited, the report said, "a little city called Havre is incomparatively [*sic*] the worst. Everything is licensed there and its most vicious forms of evil are found in broad daylight in the streets and trading areas. There is no protection for anyone against anything."

All was under the tight control of a local political boss—just like Chicago, Jersey City, Boston, Kansas City, and other less isolated and more advanced regions. He was Shorty Young, a five-foot two-inch powerhouse who, according to Wilson, had his standards. Prevailing through repeated waves of reform attempts, Young once vetoed a decision by the local mob (the "Havre Bunch") to assassinate a particularly troublesome police chief. Rather than kill him, they merely forced him to leave town. Just before he departed, Young called the former chief to his office and informed him of his narrow escape. Young told him he "respected an honest lawman; it was kind of refreshing," he said, "even though troublesome."

Incongruously, Young also had a reputation for philanthropy. When he died, he specified explicitly that his estate be used for humanitarian purposes.

Such notorious western centers of violence and corruption as Dodge City, Abilene, El Paso, and the like tended like a box of matches to flare suddenly. They were hot, but they burned out quickly. Their rough periods generally lasted no more than a decade or two. Havre's, in contrast, had staying power. Its gangsters reflected a western entrepreneurial spirit, and they maintained the town's wicked ways for decades, aided often by the closeness of an international border. Havre consistently beat back reform attempts until the 1940s.

Now, though, Havre's local government is almost depressingly clean. As Wilson put it, the height of scandal there these days is likely to be an official meeting that wasn't fully open to the public.

One of Montana's road signs just outside of town puts it this way:

Cowpunchers, miners, and soldiers are tolerably virile persons as a rule. When they went to town in the frontier days seeking surcease from vocational cares and solace in the cup that cheers it was just as well for the urbanites to either brace themselves or take to cover. The citizens of any town willing and able to be host city for a combination of the above diamonds in the rough had to be quick on the draw and used to inhaling powder smoke.

Havre came into existence as a division point when the Great Northern Railroad was built and purveyed pastime to cowboys, doughboys and miners on the side. It is hard to believe now, but as a frontier camp, she was wild and hard to curry.

Havre's university is a branch of Montana State. It has a small but useful library. The public library also has good resources. One of its librarians, Francine Brady, went out of her way to provide excellent help.

When I asked her for papers from the 1920s and for any archival materials from that decade regarding roads, I received one of my surprises. She responded, "Oh, you're working on the Theodore Roosevelt Highway!"

Whatever I might have expected her to say, that wasn't it. She said that she once had researched the Highway for someone else. It was so long ago, though, that she no longer remembered who it was.

It was good to find materials in Havre about the TRIH, even though they didn't add anything to the information I already had. Of course, I was curious about the other researcher. I still am.

The day was slipping away, and I still had more to do. I didn't want to leave without experiencing Havre Beneath the Streets, and by the time that were to be finished, I might as well spend the night. I set up camp not far away in the Clack Memorial Museum and Campground, and returned to town.

In 1904, a huge fire burned much of Havre, including most of the downtown. Undaunted, the businesses continued to operate in their basements. These basements were connected by passages under the sidewalks, and steam tunnels. Today, the area is a museum that reconstructs enterprises from Havre's past.

The range is wide. Among the exhibits are an opium den, a bordello, a saloon, a mortuary, a hideout for Chinese illegal immigrants (who needed more to evade local ruffians than law-enforcement officials), an ice-cream parlor, a bank, a post office, newspaper offices, a blacksmith shop, a Chinese laundry, a bakery, and more. Those who take the underground tour can even see Shorty Young's office, where in Havre's bygone days the diminutive boss gave orders, pulled political strings, and controlled his surprisingly far-flung empire.

In Havre Beneath the Streets, the town has a gem—even though the town doesn't own it. Creating the fascinating glimpse of a colorful past was left to a nonprofit private group. Contrasting with the small-town booster spirit that nearly always prevails, residents of Havre seem particularly unconcerned about their fine exhibit. When I mentioned that it was something I didn't want to miss, several residents said, "Oh, really? Why would you want to see that?"

I returned to camp to write up my notes, and wait for darkness. Thunderheads were building quickly over the prairie. I watched them form during the sunset, turning black then reflecting the sun's red. They towered above the plains and threatened wind and rain. As soon as it became dark, I crawled into my tent and my light sleeping bag, and listened to the strong wind and the rumbling thunder. I loved it.

On the road the next morning, the Sweetgrass Hills were ahead of me to the northwest. I could still see the Bear's Paw Mountains to the south. There were remnants of shacks—often a standing chimney—that probably marked abandoned homesteads. Grain elevators were among the most frequent landmarks.

More towns with exotic names came and went: Kremlin, Gildford, Hingham, Rudyard, and Inverness. I stopped only in Hingham, just briefly, to snap a photo of the one original building left in town. "Est. 1913," the sign said. I thought it an ironic touch— and a somewhat sad one—that the building was abandoned. Then came Joplin, which described itself as the "Biggest Little Town on Earth."

Spritzer said that all these towns grew up with high aspirations. They may not have realized those aspirations, but as he noted they "managed to hang on through the drought and depression decades." He pointed out that each "still serves an agrarian hinterland, contains a grain elevator as the economic center of town, and supports a school as the educational and social center." Many other towns that had equally high aspirations have vanished from maps, and from the landscape.

Chester calls itself "The Heart of the Hi-Line," and Spritzer must agree. He wrote that it "outshone all the other small homestead communities between Havre and Shelby." As evidence, he cited Chester's defeat of Joplin in a 1919 election to become county seat of Liberty County.

Vichorek added to the story. He wrote that after Chester won, "Jopliners had another inning." They circulated petitions to redraw county boundaries more to their liking. "In order to keep track of this treacherous activity, the Chester interests stationed a man on the water tower in Inverness to keep them informed where the cars from Joplin went with their petition. Then the Chesterites lobbied the same citizens visited by the Jopliners, and won that election too."

I found Chester interesting, but for another reason. I had heard that a Roosevelt Street there dated from the TRIH. A waitress in Spud's Café served me soup and iced tea, and disappointed me by saying, she couldn't think of any Roosevelt Street, but she referred me to another customer.

He agreed that there was no Roosevelt Street, but when I explained to him about the TRIH, he said, "Well, there is the Roosevelt Station; a filling station. Everyone still calls it that. It was named for the Roosevelt Highway. I've been here all my life and I'm 76 and it's always been the Roosevelt Station. The building's about the same as it's always been."

I found the station, on a corner on U.S. 2, facing the highway. It still is in operation, but nothing identifies it as the Roosevelt Station so I hadn't noticed it. The owner, Bob Nordstrom, said he didn't know much about its history, but he did know that it is routinely called the Roosevelt Station because it was named for the Roosevelt Highway.

I added another remnant of the TRIH to my file.

Shelby, "America's Crossroads," sits on the junction of U.S. 2 and Interstate 15. That might get it listed in geography books, but it also has a claim to fame that warrants it a place in history books. The most famous fight in Montana's history took place in

Original Troy-Libby Road/TR Highway, Montana

Shelby—I should say the most famous *prize* fight. Custer and Sitting Bull did, after all, have their own contest in what is now Montana.

The fight took place on the 4th of July, 1923. By then, the TRIH made it possible to get to Shelby by automobile. The bout was a world heavyweight boxing match between the champion, Jack Dempsey, and Tommy Gibbons. Promoters had arranged it, built an enormous stadium, promised huge sums of money, expected vast crowds, and lost almost everything.

Spritzer called it "a clear case of rampant boosterism." There had been so many bad loans to promote the contest that afterward, banks failed not only in Shelby but also in Great Falls and Joplin.

The weakness of the early TRIH, which had enabled motorists to get to Shelby, was also apparent. It was inadequate to enable them to get away. A huge rainstorm turned the road into a sea of mud. Many would-be drivers had to ship their cars out by train.

Still, there was a fight. Spritzer admitted that it did "put Shelby, Montana, in the national limelight." However brief, and however improbable it was, Shelby had its moment of fame.

The day was cloudless, but a fierce headwind had developed. I passed another segment of the old highway, this time off to the right, but it too was closed. Then, I witnessed the TR Highway's first display of REAL western mountains—snow covered ones.

Apart from distant mountain views, the scenery on to Cut Bank was typically Hi-Line. There, the display of the Rocky Mountains began in earnest. Another display greets the traveler at Cut Bank's city limits: a huge, apparently concrete, penguin standing above the greeting: "Welcome to Cut Bank MT. Coldest Spot in the Nation."

As a matter of fact, the coldest temperature ever recorded in the forty-eight states did indeed occur in Montana, but it was not at Cut Bank. The date was the 20th of January, 1954. The temperature was 70 degrees below zero. The altitude was 6,376 feet above sea level. The place was Rogers Pass, a rugged area where Montana 200 crosses the Continental Divide between Great Falls and Missoula. The instrument was an official thermometer of what then was called the U.S. Weather Bureau. Cut Bank, though, undoubtedly is cold enough.

The penguin bears the notation: "By Ron Gustafson." I asked a waitress at the Golden Harvest about it. She told me, "He had a wild hair and just decided to put up a penguin because Cut Bank should be above the Arctic Circle." I thought that with a penguin, perhaps it should be below the Antarctic Circle, but I kept it to myself. The proprietor at the Glacier Gateway Inn supported the idea that the whole project was done on a whim. "My son just decided to build it," he said. That was in 1989.

I turned off the highway to follow signs to the Glacier County Historical Museum. Thelma Rhind, there, remembered the TR Highway well.

"It's U.S. 2 now," she said, "but when I was little it was the Theodore Roosevelt Highway. It went right through Cut Bank."

She was born in Kalispell, but moved with her parents to Kevin, in the oil fields north of Shelby. Kevin, and its neighbor to the north, Sunburst, began as oil and gas towns. She has lived in Cut Bank since 1940. For a time in the 1930s, she lived near

Essex, and saw the Izaak Walton Inn being built. At first, she said, the inn was only for railroaders. Her parents at the time owned a service station and some tourist cabins at Pinnacle, on the road just west of Essex, and she recalls thinking of the inns in Glacier National Park as being the height of luxury.

She and her colleague Martha Ann Worth were unusually helpful. They eagerly dug into the Museum's archives, looking for materials on the TRIH, and their search was successful. Not only did they find county plans and maps for 1928 that clearly identified the TRIH, but they also permitted me to photograph them.

After leaving the Museum, I stopped at a farmer's market and discovered that the vendors were Hutterites. They said their farms were some twenty miles or so distant. I knew that they, along with Amish and similar groups, were likely to be sensitive about photographs, so I asked them if I could take a picture of the market. They said that would be all right. It even would be acceptable if they happened to be in the picture, but they could not pose for one, or be the specific subject.

After Cut Bank, there was no doubt that the plains were ending. Just west of the town the Blackfeet Indian Reservation begins, the flatness recedes, and the highway narrows. Twenty miles or so from Cut Bank, a Lewis and Clark Monument stands on a high bluff on the Reservation looking far over railroad tracks and foothills all the way to the rugged, snowcapped, Rockies. It also overlooks the northernmost point that the Corps of Discovery reached in its amazing journey.

The monument commemorates "Camp Disappointment." Meriwether Lewis had separated for a time from William Clark to explore north along the Marias River in an

Cut Bank, Montana

attempt to find the northernmost drainage of the Missouri. He found that the Marias flowed not from the north but from the southwest, and that there was no connection between the Marias and Saskatchewan Rivers. A connection might have enabled the Canadian fur trade to be diverted down the Missouri to the United States, and a source farther north for the Marias could have expanded the boundary of the Louisiana Purchase. He and his men stayed four days in disappointment, and named their camp accordingly.

The night after leaving Camp Disappointment, Lewis and his party met a small group of Piegan Blackfeet. Lewis had hoped to avoid the Piegan, but at first, all went well: the two groups camped together peacefully that night. Unfortunately, peace evaporated the next morning. The resulting skirmish left two of the warriors dead. It was the only case of a fatal conflict with Indians during the entire Lewis and Clark Expedition, but it poisoned relations between the white invaders and the native residents in the area.

Whether or not it reflects that lingering hostility or simple vandalism, the monument bears the marks of rough treatment. The obelisk—probably eight or ten feet high—is scarred with graffiti, chipped and spray-painted. Sadly, although it is a National Historic Landmark, there obviously is little or no maintenance. It stands not, as intended, as the proud memorial of a brave and valuable expedition. Rather it is a sorry reminder of the tragic conflict between two cultures. One might add that it also is a sad commentary on the unwillingness of the United States to spend the money necessary to keep its monuments, parks, and the like, as befits national treasures—even permitting them sometimes to become national embarrassments.

Browning, "The Home of Indian Pride," hosts the office of the Blackfeet Tribe. It also has the Museum of the Plains Indian. I found that the Museum had dedicated and pleasant personnel. I was pleased by the extent of its collection of Indian artifacts.

After visiting the Museum, I stopped at a combination grocery store and café for lunch. On the way in, I passed several motorcycles parked near the door. The leather-clad bikers, four of them, were sitting together at a table.

I struck up a conversation. Their American wanderlust took a different form from mine, but was similar. Even though they hadn't heard of the TRIH, they seemed to appreciate what I was doing.

They had decided to take some months off their various jobs to go to Sturgis, South Dakota for the annual bikers' rally, and also simply to roam the land, vacationing. They had been out to California redwood country, and were heading back east, camping along the way. The night before, they said, was too cold in the mountains, so they stayed in a motel.

They all were from the South. Denny Breland, from Hattiesburg, Mississippi was riding an antique '72 Harley. He complained that his carburetor was messed up, and was using an extra gallon per tank. Also from Hattiesburg was Dan, "Mad Dog" Bryant. Mark George, the leader, was from the small town of Purvis, Mississippi. The fourth member of the group was Rick Mize from Spartenburg, South Carolina. We briefly compared notes on our trips, and wished one another well.

The road was still under construction. I drove over gravel. Then, pavement resumed. I passed mountain lakes, and drove over a deep ravine. At East Glacier I passed the east entrance to Glacier National Park. The highway twisted through mountains that I described in my notes with one word: "outstanding."

Glacier country demanded that I spend some time and not hurry through, so I had reserved a room that night at Glacier Park Lodge, and the next night at Izaak Walton Inn. I was happy that I did. The lobby at Glacier Lodge is four stories high. Enormous logs, complete with bark, stand as pillars. Along with the other hotels in Glacier Park, it is rustic and satisfying. Lake McDonald Lodge and Many Glacier Lodge similarly are vast, rustic, lovely structures, with huge fireplaces, comfortable bars, and enormous tree trunks for pillars.

The most dramatic of all the Park hotels is the Prince of Wales, across the Canadian border in Waterton/Glacier International Peace Park. The Prince of Wales sits atop a high bluff overlooking the mirror-smooth surface of the extensive Waterton Lake. The Lake is surrounded by sharp rocky peaks that tower even above the hotel on its elevation. The Prince of Wales offers accommodations similar to the other Park hotels, but its views are the most dramatic of all.

They all require a trek to the upper floors—there are no elevators—and there is no air conditioning. In that climate with cool breezes common there generally is no need for it. The absence of telephones and television, under the circumstances, is as much a relief as a lack.

I roamed around the Glacier Park Hotel, and found a large photo exhibit just off its lobby. The scenes included vintage views of the railroad and the region, with some early shots of the TR Highway. John Chase of Great Falls, Montana, a collector of railroad antiques and artifacts, put together much of the fine display.

Across the way from the hotel was the railroad station. There I watched the train come in, discharge and collect passengers, and go on its way. I also met the Amtrak Agent, Patty Hughes. She told me that she lived in the station with Chinook, the large brown dog sleeping at her feet. She was, she said, the last Amtrak stationmaster who still lived in a station.

"When I moved in, it was like a cave in here. The setting was dark and gloomy. It was all covered with old walnut varnish. I painted everything white to make it more cheerful."

She knew about the TR Highway.

"Most of it was along Route 2," she remembered, "and from Mesaba Avenue in Duluth on west it was the Main Street through all the communities."

The next morning I drove on to Summit, on the Continental Divide at Marias Pass, which has the lowest elevation of any pass on the Divide in the northern United States, 5,220 feet. Also standing on the Continental Divide where the Lewis and Clark National Forest and the Flathead National Forest meet is the 60-foot tall Theodore Roosevelt Monument that had inspired my journey. The obelisk commemorates TR's contributions to conservation and also the completion of the highway that I was traveling. A plaque at the site says:

A 56-mile section of highway over Marias Pass was the last section of the Theodore Roosevelt International Highway to be completed. Prior to the completion of this section in 1930, automobiles were loaded onto railcars and transported from one side of the pass to the other. The Theodore Roosevelt International Highway extends 4,060 miles from Portland, Maine, to Portland, Oregon, by way of Ontario, Canada.

Fortunately, the monument no longer stands, as it did for decades, in the middle of the road.

It was still a danger to traffic when Least Heat Moon in the early 1980s drove east across Montana, unaware that he was on the TR Highway. He wrote that "in the middle of the pavement at the top of Marias Pass stood a tall limestone obelisk marking the divide and also commemorating Teddy Roosevelt. Your basic double-duty monument." Double duty it performed, but it was to honor TR and his highway, not to mark the Divide.

One side of the monument has a plaque reading:

FLATHEAD
NATIONAL FOREST
MEMORIAL TO
THEODORE
ROOSEVELT

IN COMMEMORATION
OF HIS LEADERSHIP IN
THE CONSERVATION OF THE
FORESTS OF THE
UNITED STATES
'THE FOREST PROBLEM IS
IN MANY WAYS THE MOST
VITAL INTERNAL PROBLEM
OF THE UNITED STATES[1]

THEODORE ROOSEVELT

Another side has a plaque from the other forest:

LEWIS AND CLARK
NATIONAL FOREST
MEMORIAL TO
THEODORE
ROOSEVELT

THIS MEMORIAL WAS
AUTHORIZED BY A BILL
INTRODUCED IN THE CONGRESS
OF THE UNITED STATES OF
AMERICA, BY REPRESENTATIVE
SCOTT LEAVITT, FEBRUARY I,

1930 AND APPROVED BY
PRESIDENT HOOVER ON
JUNE 2, 1930

The monument since 1989 has been in the park, with ample space for cars. Whether there or on the road, it remains the largest and most striking reminder of the TR Highway that still exists. A sign at the site says that "Congress appropriated $25,000 for the memorial in 1930. The monument was originally to have been a granite arch spanning the highway. Instead, this obelisk was built, and the 1,500 pound cornerstone was laid on August 23, 1930."

The law in question, H.R. 9412, stipulated "That the Secretary of Agriculture is authorized and directed to erect a suitable archway spanning the Theodore Roosevelt International Highway on the continental divide at the summit of the Rocky Mountains on the boundary between the Lewis and Clark National Forest and the Flathead National Forest in Montana." This legislation seems to give clear official legal recognition from the Government of the United States to the Theodore Roosevelt International Highway.

Also in the park were two other memorials. One was a statue of John Stevens, the rugged civil engineer who surveyed Marias Pass in 1889 for the Great Northern. Years later Theodore Roosevelt appointed him to play a major role in the construction of the Panama Canal. Stevens had been present at the dedication of the statue in 1925, where it stood on a bluff above the tracks. In 1989 when it was moved into the park, it had been the victim of target practice. A sculptor repaired it, and found that there were 32 bullet holes. The other memorial is a plaque and sign honoring the mountain man who donated the land for the park, William "Slippery Bill" Morrison.

I can't leave the subject of the monument to TR without mentioning a mystery surrounding it. Records indicated that a time capsule buried at the site contained several items, including a copy of the congressional act that provided the funds. There were even reports that purported to be eye-witness accounts of Eleanor Roosevelt—who as well as being FDR's wife was TR's niece—placing the items first in a copper box, and then in a hollowed out portion of a granite cube that was then sealed and buried.

As workers prepared the monument for its journey off the road and into the park, they located the heavy two-and-a-half foot cube. With considerable effort, they removed it from the earth, and transported it to the C. M. Russell Museum in Great Falls. There, it could be opened in a controlled climate.

In July of 1989, the opening took place. The *Daily Inter Lake* reported on the 27th, that "before television cameras and breathless observers, a concrete plug set in a hole in a granite block was chiseled away Wednesday in Great Falls to reveal—nothing." No one knows what happened, although the Museum's acting director, Ray Steele suspected that someone simply threw the capsule away or buried it in the ground in order "to avoid spending another couple of days drilling in the granite." Cynthia Hamlett, an archaeologist with the Lewis and Clark National Forest, said "It seems like somebody went to an awful lot of work not to have it there."

As a footnote to the mystery, Eleanor Roosevelt was nowhere in Montana at the time the "eye-witness account" placed her there. The FDR Library in Hyde Park, New

York has her appointment schedule, and there is nothing relating to a Montana trip at the time. There had been an entry that later was erased, and now is illegible. So, there is no information at all for the specific date in question, 25 October 1931, and her appointments for nearby dates make it impossible that she could have journeyed so far and returned so quickly in those pre-jet days. Such things make life—and of course history—interesting!

The road proceeds west from Summit through deep canyons, lush timberland, and ever-varying mountains. The rails on the right frequently go through long wooden snow sheds—understandable for a region that typically gets more than twenty feet of snow a season. Off to the left is Goat Lick. Pulling off into a parking lot, I walked down a trail to an observation platform. At the bottom of a deep ravine, and far across a river, was an area where mountain goats loiter, and gambol, but no one complains. Tourists—and I include myself—find it awesome. I would guess that even many of the locals do. The scene would have been spectacular even without my binoculars, but they brought it close in vivid detail.

At Essex I turned left, and within a few hundred yards came to the Izaak Walton Inn. The whole—Inn, structure, interior, and ambience—reflects the American railroad. Tracks run behind the building, and trains use them frequently. Amtrak stops nearby, and passengers can walk from the railway to check in. Across the tracks as a part of the Inn are restored cabooses; these serve as cabins for additional guests. Railroad photos, signal lights, timetables, and lore permeate the atmosphere. The rooms are comfortable, the food is good, and the abundant wildlife, mountains, and forests nourish the eye, and the soul.

The next morning I drove on to find pieces of the old road. Generally they were passable for a short distance and then required me to retrace my path. Near the west entrance to the Park, I set up camp early in the Glacier Campground. The campground is private, and outside the Park. Its facilities are excellent, and it is well-designed. The campsites are nestled into forested spaces to provide both privacy and a forest atmosphere. Signs cautioned campers to deposit their garbage in central locations. There had been trouble with bears.

I spent the day in the Park. The Going-to-the-Sun Road offers views that inspire the imagination, and stamp themselves vividly upon the memory. Other mountain views may equal those of Waterton/Glacier, but none exceed them in sheer beauty. I say that as one who has seen Mount Everest—admittedly dimly in the far distance, and from Nepal.

The Park offers vintage "Jammer" busses, red, open-topped, 1930s style (but modernized) for those who might enjoy the spectacle more without having to drive themselves.

In the morning I fixed breakfast, cleaned up, and set out early. Beyond the South Fork of the Flathead River was a spring by the side of the road. It flowed through interesting stone work, and I thought that it probably had been significant for the early travelers on the TRIH.

The Flathead River is a feast for the eyes, but Columbia Falls has no falls. It does have the *Hungry Horse News*.

I stopped at its offices to talk with the editor and publisher, Brian Kennedy. I had copies of a number of articles about the TRIH from early editions, and had hoped that there might be some archival information available. Kennedy told me that I had covered all bases already, and that as a matter of fact, he received his information from the National Park Service. He recounted to me the story of the bullet-ridden statue of John Stevens, and said that it required the services of a well-known sculptor to repair it.

The very first route of the TR Highway went on what now is Montana 40 to Whitefish, a historic community where local highway boosters met to plan the Montana segment of the TR Trail. In the early 1900s, railroad workers cut so many trees that the community came to be called "Stumptown." Whitefish has become a resort area. Its Stumptown Historical Society owns and has restored the Burlington Northern railroad depot. The depot still serves as a railroad station, but also houses offices and the Stumptown Museum.

From Whitefish for quite some distance the original route goes through wild and isolated country. It follows U.S. 93 northwest through the tiny villages of Olney and Striker, goes past Trego to Fortune, and Eureka. Everywhere I saw a dwelling, I saw animal skins and evidence of taxidermy. Eureka now is a tiny and quiet village. No evidence lingers that I could see of a violent and protracted labor dispute during the First World War that began there and spread through Northwest Montana's logging region.

As I drove, the weather turned threatening, and light rain fell, mixed with snowflakes. Just beyond Eureka, the route takes a left turn onto Montana 37 through Rexford, and runs along the miles-long Lake Koocanusa through the Kootenai National Forest. It passes the Libby Dam and Visitors' Center—where I didn't stop—and comes out at Libby.

I picked up U.S. 2 at Libby and took it east back to Columbia Falls so that I could follow the later route of the TR Highway, which went through Kalispell, rather than Eureka. The change occurred first as a temporary measure pending completion of better roads through Eureka, then before long became permanent. It shortened the distance, and ventured through more settled territory than the other way.

Leaving once again from Columbia Falls, I drove this time along U.S. 2 toward Kalispell. The road that had been narrow and winding, became flat and wide. Kalispell is a clean resort community with good restaurants, many attractive used bookstores—the oddly-named Club Algiers Bookstore is exceptionally good, thanks to Bonnie, its owner—and an impressive airport with jetliner service. The Grand Hotel is fully restored, and provides the atmosphere of bygone days in complete comfort and a spirit of fun. The mountain views are less impressive than those in Glacier Park, but are excellent even so.

Driving west from Kalispell, surveying the countryside was pleasant, although I didn't enjoy the many monster trucks. On the side of the highway by my left, was a pointed boulder. For no apparent reason, its top was painted blue. I passed Smith Lake, also on the left, which seemed to be a mountain pool in marshy land, and on the right were stone cliffs.

The earlier bad weather farther north had given way to clouds, with puffy cumulus buildups. The grasslands showed an amazing variety of greens, light and dark, all beautiful. The highway narrowed. A sign warned of range cattle. Shadow patterns appeared on the mountains. Traffic became lighter. Winds became stronger. A sense of isolation increased.

Ahead on the right I saw a sign advertising ice. The ice in my ice chest was almost gone so I stopped to get another block. It was a store, gasoline station, and campground. On the ice machine were two bumper stickers: "Ted Kennedy's car has killed more people than my gun," and "Ban Guns—Make the Streets Safe for a Government Takeover!"

As I paid for the ice and was walking out the door, I noticed three men beside a truck at the pumps. I think they had driven up while I was inside. One was filling their truck's tank.

All were loudly and irately condemning General Motors.

"I told you that On Star system was gonna spread," one said.

"How d'ya mean, spread?"

"First they said it was only on Cadillacs. Now you can get it on Buicks and SUVs. Pretty soon it'll be on every car. I wouldn't be surprised if they all got it now, only we don't know about it."

The "On Star system" is optional, and is a global satellite arrangement. If the driver's air bag deploys and there is no signal from the car to cancel it, the service can identify the location anywhere in the country and dispatch an ambulance. From a remote point the service can flash the car's lights, blow its horn, or unlock the doors if the keys get locked inside.

"Sure," the third man said, "people'r so dumb they'll pay to get this. Can you believe it? I guess it sounds good at first. That's what makes it so dangerous. When you start to think about it you're gonna realize that G.M.'s gonna be able to keep tabs on your car's location anywhere, anytime. Who're they gonna be feeding that information to?"

"Yeah, it'll be the CIA, the ATF, the FBI—you name it. You won't be able to hide anywhere. They could be all over you before you even know it."

"Well, hell," said one, "I sure won't buy a G.M. vehicle."

"You think that'll protect you? You can bet your ass every car sold in this country already has that chip in it. You just can't use it yourself if you don't pay extra. What's more, my guess is that it's gonna be in every gun that's manufactured here if it's not in 'em already. Then where'll freedom in this country be?"

I drove until I found something that demanded a stop: the Kickin Horse Saloon. It was a classic loggers' bar. The rail around the porch was made from large logs without bark, with horseshoes filling the spaces like gigantic chain mail. The "Kickin Horse Saloon" sign and the "Casino" sign each showed two horseshoes.

In the parking lot, pulled up to a rail fence with logs for posts that looked like driftwood and near a huge chunk of knotty tree trunk, was a bizarre car. It was an old convertible with the top down, black, with red and yellow flames painted on the sides. Even the tires were painted with swirls. On the passenger's door (I didn't see the other side) was a large white six-pointed star, with "KICKIN HORSE" lettered underneath.

Inside the saloon there was a large dance floor. The rustic décor included log beams and posts, pin-up posters, and a mounted assault rifle that looked to me as big as a cannon. It would have been right at home in a "Rambo" film—and was about as authentic. It was a fake; designed, said the server, for some local celebration.

Driving on, I passed the lovely Loon Lake. Later, I saw damage from widespread forest fires. There were disastrous fires around the area in, I think, 1994. The scars had lasted for years, and would be there for years to come. Elsewhere were stumps where logging companies had clear-cut large tracts. The clear-cutting made it possible to see the logging roads winding around the mountainsides.

Sprinkled here and there, usually at a distance, were rugged log cabins. These were authentic, not frou-frou vacation homes. The countryside, despite its beauty, seemed far remote from vacationland.

Beyond Fisher was very heavy forest. A small, wooden, abandoned building at the base of a mountain caught my interest. The mountains to the west were sharp and snow covered. Coming up to Libby Creek let me know that the town of Libby was not far.

On the eastern outskirts of Libby was the Heritage Museum. I was delighted inside to find that the Museum was exhibiting an antique Forest Service sign:

> KOOTENAI NATIONAL FOREST
> < ROOSEVELT HIGHWAY 1 M

In the sign's upper left corner was the old shield of the Service.

It may not have been a road marker, but after driving thousands of miles across the continent I had found a sign for the TRIH. The Museum, unfortunately, is open only for "the season," which in that part of the world means that it is closed for much of the year.

Libby is in an especially rugged mountainous and ravine-filled area called the "Montana Wilds." It sprang up as a gold-mining village and boomed for a time after the railroad reached it in 1891. It stretched out along the tracks, and ultimately settled down to become a rather attractive lumber town. Spritzer wrote that "early Libby was so isolated that even the prostitutes who usually swarmed into such boomtowns failed to show up."

I drove to office of *The Western News* to see if my luck would continue. On the way there was a sign I liked: "Starlight Electronics and Bail Bonds."

At the newspaper office, I asked the woman at the desk about the TRIH. She turned and relayed my question to the room. The editor, Roger Morris, yelled back:

"The Roosevelt Highway. Oh yes. The TR Highway wound through downtown Troy. That's how the Roosevelt Bridge got its name."

That was the beginning of an interesting conversation.

"It's an old iron bridge," he said, "still in use, but it's off the beaten path. The new highway goes straight through town to the new bridge, but the old TR Highway crossed the tracks in downtown Troy, and went across the river on the Roosevelt Bridge."

Roosevelt Highway Sign, Heritage Museum, Libby, Montana

Morris gave me detailed directions, so that I wouldn't miss the bridge. My luck seemed to be holding. I had been disappointed every time I had been told that a landmark, a sign, or some other remnant of the TRIH was in a certain location. This time, though, the information came from someone who obviously knew the area, had some detailed knowledge of the Roosevelt Highway, had unmistakable knowledge of local history, and provided me with a specific location. It sounded as though this might be the real thing.

The road to Troy climbs high and brings a rush of enthusiasm. A few miles west of Libby I came to the Kootenai Falls overlook. I walked along a short trail—perhaps a half mile or so, including a bridge over railroad tracks, then down sixty-four steps— and came to the tumbling water. I had not been there before, but it looked familiar. Much of the filming for the movie, "The River Wild," took place there, and I remembered it from the film.

Finian McDonald built a British trading post near the falls shortly after David Thompson in 1808 became the first white man to visit and explore the region. In the first few years of the twentieth century, the railroad was the only practical method of travel between Libby and Troy, although there was an old Indian portage trail that Thompson had used a century earlier.

In 1915, the Troy-Libby Road opened. Later, it became a part of the original TRIH. It was an especially difficult road to travel, even though it had been publicized as a marvel. Glowing reports had described it as "the connecting link between the Atlantic and Pacific oceans in the great national Parks automobile highway. One of the greatest scenic routes on the globe." People were excited, because for the first time it became possible to drive across Lincoln County—possible, yes, but dangerous.

Despite the puffery of the time, I have been told that locals knew enough to avoid the road when possible. Often when they had to drive it, they would tackle it in pairs, with one person driving, and the other walking to the sharp curves to be sure that no one was coming. Most of the traffic consisted of outsiders, tourists going between Spokane and Glacier National Park.

Clare Hafferman some years ago reported on the road's rigors in "Libby to Troy Road," for *The Western News*. (How many years ago I couldn't find out—I found an undated reprint of her article in the archives of Montana's Transportation Department.)

"People and objects are more interesting when you know something about their history," she wrote. "There is a short section of the old Theodore Roosevelt Memorial Highway still existing between Libby and Troy in northwestern Montana which is worth seeing even now because of its scenic value (rock cliffs patched with alum root and fern, crumbling stone guard walls, and a good view of the Kootenai River) but also worth investigating for its place in the annals of Montana road building."

She was interested in seeing what had happened on the day she was born, so she checked the paper's files for the 30th of January 1930. She discovered that on the day she came into the world, "another soul left it via a spectacular accident on this path cut out of the rocks. The victim's name was E. L. Torr, a salesman from Missoula."

He left by way of an accident on the TR Highway—an especially bizarre accident. The road had been covered with ice, and a telephone crew had dug trenches through the ice to serve as ruts for their car. Unfortunately for Torr, water from a spring had filled the ruts and frozen. It was apparent from his tracks that he had stopped his car to look the situation over.

"It was also apparent," Hafferman wrote, "that he had attempted to fasten the car with a log chain to a small tree on the uphill side and then had driven onto the ice, with the result that his vehicle left the road and tumbled down a steep incline of some 400 feet, killing him and demolishing his car." The sheriff and a deputy hiked up the steep mountainside to investigate, and "saw parts of the inside finish of the car hanging in the tops of trees."

Hafferman understandably asked in wonderment what sort of road it was "where one had to chain a vehicle to a tree and then inch out, cautiously?" From a 1915 account, she found a description that said it ran through the Kootenai Canyon from Troy to Libby, and had "been cut out of solid rock in several places and climbs to an elevation of about 400 feet above the falls and canyon." Heavy rocks had been left on the roadside and "generally" a sufficient ridge had "been left along the outer edge to make it perfectly safe." The road was graded earth, 20 feet wide with a right of way 40 feet in width. Early predictions were that the "Libby-Troy section would be known all over the nation for its spectacular scenery." Even more ambitious was the boast that "this road will last longer than the Rock of Gibraltar."

Hafferman cited the Montana Department of Transportation as to the significance of this section of the TRIH. "This road was so important in the days when it was built because it was Montana's first transcontinental route and linked Portland, Maine and Portland, Oregon," a Department release had said. "It followed present-day Highway 2 along the Hi-line and crossed the continental divide at Marias Pass in Glacier Park. Ceremonies were held Aug. 23, 1930, at Summit, and a monument was dedicated to President Teddy Roosevelt, honoring him for his timberland conservation leadership."

The old Troy-Libby Road is still there, in a sense, although it is exclusively a foot-path for hikers. Drivers now are confined to the faster, safer—but considerably less exciting—new highway far below the original. They can park in a number of turnouts between Libby and Troy, though, and get out to walk for miles along the path of the original "highway." On the trail they can appreciate fully the challenges that the early TRIH posed for the hardy travelers who dared to take their autos across that stretch of "perfectly safe," narrow, steep, treacherous road.

Those without the time or energy can get some idea of what the road was like even without hiking. Parts of its infrastructure are still visible from below. Considering everything, the cuts into the rock and the retaining walls that prevented the roadway's collapse are impressive even viewed from underneath.

Troy is at a low elevation, for Montana, just under 1,900 feet. It has the look of a typical western town. It also, I discovered, does indeed have the Roosevelt Bridge.

U.S. 2 now follows a straight path through town, deviating from its original course. I followed the directions from Roger Morris, turned right, and drove directly to the bridge. As he said, the old iron bridge still is in use. The road crosses it, turns left, and winds up the mountain before reconnecting with today's U.S. 2.

The bridge is fairly long, with a concrete support in the middle. Its superstructure has two arches, each from the support to the respective bank. The floor is made of wooden cross pieces, but with wooden tracks running the bridge's length to provide a smooth trip across. A conspicuous sign posts weight limits, but they are sufficient for reasonably large trucks. The bridge seems quite sturdy.

Near the center support where the arches meet, but high on the superstructure, is a most dramatically-placed nest. At first I thought it belonged to eagles. Roger Morris later corrected me, though, and saved me from a mistake. The nest belongs to a family of ospreys, and the large, graceful birds delight Troy's residents by swooping along the river to catch fish.

The Roosevelt Bridge is near downtown Troy, but it sits in a wooded setting. From many viewpoints it could be in a completely rural area. Only the passage of a car or truck every two or three minutes as I watched suggested that it serves a settled community.

Sandra Johnson, Troy's City Clerk, had more news for me. The city is planning to place large "Roosevelt Bridge" signs on the bridge, and is constructing a Roosevelt Park at the bridge on the Troy side. Plans are for the park to include a picnic area, a boat ramp, and walking paths. The purpose is to honor Theodore Roosevelt, and to commemorate his memorial highway.

She also pointed out to me something I had searched for all the way across the continent: an original TRIH road marker. On one side of the Troy City Hall is a painted square enclosing the initials "TR," the Theodore Roosevelt International Highway's symbol that appeared across the country to guide travelers on the TR Trail. The city has maintained it carefully.

Troy, Montana—at least in connection with my search for remnants of the TRIH—turned out to be a treasure trove. There were three more states to cover before my journey was over. I expected to learn more about my own country as I continued, and I hoped to find more about the Highway. But, I would have been happy even if my trip had ended in Troy.

West of Troy, U.S. 2 was unpaved as late as 1939. After crossing the Kootenai in town, it ran north of the river into Idaho. The re-located U.S. 2 still follows the Kootenai, and is a modern road, although it remains two-lane. The new route for most of its way to the state line stays south of the River. It still winds up, down, and around but it is civilized—presenting nothing close to the rigors of the old Troy-Libby Road.

I drove to the state line, crossing over the Kootenai and Yaak Rivers, to cover the new route. Then, I turned around and backtracked a short distance to locate a segment of the old road that I knew still existed. It begins a few miles inside Montana, and continues on the old path, winding north of today's U.S.2, into Idaho. It's still designated "Old U.S. 2," but there is no marking at the Montana end. I wouldn't have known which turnoff to follow, except that I received help.

Lorna Bandimere, a local resident, noticed that I was from far away and seemed to be looking for something. She pulled up beside me and I explained what I was doing. I could follow her onto Old U.S. 2, she said. She happened to be going that way. Because of her help, it was simple to follow the old route through quite isolated country past the state line.

All the way from Maine to Idaho, people had been interested in what I was doing, and eager to assist me however they could. My project seemed to have struck a responsive chord everywhere. It was simply a more intensive version of something I have noticed for years during many trips all over the country. In spite of regional

Only Remaining TRIH Marker, City Hall wall, Troy, Montana

stereotypes most people—regardless of where they live, whatever their race, and without regard to social and economic class—unless they feel threatened in some manner, are usually anxious to help others.

Many current maps do not show these few miles of original highway—TRIH and Old U.S. 2—that still exist. I knew roughly where the old route went from antique maps, especially from a 1939 Standard Oil map, but both my new road atlas and Montana's official state map left me in the dark. Ms Bandimere's help enabled me to put it all together.

Along the way, I appreciated a log cabin secluded in the woods. A stone fireplace chimney graced one side, and a bearskin almost covered another. Also on the way, fully meeting an American stereotype, was literally a "little red schoolhouse." The building was bright red, and it may have had more than one room, but if so not many more. It was the McCormick School. It dated from 1909, had a bell tower on the roof, and—as indicated by a yellow school bus parked at the side—still operated to educate rural Montana children.

I drove the few miles along the portion of the old highway, and within a short time came back to U.S. 2. Then, having covered the length of the largest state on the Theodore Roosevelt International Highway, I crossed into Idaho.

Chapter Twelve

Idaho Isolation

The first order of business was to find somewhere to spend the night. I had gained an hour when I crossed into Idaho. As timepieces measure it, darkness comes earlier at the eastern edge of a time zone.

Quickly, I found a nice campground, nestled deep into the woods. The camp store was already closed. I left my registration and fee in a locked box.

I selected a tent site among trees on a riverbank. Working quickly, I set up camp and prepared dinner. There wasn't much time remaining before mosquitoes would be out in force, so I hurried to finish.

During the night, the temperature dropped sharply. I awoke around midnight when my head became cold. I pulled up the sleeping bag's hood, and slept in comfort until morning.

U.S. 2 continued on through heavy forest. Idaho has almost as many acres of forested land as its huge neighbor Montana, which is nearly twice as large. Both states are rugged, but Lewis and Clark said they found Idaho's terrain to be the most rugged of any in their entire journey. Idaho still has more acres of wilderness than any other state except Alaska.

After Lewis and Clark, trappers invaded the wild country. They shipped a steady stream of furs to Europe and the United States, but the fur trade was brief. Changing fashion lessened the demand, and the trappers had severely depleted the animal population. With unconscious irony they killed not only the animals but also the fur trade itself.

The trappers moved out, and missionaries rushed in. Among others, Father Pierre Jean De Smet worked with the Coeur d'Alenes, and Henry Spalding founded missions among the Nez Perce. The first permanent white community in Idaho arose in 1860, in Franklin County near the Utah border, when Mormons emigrated from Utah. Today, Latter Day Saints constitute some 25% of Idaho's population. They now have powerful influence there, but for years the state denied them even the right to vote.

California's gold rush in 1849 brought only traffic; Idaho's own gold rush of 1860 brought settlers. In 1863 President Lincoln formally organized the Idaho territory.

Lewiston was the first capital, but the new upstart Boise soon replaced it. Idaho became the 43rd state in 1890.

A century after statehood, yet more invaders came: high-tech industries fleeing high-cost California. They supplemented the traditional economic mainstays of lumber, potatoes, and mining. During recent decades, other changes unrelated to high technology have sharply revised Idaho's politics.

The state had entered the Union in the midst of bitter labor disputes that in 1905 led to the assassination of a former governor, Frank Steunenberg. Carlos Schwantes in his fine interpretive history, *The Pacific Northwest*, graphically lays out the events that led up to the assassination.

When miners organized, powerful mine owners in the Coeur d'Alenes responded by forming a "protective association." In late 1891, they hired a Pinkerton detective, Charles A. Siringo, to infiltrate the union and spy on its meetings.

Calling himself C. Leon Allison, he worked at the Gem Mine and joined the union. Siringo impressed the miners, who elected him the union's recording secretary. In this position he learned everything about the union's plans. With their steady flow of confidential information, the owners were able time after time to thwart the union. Ultimately, the miners became suspicious. Siringo had to flee for his life, and escaped by sawing a hole in the floor of his room, and crawling out underneath. The ensuing outrage led to violence and martial law, but eventually it brought union-scale wages to most large mines.

The Bunker Hill and Sullivan Complex was an exception. In 1899, an armed group seized a train, picked up nearly a thousand miners, and descended upon the Complex. They burned and dynamited at will before returning home. One young miner warned, "You can't steal railroad trains, dynamite mines, and burn villages without some reaction."

He was right. Governor Steunenberg declared a state of insurrection, and called in federal troops. Until the end of his term, no miner could be employed in the region without displaying a state permit, and without proving that he had not participated in the bombing.

Later, one Harry Orchard, whom Schwantes called a "strange and violent man," planted a bomb that killed the former governor. Orchard confessed, and escaped the death penalty by accusing the leaders of the Western Federation of Miners of having hired him. He received a life sentence.

Idaho sent agents to kidnap three of these leaders in Denver, and brought them to trial. They were William Dudley "Big Bill" Haywood the union's secretary-treasurer (who was one of the founders of the I.W.W.), Charles Moyer, the Federation president, and George Pettibone, a former miner who had been blacklisted and was then a hardware merchant.

The trial opened in Boise in 1907. Newly-elected Republican U.S. Senator William E. Borah was the prosecutor. Borah appears to have prosecuted the case vigorously but fairly. The defense attorney, Clarence Darrow, won acquittal for all three.

Orchard had hardly been credible. On various occasions he had claimed to be a bigamist, an arsonist, and a mass murderer in addition to being an assassin. Moreover, Idaho law required corroborating witnesses, and there were none.

Borah rose to national prominence, serving from 1907 to 1940 in the U.S. Senate. Time and again "the Lion of Idaho" demonstrated his independence, even from his own party. Borah supported civil liberties and the Bill of Rights during World War One, when they were decidedly unpopular. He supported President Wilson's conduct of the war, but opposed the Versailles Treaty and American membership in the League of Nations. During the 1920s he supported aid to hard-pressed farmers.

Ultimately he became Chairman of the Foreign Relations Committee until the Democrats took control of Congress during the New Deal. Even though President Hoover was a fellow Republican, Borah had refused to support his re-election because of Hoover's opposition to aid for the needy.

During the New Deal, Borah supported some of Franklin Roosevelt's reforms, but became the "great opposer" on others. Most notably, he opposed participation in World War Two and became a prominent isolationist.

The Republican Party had dominated Idaho and much of the Northwest during the early twentieth century, but Idaho became solidly Democratic during the Depression. This didn't change its affection for mavericks such as Borah.

It sent Liberal Democrat Glen Taylor, "the Singing Cowboy," to the U.S. Senate from 1945 to 1951. While in the Senate, Taylor opposed fellow Democrat Harry Truman's bid for re-election in 1948, running for vice president on Henry Wallace's Progressive ticket. The Wallace-Taylor team attracted most of the votes of the far left.

In 1956, Idaho elected liberal Democrat Frank Church to the Senate, and kept him there for twenty-four years—he, too, rose to chair the powerful Foreign Relations Committee. Church became a major critic of the C.I.A. and of the war in Vietnam. Idaho loved him.

Then, with Reagan's victory in 1980, Church narrowly lost his seat. His successor, Steven Symms, followed in the Idaho tradition for flamboyant senators and remained in the Senate for twelve years. He once appeared with two revolvers at an anti-gun control news conference, saying "They can call me a right-wing kook, but I'm out there on the fringe with Ronald Reagan." Just so.

Now, Idaho arguably has become not only the most Republican state in the country, but the most conservative as well. Among the 35 members in its state senate, at the century's close only four (no doubt very lonely) Democrats remained. What happened?

For years staunch conservatives had fled California to the Rocky Mountain states, especially Idaho, seeking rural quiet. Lightly-populated areas promised an additional advantage: the possibility of creating the political climate they desired. Their political broom swept out many moderate Republicans along with Democrats.

In moving to an environment where they could be isolated, they also made their new dwelling places much more conservative simply by their presence. A relatively small group can loom large in a rural area. Their effective organization and keen political skills soon brought them into control of Idaho's politics.

As an influence on national politics, though, the migration cut both ways. To be sure, population shifts brought staunch conservatism to the mountain states, but conservatism weakened in the regions left behind, especially in California. Even that mainstay of tradition, the South, wavered from the totality of its conservative commitment at the same time that the Rockies embraced it more fervently.

Reflecting the rapid shifts that make American politics so interesting, however, that Rocky embrace, too, may be less than it appeared. After the elections of 2004 Democrats had made great gains in Colorado, had taken the governorship and both legislative houses in Montana, and in Idaho's Senate had increased their total dramatically (in percentage if not in overall numbers), from four to seven.

I followed U.S. 2 across the Moyie River. It took me across a bridge high above a dam, and then on past the town of Moyie Springs. Soon I was in Bonners Ferry, named for a Civil-War vintage ferry service across the Kootenai River. Much later the area became the site of America's last Indian war. The Kootenai Tribe there in 1974 declared war on the United States. The Tribe came out a winner of sorts. After non-violent negotiations it received an 18-acre reservation.

U.S. 2 did not proceed west of Bonners Ferry until after the TRIH had begun to fade from existence. It was 1948 or so when the American Association of State Highway Officials recommended its extension to Everett. The first listing of the extension appeared in the log of U.S. numbered highways for 1951.

I had hoped to meet editor of Bonners Ferry's newspaper, the *Herald*, but I arrived on Saturday and it was closed. At the Visitors' Center, I found what I wanted. A volunteer, Margaret Monat, knew exactly what I meant when I asked about the TRIH.

"You asked the right person. I live on the Roosevelt Highway. They call it Old U.S. 2, but the real name is Theodore Roosevelt Highway," she told me. "That's what still appears on my water bills. In the early 30s it was dirt, and went down a steep hill, but it still was 450 feet from the water. In the winter it was impossible to get up that hill."

She told me I could find the road back in Moyie Springs. I had passed it on the way to Bonners Ferry without noticing.

I retraced my path there and found a turnoff to the south, but it had no marking. I stopped at a store to ask directions. The turnoff was the right road.

"The TR Highway went down to the river in a canyon," the storekeeper told me. "There's no crossing now, but if you go down there, you can see where the bridge was. Then it came back up to the new road on the other side."

It soon became clear that I was indeed on the TRIH. At every intersection street signs identify the road as "Roosevelt Street." The road continues for some distance. Along the way I was amused by a unique piece of folk art, or "mailbox art." Constructed from old mechanical parts, a fierce metal skeleton supported the mailbox that protruded from its loins. The full length of the road was about three miles, and the old bridge site was visible.

Back in Bonners Ferry, I turned off the highway to look around. A "Pink Lion Launderette" sported a brilliantly colored big cat: the Pink Panther. A barbershop looked like a wrecked ship, tilted toward the sky. A covered-wagon parade of Mormons headed cross-country toward Utah. At the western end of the city in a residential area were crisply arranged patches of tulips—a perfect farewell from Bonners Ferry, or a warm welcome to others traveling east.

Mailbox art on TRIH (Roosevelt Street) Moyie Springs, Idaho

On the way west I followed Mountain Meadows Road to a stretch of Old U.S. 2. Back on the new U.S. 2 I also was on U.S. 95; the two run together for a time. The road paralleled railroad tracks, and I was surprised to see a train pulling a caboose. I had thought cabooses were all museum pieces.

The highway crossed a bridge high above a creek. Meadows became as scenic as the mountains that punctuated them as decisively as exclamation points. I passed tiny towns, Elmira, Samuels, and Colburn. Several signs announced that this was "MOOSE AREA." These were worded signs, not silhouettes. I saw no moose, though. A long bridge over Pack River carried me into Sandpoint.

Sandpoint felt urban after my long time in the mountains. It also has the attractive Bonner County Historical Museum. The collections included geological exhibits, Native American artifacts, materials relating to dam construction in the Pend Oreille region, small reproductions of the Smithsonian's display of First Ladies' gowns, and a fascinating photo gallery. An outside exhibit includes a caboose and a homesteader's cabin. The Museum's research archives contain a wealth of material on local history, including photographs, newspapers, and various interesting documents.

It is a splendid resort area, but one that has gained notoriety. Former police officer Mark Fuhrman put Sandpoint in the headlines by moving there after the O. J. Simpson trial. Many residents and others had already been nervous about survivalist groups, as well as neo-Nazis and various other white supremacists that had settled some miles to the south. *Sandpoint* Magazine highlighted an interview with him in its Summer, 1997 edition. Fuhrman had objected to a story in the magazine's previous Winter issue.

The point of that story had been that the media were creating an image of northern Idaho as a haven for racists. It called sensationalistic the treatments of Fuhrman's move to Sandpoint and the presence nearby of "white separatist Randy Weaver and avowed racist Richard Butler of Hayden Lake," citing these as examples of unfair coverage. In contrast, it pointed to the positive work of the Bonner County Human Rights Task Force.

Fuhrman objected to being classed with Weaver and Butler, saying that he considered them "two kooks overtly going against the government and everybody else." He also questioned why there was a need for a human rights task force, and said he had seen no evidence of human rights violations. Local media, he said, should stop being defensive. "You almost create a negative image by trying to justify a positive image," he said.

U.S. 2 heads southwest at Sandpoint, and after a short distance veers west once more; this time into the State of Washington at Newport. Some maps showed the TRIH as doing the same, but most indicate that it went south for several miles before turning west and entering Washington near Spokane. I took both routes.

First, I proceeded southwestward to follow U. S. 2. I drove through the small town of Dover, then Laclede. In Priest River a campground displayed a sign announcing that it was filled. Signs promised a "Historical District," and a traffic jam made me creep along for a time, then I passed a lumberyard of impressive size. I passed up the chance to stop in at the River Pigs Restaurant, although I'd heard it was good. After seeing the Abeni Falls Dam, a hydroelectric project, and crossing the Pend Oreille River a sign greeted me, saying "Welcome to Washington, the Evergreen State."

Although Newport is in Washington, it has the distinction of once having been Newport, Idaho. Originally it was on the Idaho side, beginning as a small trading post in 1889. With the coming of the Great Northern in 1892, it moved across the border. Now it actually spills back into Idaho where mall shopping will be found near the original site overlooking the Pend Oreille. The main part of town has the Pend Oreille County Historical Museum, which occupies the old railroad depot. It was another small western museum that was excellent and entertaining.

I stopped at the Pend Oreille County Library and asked the librarian about the TRIH. "That's interesting," he said thoughtfully, "The Theodore Roosevelt Highway, you say? I used to live in New England and it went north of my house. I think the name's pretty obscure now, though."

He knew nothing about the Highway in the west, but cranked up his computer to check it on the Internet. While he was looking, I asked him how he liked the area.

"I love it here," he said. "I wouldn't move for anything. Wait a minute, here's something."

He had found a piece about another TR Highway, not the TRIH. Then he came across a small bit about U.S. 302 in Maine. He was pleased to have found it, even though I told him I'd already driven it at the beginning of my journey.

Following U. S. 2 toward Spokane, I passed Diamond Lake and drove through a marshy area. Prosperous-looking farms came next, then an African theme park on the left. I halted while an emergency crew cleared an accident from the road ahead of me, and then drove into Spokane.

Spokane would have to wait. I would be approaching it again by the other route, and would see the city and spend the night there when I returned. The day was still young. I turned east on Interstate 90 back into Idaho, then turned north for the quickest way back to Sandpoint.

There was little traffic, and after a while the area became quite isolated. It was there that I encountered something I would never have expected anywhere, let alone in Idaho. Ahead there were two cars, and as I began to pay attention to them, something seemed strange. One, a large red Buick several years old, kept passing the other, a Camry, and then slowing almost to a crawl. The Camry itself would then pass. Every time the Buick passed, a banner would billow from its roof. This happened two or three times.

As I drew nearer, I could tell that the billowing banner was a Confederate battle flag, the stars and bars, held up through the Buick's open sunroof. Then I noticed that the driver of the Camry was black. I didn't want to leave him alone with his tormentor in that isolated area, so I pulled in between him and the red Buick. When the Buick slowed, so did I. The Camry stayed behind us both.

Finally, the Buick pulled to the side of the road. The Camry passed me as I passed the parked Buick. The Buick's driver was a fat white man, probably in his early twenties. He glared at me with a look that I've seen before, but fortunately not often, and never in a person I thought sane. I watched him in my mirror, and saw him pull back onto the road, probably a half mile or more behind.

The Camry then accelerated, and sped far down the highway. I stayed back to keep the Buick in sight. It came no closer, and within a few minutes turned off down a side road. I then sped up myself, but didn't see the Camry again—nor did I see the Buick.

I had hoped to give the Camry's driver a thumbs up gesture just to let him know that someone was on his side. Unfortunately, he may have thought that I was intimidating him too. I was glad to have been there at the right time anyway.

At Sandpoint once more, I took U.S. 95 south toward Athol. The scenery was pleasant, but without the dramatic stabs toward the sky and sudden deep ravines that I had come to expect from Idaho. Athol is a tiny village of some 350, but it is near the Silverwood Theme Park, at the juncture with Idaho 54.

I took that road to the west to connect with Idaho 41. The routes have been changed slightly from the graded or gravel road that constituted the TRIH, but 41 is a close approximation. It goes through Rathdrum, and on to the state line with Washington.

For many reasons, Idaho is exceptional. Rather than class it with any other state or region, simply consider it unique. For me, it was intriguing. Apart from one episode, I found no unpleasantness there—not near Hayden Lake or anywhere else.

I also had found no TR signs. I had been looking even more carefully ever since the trucker Art Jensen back in Williston, North Dakota told me he had seen one, and thought it was in Idaho. Look for "Case Crow Motors," he had said. I did, but found nothing. This fit the established pattern. Nevertheless, I couldn't be too disappointed. In Montana I already had discovered both a museum display of a Forest Service sign giving directions to the Roosevelt Highway, and an actual TRIH marker still in place.

The main impression I had during my brief time in Idaho was of wilderness and grandeur. I left its magnificence, once again to pass a sign welcoming me to Washington, the Evergreen State.

Chapter Thirteen

Wandering Within Washington

Until it enters Oregon, the TR Highway never strays far from Washington's eastern border. Spokane itself is only a few miles from the state line. I arrived there within minutes.

Few cities anywhere can boast of accomplishments equal to Spokane's. Almost no city anywhere near its size, somewhat shy of 200,000, can do so.

The city's accomplishments began early. After its incorporation in 1881, it soon (1885) had the first hydroelectric plant west of the Mississippi. Before the end of the decade it had major links to the East, taking the form of five different railroads.

In 1889, the same year that Washington became a state, a raging fire consumed much of Spokane Falls—the city's original name. In the business district, only one significant building remained standing, the 1880 Crescent Building, which still exists. The town quickly re-built, voted in 1891 to re-name itself simply "Spokane," and set about prospering.

For years, the riverfront along the Spokane River was, in the words of historian Carlos Schwantes, "an unsightly thirty-eight hundred-acre complex of warehouses and railroad tracks." Riverfront Park, recreation facilities, and a revitalized central city have replaced the previous eyesores. Downtown Spokane now has one of the most appealing urban areas in the United States. Among its preserved architectural landmarks are the old Great Northern Depot's Clock Tower, dating from 1902, the 1914 Davenport Hotel, the 1891 Spokesman Review Building, the 1908 Matador Restaurant, and the Spokane County Courthouse as well as the Crescent Building. Several blocks along Riverside Street are known for their magnificent old buildings.

Riverfront Park resulted from Spokane's 1974 World's Fair. People had jeered when Spokane proposed the fair. But the city forged ahead and has benefited ever since. Frederick Law Olmstead, the foremost landscape architect of his day, had laid out much of what became the park's design a century before the park actually materialized. In returning to his plans, Spokane demonstrated civic consciousness, and its long memory.

Certainly the city had a great advantage because of its splendid natural setting. In 1873, James N. Glover discovered the falls, and decided that he had to live there amidst the "beauty and grandeur of everything." He bought a sawmill that Seth Scranton and J. J. Downing had built alongside the river, and set himself up in business with a stable and store. Glover became celebrated as the "father of Spokane."

Riverfront Park includes those same Spokane Falls. Fortunately, Spokane had the good sense to restore and emphasize the setting. Spokane built its park around the falls, constructed a gondola ride over the river, and placed a carousel and other attractions to amuse children.

One of those attractions is certainly the most odd. It is an eye catching red, old-fashioned, "Radio Flyer" child's wagon—but it is some two stories tall. Its wheels are taller than a man's head. Children can climb up a stairway to its insides, and then slide down the "handle."

Near the park is a Museum of Native Cultures. The Cheney Cowles Memorial Museum also is downtown, and has a wealth of materials on local history. Gonzaga University is nearby.

Not far from the business district is Browne's Addition, a rather stately residential area featuring impressive Victorian homes. Some are splendid. Also nearby is "The Hill," a residential district that also includes Cliff Park. The Park provides Spokane's highest lookout point, on Review Rock.

The city has excellent accommodations. Cavanaugh's Inn at the Park, which offers comfort consistent with its setting, is especially inviting. But I wouldn't be staying at Cavanaugh's this time. Riverside State Park, just north of the city, has campgrounds, so I opted to camp as more in keeping with the experiences of a TRIH traveler.

I located the park easily. Two rangers were on duty as I checked in, Ken Karg and Frank Dorman. When I explained about my journey along the TRIH, Karg took an immediate interest, and told me he had read an article about the Highway in *Columbia* magazine.

Dorman expressed keen interest also. "That's a great project," he said. "I'm not a liberal—in fact, I'm the farthest thing from a liberal—but I really liked Charles Kuralt."

While the three of us talked about the TRIH, I asked if either of them had ever seen anything resembling a TR marker. Neither one had, but Dorman suggested something I hadn't considered. "With the desert climate you're going into, you may find some of the original markers preserved."

The camping area was just what I had hoped. I found a secluded spot among trees by the side of a river. As an added benefit the restroom and showers were nearby.

The next morning was cool, but bright and beautiful. After breakfast, I packed most of my gear, and went to the restroom to shave and shower. When I finished and stepped outside, I saw that I should have packed the tent also. The sky had been clear less than a half hour before, but had become heavily overcast. Worse, it was sleeting heavily. I packed the tent as quickly as possible, taking care to brush as much of the ice as I could from it so that it would be relatively dry when folded into its bag, put the remainder of my things into the truck, and drove back to downtown Spokane.

Although it was early rush hour, the traffic moved smoothly. I meandered around to get a better look at the city, and found another small slice of the Americana that enlivened my cross-country journey. On the corner of Post and Garland, I stopped to take a photo of "The Milk Bottle," a diner in the shape of a large old-fashioned glass milk bottle.

The rest of the morning I spent in the Public Library's Northwest Room, finding enough in its excellent collection of materials on the region to absorb me for hours. The library personnel were most helpful. In *Columbia* magazine, though, the only related article I could find was about the Yellowstone Trail, not the TRIH.

For lunch I drove to Frank's Diner. Part of Frank's occupies a 1906 railroad car, which I understand was brought from Seattle in 1991. Frank's sits at the point where U.S. 2 (the TRIH) turns left, going west through Spokane.

This was the classic railroad car diner, reminiscent of those that were sprinkled throughout the country in times past. It was clean and reasonable in price, the service excellent, and the food quite good.

The "Milk Bottle," Spokane, Washington

It would have been easy to spend more time in Spokane, but I needed to be on my way. Departing the city, U.S. 2 and U.S. 195 run together briefly on Interstate 90. The original trail out of town lies buried under the Interstate. The route now is labeled U. S. 195, and at Spokane the TRIH traveler can forget about U. S. 2. There, the TR Trail departs from U. S. 2 permanently.

Washington was one of the states that responded quickly to my early requests for information. It also was among the most helpful. Janette Ingham of the state transportation department's Ombudsman Office sent me comprehensive materials, and even went to the trouble of providing a state map with the TRIH route highlighted not only through Washington, but all the way to Portland.

Exiting Interstate 90, the TRIH heads south on U. S. 195. The highway remains divided, and takes the traveler through a deep expanse of evergreens, reflecting the nickname of the state. Despite the broad vista of greenery, though, the earth itself was brown. After several miles of rolling hills, the road narrows to the two lanes that travelers on the TR Trail have come to expect.

I passed a turnoff to Cheney, 14 miles distant, the location of Eastern Washington University. The hills had become treeless. They were an extraordinarily deep green, mixed with brown and yellow. I could see mountains in the distance.

At Rosalia, I drove into town on Business 195, the original TRIH. When I stepped outside the air-conditioned truck, a wave of heat hit me. I had awakened that morning in chilly hills not far away, and had even encountered sleet. The desert heat in Rosalia was startling.

There was a library of sorts, and a small museum also, but both were closed. The place had a look of hard times. Bits of litter lay in the streets, and many shops were vacant. The homes, though, appeared to be neat and well-kept. Rosalia distributes a nice little brochure pointing to local virtues.

The little town has been there since 1872. According to its brochure, it sits in Whitman County, "one of the largest wheat producing areas in the world." Another boast is that "we are also among the largest exporters of peas and lentils."

A block or so from where I parked I stopped to admire an elegant clock on a tall pole at the curb. In one sense, such a splendid object seemed out of place in its rather shabby surroundings. From another perspective, though, it was perfectly matched to its setting, and recalled an earlier time—a time when travelers were wending their way within Washington on the TRIH. Rosalia's brochure highlights the clock, saying it symbolized "old fashioned values and friendly service."

As I stood looking, a man walked up and began talking. I barely had noticed him when I had first seen him down the street.

"There used to be a jewelry story on this corner. That clock still keeps good time," he volunteered. "A guy comes out and winds it every day."

"I'm impressed," I told him. "It's certainly a beautiful piece. Who does the honors, is it the mayor, or some other official?"

"No," he said, "it's just a tradition. It's all informal. One guy takes the responsibility, and when he can't do it, someone else fills in. One fellow did it for years. When he died another just stepped in and took his place. I'm Melvin Hofmann," he said. "I'm the town artist. What brings you to Rosalia?"

I explained about the TRIH.

"I've never heard of it," he said, "but I know this used to be an old stagecoach road. I was born here, and I've lived here all my life."

"You say you're the town artist?" I asked.

"See the mural on that building over there? That's my work." He pointed into the next block at an abandoned building. The front wall contained a painting of a steam locomotive, sitting on a track. Smoke poured from its stack. A bit of a building was visible in the background. In front of the engine was some grass and another railroad track.

We walked into the next block to get a better look at Hofmann's work, and he posed in front of it for a photo. He thanked me, and seemed pleased when I told him that I would mention him and his painting.

It seemed to be hotter than ever, and I was thirsty, so I walked across the street to the Brass Rail Tavern. I relaxed briefly at the bar with a diet cola.

A sign over the bar said, "Football is not a matter of life and death. It's much more important." Another large sign, a poster, advertised "One-Eyed Jack Alcohol Lemon Brew." That was new to me. In huge letters it said, "Drink This Product Responsibly [Or We'll Come to Your House AND KICK YOUR ASS!]."

The place was friendly, and the bartender asked around if anyone knew about the TRIH. It was a biker/geezer bar. There were a few tattooed, leather-clad men and women with Harley symbols, and a few grizzled, elderly, men; nothing in between. Each group seemed to have its own section, and occupants of each spoke up about my trip.

"Flying A" Drive-in, Dayton, Washington

A geezer said, "Yeh, I've heard of that." Another said, "It was a big deal at one time." An enormous biker with his arm around a woman almost as big as he was surprised me by saying "I've heard of it too. People don't care much about history anymore, but it's interesting to roam around and explore, just to see what's left. Have you come all this way from Maine by yourself?"

"Alone all the way," I told him. "My wife is going to join me in Portland, and we're going to vacation on the way back home, but she has a limited tolerance for long road trips."

"So does his wife!" the woman yelled, punching the biker. At that, the whole bar broke up in laughter, the biker laughing loudest of all.

The bartender said, "Say, there's something that might interest you. Have you met our town artist?"

"Right outside, just before I came in," I responded. I thanked him for his interest, and finished my cola.

"Gotta get on the road," I said to the patrons. "Have a great trip," several of them yelled and waved. I waved back, and stepped out into the heat again. I wanted to wave goodbye too to the town artist—the only town artist I've ever met—but he was nowhere in sight.

I drove on south on U.S. 195 for some time. After a while, I turned off on a segment of the old highway. "Thornton Road," it said. It was paved, but so narrow it reminded me more of a footpath. It had no shoulders. The isolation was palpable. Then the old road rejoined 195.

The terrain was unlike any I had ever encountered. It was hilly, absolutely treeless, and resembled dunes—although it wasn't sand, it was wheat. I have seen treeless prairies countless times, treeless barren hills countless times, wooded or grassy hills countless times—but never hills of such color, and never with such constant movement. I was in the Palouse country, a fertile wheat-producing area in Whitman and Garfield Counties, which flows across the state line into Latah and Benewah Counties in Idaho.

Heat Moon had given us the classic description. The "treeless, rounded hills, shaped by ice and wind and water to a sensuous nudity," when he saw them were "sprouting an intensely green fuzz of winter." He called the fertile highlands "the steepest American cropland," and wrote that they were so "vast and rich, special machinery has been built to work them: twelve-wheel, self-leveling tractors and combines that can ride the thirty percent gradients."

A drive of no more than a mile takes one over hill after hill. Some are as high as 200 feet. My guess would be that most of what I saw had changed little if any from the days of the early travelers on the TRIH. The towns, too, had changed little. They remain friendly, as no doubt they were then, but hardly more oriented to tourists than I suppose they had been in the 1920s.

Metaphors from the sea describing wheat fields have become clichés, but there are good reasons for them. Speaking of waves and billows when looking out over acres or miles of growing wheat results less from verbal inadequacy than from the striking resemblance to an ocean, never still, always changing, an ocean of bright emerald or sandy gold, depending upon the season.

Carlos Schwantes described the Palouse country as "one of the most productive wheat-growing regions in the United States." It was easy to believe. From horizon to horizon, there was nothing to see, nothing under the endless sky, that is, but wheat and highway.

The best view of how thoroughly wheat blankets the land is from the top of Steptoe Butte, which is also a state park, just east of U.S. 195. The butte is an outcrop of the Selkirk Mountains. It takes its name from Col. Edward J. Steptoe, who in 1858 met a humiliating defeat at the hands of several Indian tribes in the area. A Steptoe Battlefield Memorial stands today marking the conflict. Early maps list the butte as Pyramid Peak. The army returned after Steptoe's defeat with a large and well-armed force. Under the command of Col. George Wright, it slaughtered Indians and their horses with new long-range rifles, and then marched through the territory hanging chiefs and others.

The next settlement was Colfax. It was a typical western small town. All the way from the east I had seen espresso and cappuccino signs, and Colfax had them too. It also had several recreation areas—the largest being Schmuck Park.

James Perkins, from Illinois, founded Colfax in 1870. The Perkins House, standing at 623 N. Perkins Street, remains as a historical exhibit. It was the first house in Colfax, a squared log cabin dating from the middle 1880s. Behind it the first Republican convention in Whitman County took place.

At Colfax, the TRIH departs from U. S., 195, so I turned right on State Highway 26. I drove by the tiny Palouse Fairgrounds on my right, and followed the road to Dusty, where I took State Highway 127 to the south. The road wound back and forth, but its surface was good. The vistas remained vast.

I pulled off at Central Ferry State Park to look things over. It sits by the side of the Snake River and Central Ferry Bridge. There are ports there, but I saw no activity. What I did see was space. I had an intense feeling of solitude. In every direction the horizon seemed farther even than on the Great Plains. Back on the highway, I drove toward it.

At Dodge, I turned right onto U. S. 12. The road took me over a small bridge, which looked so old it appeared almost tired. The road itself was black. It had the appearance of oiled gravel. Viewing the country ahead, I could have been back in the Badlands. Even farther beyond were mountains. The scenery was interrupted by a succession of logging trucks.

Dayton greeted me with a sign saying, "Welcome to Historic Dayton Home of the State Champions." The main street was broad and boulevard-like. The town was beautiful and manicured, boasting that it was the "Gateway to the Blue Mountains and the Umatilla National Forest." Dozens of 19th and early 20th century houses grace its streets.

Several local attractions are "the oldest." The Oregon Railroad and Navigation Company built the Dayton Historical Depot in 1881. Today it is the oldest railroad station extant in Washington, and earns a mention on the state's official highway map.

"Flying A" Drive-in, Dayton, Washington

The Depot now houses an interesting museum. Dayton's Columbia County Court-house, an 1887 structure, is Washington's oldest courthouse.

Certainly not the oldest, but among the most interesting was the "Flying A Drive-in." Anyone interested in the development of automobile tourism would recognize the "Flying A Gasoline" emblem perched on the roof, or its companion, the Socony-Mobil "Flying Red Horse." In front of the building is a large replica of a gasoline pump, but the key to it all is an antique motor coach—a real bus, big and red—with its front half embedded in the building. It serves as an adjunct dining room. Those who choose to eat inside may elect a seat in the building proper (a converted gas station), or they may step up into the body of the bus and take a table there, dining in style.

Beyond Dayton are Lewis and Clark State Park, and markers for the Lewis and Clark Trail. On the way to Waitsburg was a small river on my left. Minutes later I passed "Poverty Lane." Waitsburg proclaims itself to be "One of a Kind. Settled in 1859. Still Governed by Original Charter."

The town was tiny, and quite pleasant. I walked around its main street briefly, and then headed into the Bullseye Tavern to use the restroom. Other than the bartender, who paid no attention to me when I walked straight to the men's room, no one else was inside. A distinct bit of graffiti said, "I just stepped out for a beer—be right back!"

I set off again on U.S. 12. The highway turns sharply left, and proceeds south out of Waitsburg. The next village was Dixie. Although the current maps that I had didn't show them, there were old roads where the original TRIH diverged from today's U.S.

12. I followed Pettybone Road through rich croplands waving their crops. Other than cultivated fields, I saw little sign of inhabitants.

The road became blacktop, then gravel. It was marked "Middle Waitsburg Road." I passed a farm marked "Stonecipher and Sons," and at a fork found that the road there was marked "Stonecipher Road." At the end of the road, though, where it re-joined U. S. 12, it again was marked "Middle Waitsburg Road."

Then I was in Walla Walla. Its name inspires jokes from comedians and red lines from spell checkers, but it rolls off the tongue in a lilting way. In common with many American names, it has an Indian heritage, and means "many waters" in Nez Perce. Residents are fond of saying that they live in an "oasis in the desert," which has some truth to it. Walla Walla, located near the Blue Mountains, has beautiful trees, streams, and rivers but most of the surrounding country is arid and much less inviting.

Even less inviting is the Tri Cities area, west of Walla Walla about 50 miles along U.S. 12. The Tri Cities, Richland, Pasco, and Kennewick are not on the TRIH, but are close enough to be an attraction of sorts. The area is the base for the Hanford Site— or the Hanford Nuclear Reservation. In 1943, the government relocated residents from an extensive area and created a huge top-secret installation to produce plutonium. Richland, the nearest town, actually arose to house workers imported for the nuclear industry. Hanford itself now houses huge tanks of nuclear wastes. Through the years contamination of soil, water, and air has been catastrophic.

Schwantes reported that since the mid 1940s there have been many atmospheric releases of radiation, each of which was thousands of times greater than the amount causing such concern at Three Mile Island. Dayton Duncan followed the Lewis and Clark Trail, and in *Out West* wrote compellingly of his adventures. He followed the Trail through the Tri-Cities, and found that life "still revolves around the atom." In 1949, he said, officials at Hanford *deliberately* released 5,500 curies of radioactive iodine into the atmosphere. That was some 500 times the Three-Mile Island amount, he said, and officials still refuse to say why. He interviewed one of the many local residents who had thyroid cancer. The man attributed it to chance.

The potential is even worse. A physicist colleague of mine who has done nuclear regulatory work tells me that a former official at Hanford has told him—off the record, of course—that the tanks contain millions of boiling gallons of the most toxic radioactive substances imaginable. No one has even the slightest idea how many different materials are in the mix, or what they might be. What is known is that a hard crust covers the tops of the liquids in the tanks. What is unknown is just what the crust consists of, or how thick it is.

One thing is certain, however: piercing the crust would be a big mistake. Possibly— again, no one knows—the crust is holding in highly explosive hydrogen gas under enormous pressure. An explosion would fling the unimaginably radioactive garbage every which way. In terms of radioactive release, it could be much worse than any nuclear explosion or possibly even a series of nuclear explosions. It might have the potential ultimately to contaminate the entire world.

Duncan had driven to the Nuclear Reservation to see what he could see. What he could see amounted to buildings and reactor domes beyond guarded gates, and a police car that followed him closely. When he turned around and left, he said, the "cop car follows me until I reach the city limits." This is another by-product of a nuclearized state.

Many residents have been fiercely defensive regarding the nuclear activities, the foundations of the local economy. They were pleased to hear that their area might be chosen to dump all nuclear waste from the country's power plants (sadly for them, it wasn't). They proudly and defiantly named their high school teams "the Bombers."

Columnist Dave Barry discovered in May of 1999 that local leaders are humorless. He wrote that radioactive flies, ants, and gnats had been discovered near the "contaminated nuclear dump site," and said that they might mutate and attack Los Angeles. The response was vigorous. The Tri City *Herald* published an article criticizing Barry for failing to point out positive things. Included—he said he was quoting directly—were "the winning Tri City Americans hockey team," and "the booming construction going on behind Columbia Center Mall."

A "communications specialist" at Hanford, according to Barry, also protested as inaccurate his statement that "the dump site 'glows like a Budweiser sign'." Moreover, said the specialist, it was preferable not to call the insects radioactive, but "contaminated." The same applied to the tumbleweeds that Hanford "produces on a regular basis." Barry swore he wasn't making that up.

To make amends, Barry conceded that he failed to honor one of the most important rules of journalistic balance: "Before you report that an area has radioactive ants, ALWAYS check to see if it also has a winning minor-league hockey team." So chagrined did he feel, that he attempted to help tourism by developing new slogans: "The 'Tri Cities' Area . . . contaminated NOT radioactive!" or "Relax! That Booming Sound You Hear is Nothing More than Construction Behind the Columbia Center Mall."

The Federal Government has gradually relinquished the territory and its activities to other, largely private, interests. Among these is the Washington Public Power Supply System (Whoops). That hardly provides grounds for optimism, given the mismanagement that has brought Whoops such notoriety.

Walla Walla has a much longer and less frightening history than Richland. It reaches into the early 19th century. Missionaries arrived as early as 1836, and the first wagon trains over the Oregon Trail stopped there in the 1840s. It grew as a raucous settlement, supplying miners from as far away as Montana and California, and then thrived as a trading center for agriculture. Dozens of historic buildings remain, and attractions are more than enough to justify the well-structured Downtown Walking Tour. Walla Walla today is a gracious city that seems larger than its population of somewhat less than 30,000.

Before looking around, I drove to Fort Walla Walla Campground and set up my tent. It was a unique place to camp. The city maintains Fort Walla Walla and its campground, but the Fort also offers a museum complex including a village of 14 pioneer buildings dating back to 1859. The excellent campsites were grassy and shady, and the showers and restrooms were adequate.

Among Walla Walla's sights on the way to the campground were the attractive Carnegie Art Center, and some distance later a railroad exhibit by the side of the street. A battered Union Pacific steam locomotive sat in front of a brilliant yellow railroad car with a red roof. It was not a passenger car or a standard caboose, but had windows and a brightly-lettered "UNION UP PACIFIC" above, and "24550" below.

For sheer fun, there was a display of folk art facing the traffic in front of the Melody Muffler shop. From left to right, a saxophonist, drum set, and guitarist looked ready to play. Next was a skier, a fisherman, and a motorcycle beside a family—parents, child, and dog. A reindeer, a goat, and a dinosaur skeleton completed the decidedly mixed crowd. All this was sculpted from mufflers.

Walla Walla's downtown streets are broad, and clean. There is a neat, tailored, appearance throughout the town that is part of its charm. For bicyclists, a major attraction would be the bicycle lanes—they seem to be everywhere. The city even distributed a "Walla Walla Valley Bicycle Route Map."

Whitman College, a well-known liberal arts institution, has a lovely campus. A traditional ivory-tower ambience graces the school, which carefully maintains its gardens and ponds. I went to its Penrose Library, hoping to find TRIH materials. Larry Dodd, the library's archivist and expert on local history, looked carefully into the archives while I reviewed the general collection, but we found nothing relevant.

"Whitman" is a prominent name in the region. Marcus Whitman and his bride Narcissa Prentice were Protestant missionaries who had come to the area in 1836. Schwantes credited Narcissa and Eliza Hart Spalding as being the "first white women to cross North America from coast to coast." The Whitmans settled twenty-five miles upstream from the Columbia on the Walla Walla River to minister to the Cayuse, thus disappointing the Nez Percé who apparently had expected the missionaries to settle among them. The Nez Percé warned the Whitmans that they would have trouble with the Cayuse.

After a time, troubles did begin. The Cayuse resented the Whitmans' efforts to "civilize" them by destroying their hunting and gathering culture. They also took offense when the Whitmans laced garden melons with emetics to prevent "theft" by the Indians, who had been accustomed to helping themselves to the mission's crops. The Cayuse were outraged that anyone would poison the earth's produce, which should be available for human use.

They became increasingly concerned when huge numbers of white immigrants flowed through and into their territory along the Oregon Trail. When a measles epidemic struck with devastating results it fanned their resentment into fury. They noted that white children usually survived under Whitman's treatment, but Indian children rarely did. In late November of 1847, they attacked the mission, killing most of its personnel—both Whitmans and eleven others. In response, Congress in 1848 created the Oregon Territory, the first territory west of the Rockies, and the settlers launched a punitive expedition that resulted ultimately in the conviction and hanging of five Cayuse tribesmen.

Schwantes observed that the term "Cayuse" now is rare. "Tribal descendents have been incorporated into the Confederated Tribes of the Umatilla comprising the Umatillas, Cayuses, and Walla Wallas who live on a small reservation east of Pendleton, Oregon." Today, just seven miles from Walla Walla on U. S. 12, a Whitman Mission National Historic Site commemorates the tragedy. Its 98 acres contain a visitors' center with a museum, excavations of the original burned buildings, and various trails and restored features. They stand as a reminder of the result of cultural conflict and misunderstanding.

Having struck out at Whitman College's library, I went to Walla Walla's Public Library. Personnel there were also eager to help, but neither the reference librarian nor I could find anything.

A nearby library patron became attentive at the mention of the TR Highway, and asked:

"Is it going to be an article, or a book?"

"Both," I replied.

"Cool," he said.

He told me that now he is a "movement therapist," now living in Los Angeles, but is moving back to Montana. Originally he was from Whitefish. He had heard of the TRIH, but had not known that it ran along the Hi-Line.

"I don't know how many times I've seen the TR monument at Marias—I used to drive by there all the time," he said. "I've never stopped to look at it, but I will now. I've always driven a lot. I'll be sure to look for *Moose Crossing.*"

Mentally waving goodbye to Walla Walla, I set out south on state highway 125. For a short distance it was divided. After passing Yellow Hawk Creek and the Walla Walla River, I came to State Line Road. Washington Highway 125 became Oregon 11.

I had crossed the line into the final state on the Theodore Roosevelt International Highway, and was in Oregon.

Chapter Fourteen

Ending in Oregon

The end of the TRIH is in Oregon, but still more than 200 miles distant. Along route 11 signs for corn, "Walla Walla Sweets," or "W W Sweet Onions" were plentiful. As late as the 1940s, I would have gone through Freewater, then Milton. Now there is only "Milton-Freewater." I passed Athena and then Adams before I came to Pendleton, the home of Pendleton woolen goods.

Few cities bear the names of vice presidents—Dallas is named for Polk's vice president George M. Dallas; Fairbanks for TR's vice president Charles W. Fairbanks (TR no doubt would have been pleased if the ultra-conservative Fairbanks himself had relocated to Alaska). Pendleton's distinction is even rarer: its name honors a *defeated* vice presidential candidate.

George Hunt Pendleton of Ohio was the Democratic nominee for the vice presidency in 1864, the year Abraham Lincoln won re-election. Oregon's Democratic state convention for that race actually instructed its delegates to the national convention to support Pendleton for president. The town took his name in 1868.

Beyond the Umatilla River the TRIH route follows U. S. 30. That brought me into Pendleton across a viaduct, and then took me past the rodeo grounds, Blue Mountain Community College, a prison and psychiatric center, and a railroad center and museum. Trains are still frequent. The rodeo grounds were quiet, but each September they roar with activity from the Pendleton Round-Up.

For those four days, Pendleton is crowded. Each afternoon it has a rodeo. Visitors from far away come to see the Westward Ho Parade, a Happy Canyon Indian Pageant, and a teepee village. Tribes from throughout the Northwest participate.

The "Working Girls' Hotel" was perfect, so I checked in. The former turn-of-the-century brothel was nicely restored, and I had my choice of rooms. In fact, I had the whole hotel to myself. I was the only guest, and was free to choose any room—or even any combination of rooms.

Around the corner was the "Westward—Ho." Its sign offered "Fine Dining," and "cocktails." I decided to return for dinner.

Pendleton, Oregon

In the meantime, I explored. I visited the Railroad Center and the Umatilla County Historical Society Museum. I spent some time reviewing the Museum's files and they gave me a good feel for the area and its background.

Pendleton had an underground tour, which I was eager to take after having enjoyed Havre Under the Streets. It was after hours, so I had to book the tour for the next morning. That fit my schedule perfectly, so I went for some fine dining at the Westward—Ho.

Inside, I was startled to see not only that it was run down, but that it hardly came up to the standard of a coffee shop. There was no dining room. Rather than turn abruptly and walk out, I ordered a beer to be polite. "Don't have beer," the counterman said. "Haven't got a liquor license." A congenial little Italian restaurant nearby more than compensated for the disappointment.

The Underground tour was fun—even though it wasn't all underground—and the skilled guide gave an interesting presentation, describing the Shamrock cardroom, the meat market, the laundry, the jail, various living quarters, and the inevitable brothels. It was longer and more commercial than the one at Havre, but less well developed.

After completing the tour, I continued on U.S. 30, which also was Interstate 84. A sign warned, "Blowing Dust Next 40 Miles." Another informed me that I was approaching Stage Gulch. At the Echo/Lexington exit there was a large truck stop where I pulled in to fill my tanks. I discovered that there is no self-service. Oregon law forbids it.

I drove to Stanfield, which was just barely out of sight of the Interstate. It appeared to be typical of small towns isolated on arid prairies. Its streets were dusty and almost deserted. There was a tiny and cheerful public library, but it had nothing of relevance.

At Boardman, I stopped for a picnic lunch. The route by then was nearing the Columbia River. I settled briefly at a table in a lovely city park off the business route and across the railroad tracks. In addition to picnicking, it provided swimming, boating, and camping. I enjoyed the scenery while I baked in heat so dry it felt comfortable.

Around 1960, Boardman residents discovered they had to move. The new John Day Dam would cause their town to be flooded. The Boardman of today is in a new location, out of harm's way. The former site is deep under water.

So is much of the original TRIH. When the Highway became U. S. 30, it generally held to the old route, but damming the river changed that. Flooding new areas made it necessary to relocate much of the highway, and when Interstate 84 came into being, it rolled over much of the rest.

Very little of the original road is available across Oregon. The traveler seeking to stay as close as possible to the original route of the TRIH will have to drive more Interstate miles here than in any other state.

I passed the turnoff to Three-Mile Canyon. The country was rugged and visually stimulating. "Semi-badlands" seemed to be an appropriate description.

On the right was a section that had been burned over. Then, the Columbia River burst into view. Far below was a paddle-wheel boat, so large that it gave the illusion of being designed for the open ocean.

The river is huge, especially to be so far from the Pacific. The road runs high above it. Towering above me were even higher bluffs and mesas. Across the Columbia on the opposite bank were more bluffs.

At Arlington, I encountered another community that the John Day Dam had caused to move from its original, now submerged, location. I also was across the river from Roosevelt, Washington. There was no bridge and Roosevelt was not on the TRIH, so I gave no thought to visiting. Even though it bore TR's name. The Automobile Blue Book maps show that it existed as "Roosevelt" at least as early as the 1920s.

Heat Moon came closer to the settlement of Roosevelt than I did. Traveling his Blue Highways, he drove through it searching for a gas station. He described Roosevelt only as "a cluster of closed buildings."

Those closed buildings may not have shown it, but they reflected the same tough, persistent spirit that Americans have demonstrated throughout their country's history. In 1960, according to the *Sunday Oregonian* for 24 May 1964, there was despair and confusion in the town. The dam would cause it to be inundated, "but unlike the much-publicized relocation of Arlington, Roosevelt could not expect the massive federal aid the Oregon community has received in relocation. Residents were told bluntly that there is no provision for replacing facilities in an unincorporated town." The government did pay each owner for land and buildings, but it would not install utilities because there had been none in the old town where each family had its own well.

The people determined that Roosevelt would continue, so they voted to create a planning commission, and chose a new townsite. Previously, they had not even had a formal government. At the new site, a mile west of the old town, they platted and bought lots. Five families cooperated to hire a well-driller for a public water supply. River passengers, said the *Oregonian*, would look south at Arlington and see a "city largely relocated by federal funds." At Roosevelt, however, they could admire a community that existed because its people refused to let their town die.

A few months later, the *Oregonian* reported on excitement in the quiet settlement. The "population had itself a ball," it said. A Seattle, Portland, and Spokane Railway train pulled into the town at 10:00 a.m. just before Christmas, on the 22nd of December 1964. The train could go no farther because a severe storm had caused flooding and washed out a segment of the track.

The train's chef, William Graves, walked into William Clark's Roosevelt Market and "placed his first order: 20 dozen eggs." Later, he bought everything in the meat cooler. The Air Force dropped additional food, and added a Christmas tree. Chris Miller, steward of the dining car, said, "it gave everybody the Christmas spirit—and the passengers had plenty of spirit to begin with."

The day before Christmas Eve, the children among the passengers went from car to car singing carols. Then, at 3:00 the next morning, busses arrived from Portland to rescue the stranded passengers. "The town," said the *Oregonian* "had its Christmas spirit, too." Mrs. William Clark said, "that train really broke the monotony around here."

I drove past the Blaylock Canyon turnoff, and into Philippi Canyon. I continued across the John Day River, and was confronted by the immensity of the John Day Dam, a huge concrete presence amid the variegated hills and bluffs with glowing reds, purples, and yellows punctuated with greens. Judy Jewell wrote in *Oregon* that along the John Day, "the colors are as soft as the eroded hills. Dusky green willows grow along the bank, where the river roars and birds call."

Day, she noted, had been a woodsman from Virginia. On the way to Astoria in 1811, he and a companion became lost near the Snake River. They crossed the Blue Mountains in winter, and suffered incredible hardships. They received help from Indians, but lost their clothing to others. Some Astorians ultimately found them along the Columbia River, naked and starving. "John Day," she wrote, "went crazy, and died in Astoria." The silty river, "one of the longest undammed rivers in the lower 48," took his name, as did a town, a valley, and a Fossil Beds National Monument—none of which is on the TRIH—and the Dam, which is.

The Maryhill Museum sits across the huge Columbia River. That puts it off the TRIH; it even is in a different state. Still, it is close enough to be considered one of the major attractions along the TR Trail—especially since a bridge crosses the Columbia at Biggs.

Samuel Hill, road builder and associate of railroad magnate James Hill, bought 7,000 acres of land and created the Maryhill community in 1907. He had hopes that it would develop into a Quaker agricultural utopia, but his vision was realized no more than those of most utopians. He built his own estate with a magnificent mansion high above the community. Queen Marie of Rumania journeyed to Maryhill in 1926 to dedicate the partly-completed mansion. Apparently, Hill never did really live there. Nine years after his death, under the guidance of his friend Alma Spreckels it became the Museum of Art. The Museum opened to the public on the 13th of May 1940.

The two Hills were unrelated—except that Sam married James's daughter Mary. Bill Gulick described the unusual circumstances in *Roadside History of Oregon* (1991). Sam had been highly effective as a Minneapolis attorney representing local farmers in lawsuits against James Hill's Great Northern Railroad. Tired of losing, James offered Sam the post of attorney for the railroad. Sam, Gulick reported, said, "No, I won't work for you, but if you'll teach me the railroad business, I'll work with you." He became an expert on railroads, and also on roads. He left his imprint on Oregon by spearheading the Columbia Gorge Highway, one of the most ambitious roadways in the world.

Hill hired Samuel Lancaster as his engineer, and took him to Europe to study road-building techniques. He then sought $65,000 from the Washington State Legislature to "lay out a seventy-five mile stretch of highway through the Columbia River Gorge that would be the wonder of the world." He would save vast sums for the taxpayers by using convict labor.

Washington's legislature gave him "cautious approval," but recoiled in horror when it discovered *which* convict was his dynamite expert—an imprisoned IWW terrorist who had been convicted of using a bomb in an attempt to assassinate a public figure. The legislature decided that Hill's expert was far too familiar with explosives, and cut off Hill's funding.

"If you don't want the highway on your side of the river," Gulick reported him as having said to Washington's officials, "I'll take it across the Columbia to Oregon, where you can see it and regret your decision for the rest of your lives." In 1913, he did just that.

Oregon had no highway commission, but it quickly formed one and approved the project—convict labor and all. According to an information sheet from the Museum, "The Good Roads Movement and Samuel Hill," it was completed in 1915. *The Historic Columbia River Highway* traveler's guide described the Highway's dedication ceremonies. They took place at Crown Point and Multnomah Falls on the 7th of June 1916. At 5:00 in the afternoon, President Woodrow Wilson (TR's nemesis) had pressed a button in the White House, causing a flag to unfurl by remote control.

A Museum brochure, "Historic Columbia River Highway: 1913-1922," tells the Highway's story. Its author was Robert Hadlow, Curator, Oregon Department of Transportation. "In 1913," Hadlow wrote, "work began on the highway. It was constructed through county-state cooperation. It became a state-owned trunk route, part of a growing system of highways criss-crossing Oregon. By 1922 it was completed and covered in Warrenite, a patented long-wearing and smooth-riding asphaltic-concrete pavement."

Although Hadlow does not mention the TRIH, it was at this time that the TR Trail utilized the route of the Columbia River Highway to complete its connection of the two Portlands. After highway numbering began, it became part of U.S. 30.

As Gulick described it, "If ever a highway could be called a work of art, the 73.8 miles of Columbia River Gorge Highway designed and built by Samuel Lancaster qualified. Lancaster loved nature and believed that it was good medicine for the ills of urban life," and the highway would enable modern Americans "to enjoy the wild beauty of nature's gallery and recreate themselves."

At his death in 1931, both regional and national highway systems bore Sam Hill's imprint. He encouraged the formation of state highway departments, and adopted as his motto: "Good roads are more than my hobby, they are my religion."

He had no direct connection with the TRIH, however. Given Hill's pacifism, it came as no surprise when Colleen Schafroth reported to me that "Theodore Roosevelt was . . . . not a favorite of Samuel Hill. In fact, Hill seems to have gone out of his way to encourage his friends and associates not to vote for Roosevelt." Ms Schafroth is Maryhill Museum Curator of Education.

Within a few years, dam construction was responsible for changes in the routing of the Columbia River Highway, hence, of the TRIH. According to Hadlow, by the 1930s the Bonneville Dam had "caused a realignment of a portion of the Historic Columbia River Highway near Tooth Rock and Eagle Creek in eastern Multnomah County." Other changes resulted from the need to accommodate greater traffic. "By 1954, a new water-level route, founded largely on fill material dredged from the Columbia River, bypassed the entire highway from Troutdale to the Dalles. This road was subsequently upgraded to a four-lane divided roadway and eventually became Interstate 84."

Today, Hadlow wrote, about 55 miles of the Historic Columbia River Highway's original 74 miles remain. They are "cut up into several secondary highways and country roads." Fortunately, the state of Oregon now has restored many of these miles, and is working to reclaim others. Some are available only as hiking trails. The Columbia River Highway now is I 84. The old route, from the Dalles to Troutdale, is officially the *Historic* Columbia River Highway. It was listed in the National Register of Historic Places in 1983. In 1984 the American Society of Civil Engineers declared it a National Historic Civil Engineering Landmark, and the National Park Service lists it as "the oldest scenic highway in the United States."

I had begun to see mountains in the distance by the time I reached The Dalles— so named, because the French Canadian *voyageurs* from the Hudson's Bay Company who explored the area saw rocks that reminded them of flagstones (*les dalles*) along the river. I saw no flagstones, but did see wind surfers, fast and colorful upon the water.

Proceeding to Rowena, I found the first piece of the Historic Columbia River Highway. This also had been both U.S. 30 and the TRIH. I followed it back inland to the Wasco County Historical Museum. The Museum is new, large, and impressive, but had nothing relevant.

I left the Museum, and followed the historic road. It was narrow, twisting, and very dangerous. It also is worth every minute spent driving it. Spectacular is the most appropriate word—"awesome," taken literally, applies as well. At the Rowena Crest Viewpoint, I saw the snowcapped tip of Mt. Hood both peaking and peeking over a distant ridge.

When I reached the Rowena Plateau, I stopped to photograph a windswept tree, tilted away from the prevailing wind. It had full branches on the leeward side, and an absolutely bare trunk to windward from the ground to its tip. On down the road I passed something unexpected, an apricot orchard. It was clear that I had left the desert behind me. Next came Mosier, where originally the TRIH had gone through twin tunnels. They have been abandoned since the 1950s, but there are plans to restore them. Almost before I knew it, I was back on the Interstate, I 84 and the new U. S. 30.

Hood River came next. I was in the heart of the Columbia River Gorge, near where the Lewis and Clark Expedition had sent armed men after a band of Indians who had kidnapped Scannon, Lewis's dog. They were successful, rescuing the large Newfoundland without a fight.

The town is the site of one of the first bridges ever to span the broad Columbia. The "Bridge of the Gods," has carried traffic since shortly after the beginning of the twentieth century. An ancient Indian legend was the source of the name, and was also the basis for a popular novel of the same name by Frederic Homer Balch.

West from Hood River, views of the Columbia River were especially dramatic. Fjords rose majestically, their attraction rivaling that of the distant mountains. The change from desert scenery was so abrupt as to be almost startling.

Cascade Locks came next. Farmers long had protested price gouging by the railroads, and in the late 19th century lobbied for a canal around the rapids at the Cascades to make riverboat shipping possible. With the completion of a 3,000-foot canal in 1896, they prevailed.

The canal permitted boats to bypass the rapids, and used locks to lift or lower them as much as 24 feet. These Cascade Locks permitted boat traffic to proceed upriver to The Dalles without impediment, and they also became a tourist attraction.

I arrived next at the Bonneville Dam. It became operational in 1938, and was the first of the huge power-generating dams on the mighty Columbia. This New Deal project had its critics, but it was enormously popular. Much of its popularity resulted from the thirst for jobs during the Depression and the prospect of cheap electricity, but shrewd public relations no doubt also played a part. As Judy Jewell explained it, "the Bonneville Power Authority hired Woody Guthrie for a month in 1941 to popularize the dam-building project. It turned into a song-a-day marathon."

Historian Carlos Schwantes pointed out that the Indian chief who said to Richard Neuberger (later U. S. senator) that the dam would mean no more salmon was partly correct. But it "could have been far worse, because the original design for Bonneville Dam did not include fish ladders and thus would have blocked all salmon and steelhead from spawning farther upriver. Only a public outcry," he wrote, "prevented that tragedy." Previously, the magnificent river had flowed without obstruction from its sources in the mountains to the Pacific, but now one dam after another has become a part of the landscape. Dams or no, though, the scenery was rugged and striking.

At Dodson, I took Exit 35, and left Interstate 84. Once again, I was on the Historic Columbia River Highway—and the original TRIH. The scenery became a fairyland of mountains, forests, cliffs, and waterfalls. Ainsworth State Park is located here, on land donated by John Ainsworth, the son of Captain J. C. Ainsworth for whom the Park was named.

Ainsworth had been captain of the Oregon Steam Navigation Company's Mississippi River-type steamboat *Oneonta*, and once in the 1860s piloted his boat at such a speed that it placed him among the world's fastest human beings. This required a spe-

Horsetail Falls, Columbia River Gorge, Oregon

cial set of circumstances. His craft was very fast for its kind, its reported top speed was around thirty miles an hour, but many locomotives could travel faster than that.

The *Oneonta* made runs on the middle part of the river, between The Dalles and the upper Cascades. Company officials decided that it should be moved to the lower river, which would require Ainsworth to navigate six miles of rapids. He attempted the run when the river was at full flood stage, with a current of nearly thirty miles an hour. Ainsworth built up a full head of steam and charged on. His velocity combined with the current to make him fly past objects on the shore at about sixty miles an hour—the legendary "mile-a-minute," a speed that few human beings in history (and certainly no one in a Mississippi-type riverboat) had achieved up to that time—making him a local hero.

I wanted to see as much as possible in the daylight that was left, so I did not stop at Ainsworth Park. Instead, I drove on to Horsetail Falls. The 176 foot waterfall tumbles alongside the road, spraying it and the Horsetail Falls Bridge, built in 1914. Two beautiful miles ahead I came to Oneonta Bridge and Tunnel, in Oneonta Gorge. Originally both rail and auto traffic used the tunnel, but both now bypass it.

The next bridge, also built in 1914, brought me to viaducts hugging the cliffside, but not cut into it. They led to Multnomah Falls and Lodge. The Falls, with a drop of more than 600 feet, are among the tallest in America.

The road leading west from Multnomah Falls continued on reinforced viaducts. They coursed alongside the cliffs that rose high above me. As with those east of the Falls, they were not cut into the cliffs themselves. Lancaster, designed them this way in order to discourage landslides.

Wahkeena Falls and Park are only about a half mile from Multnomah, I stopped to walk a short distance to the upper falls. From there, on a footbridge, I could look up at the falls spilling down the mountain, or look down at the craggy depths of the gorge below.

Another three miles brought me to a different kind of beauty, one that I had not expected. I passed an estate and what appeared to be an Italian villa. I found that originally it was the Jacobson Estate, which the architect of the Columbia Gorge Hotel, Morris Whitehead, had built in 1916 for Dorothy and Clarence Jacobson. Today, it remains closed to the public. There are no more Jacobsons there, only the Franciscan Sisters of the Eucharist.

Passing through Bridal Veil, once a prosperous lumber town, I came to Bridal Veil Lodge. The 1926 Lodge now is a bed and breakfast, and its ambiance seems to have changed little from the days of the TRIH. Bridal Veil also offers a tiny, and ancient, post office, popular for obvious reasons among newlyweds. Bridal Veil Falls State Park contains another spectacular waterfall. A footpath meanders down a slope to a footbridge, and beyond it is a viewing area. Again, the short walk is a must, and the views are splendid.

A mile or so beyond, I passed a large white house reminding me of something from *Gone with the Wind*. Continuing on, I came to a sharp curve where the road was cut into an overhanging cliff. I later learned that the cliff was Bishop's Cap, and the undercut is called the "half tunnel."

Multnomah Falls, Columbia River Gorge, Oregon

Just around the curve was Shepperd's Dell Falls and Bridge. An observation platform affords a view both of the falls and of the bridge over the canyon. It is only a few steps away from the parking area.

A mile or so more brought me to Latourell Falls on the left and Guy Talbot State Park on the right. There is a nearby observation platform for the falls. The small Park offers restroom and picnic facilities set within deep forest. It sits between the road and the town of Latourell, which also is in deep forest. The town is tiny, and is still occupied.

Soon, I entered into the "Figure Eight Loops." Through five switchbacks I climbed some 700 feet in less than three miles and arrived at Crown Point. Lancaster designed the road in this way to keep the grades relatively gentle and to avoid excessively sharp curves.

The Vista House Observatory sits within Crown Point State Park atop a point overlooking the Columbia River from a height of 733 feet. As from a tower, there is a 360 degree unobstructed view. The structure opened in 1918, and at first there were scornful comments. Jewell quoted one, that it was a "$100,000 outhouse." The indescribable beauty of the site and its unique views soon stilled critical comment, and it has been a major tourist attraction ever since. As a matter of fact, the two-story domed structure actually is quite handsome.

In the relatively short trip through the Gorge, there had been almost too much to absorb. Now, as I passed buildings, some new and some quite old, I felt as though the major sights were behind me; that nothing more could attract my attention. I knew the feeling would be temporary, but I couldn't shake it off as I drove through the towns of

Vista House, Columbia River, Oregon

Corbett and Springdale. Part of the feeling, I knew, was that I had left the mountains—I always have a pang of regret when I have been in the mountains, and then recognize that they are all behind me.

My interest perked up, though, when I crossed the Stark Street Bridge. Immediately beyond it was a building that the Portland Auto Club built for its headquarters in 1913. It still has the look of an old rest stop for travelers, but now is a private home.

After driving through more woods I came to the Stark Street Junction, then crossed the Sandy River, and found Troutdale's picturesque downtown. Ultimately, I came to Interstate 84. I drove along the Interstate for a short distance until I reached Exit 15, which was U. S. 30 By-Pass.

It also was N. E. Sandy Boulevard, the street along which the TRIH entered Portland. After some distance, Sandy veered left, and became U. S. Business 30. I was on the original route, entering the terminal city of Portland, Oregon, after more than 4,000 miles spent crossing the Continent, originating in Portland, Maine.

History and name both reflect the kinship of the two cities. Asa Lovejoy and Francis Pettygrove were New Englanders who hoped to establish a New England outpost in the Far West, although they were not the first white settlers in the area.

At first, they called their settlement "Stumptown" (another former "Stumptown" on the TRIH) because of the tree stumps everywhere. In 1845, each wanted to name it after his home city. Pettygrove, from Portland, Maine, won the toss. But for the random fall of a coin, it would have become "Boston, Oregon."

I gave up the idea of camping. Portland has campgrounds, but it forbids tent camping, approving only RVs. In any case, I welcomed the convenience of a motel.

I wanted to experience Portland before I drove on in to the actual terminal point of the TRIH, so the next morning, I left the truck in the motel's parking area, and rode downtown on the MAX. It crossed the Willamette on Steel Bridge, and a few blocks later went through Skidmore Square.

Portland's light rail system is efficient, faster than traveling by auto, and comfortable. With unbelievable common sense, the city has made Max free to riders within its central core.

Some skeptics question the value of light rail. Somehow, they think it unacceptable since mass transit in general and light rail in particular rarely operates at a profit. They prefer freeways—which no one expects ever to show a profit. One would think that experience of cities that have committed themselves fully to rail systems should change their minds. Such cities come alive. But minds are fiercely resistant to change, and find it easy to ignore even so superb an example as Portland.

The counterculture was alive and well in Pioneer Courthouse Square. Pioneer Courthouse, itself, as one of Portland's oldest buildings, has sat across 6th Avenue from the Square since 1869. The Square had drinking fountains and shops, and was surrounded by energetic and attractive businesses. A number of people, young and not-so-young, were darting inoffensively around on skateboards.

Not too many years ago, Pioneer Square was a parking lot. Before that, it was where the Portland Hotel stood. I am told that the hotel had been a splendid building, but developers preferred that it be demolished to park cars. As happens nearly everywhere, they had their way—until at last saner heads came to prevail.

Oregon History Center, Portland

An "antique" trolley made to look authentic by polished wood and shiny brass rolled quietly by on the MAX rails. Interesting delis and small cafés dotted the area.

It was heartening to see the center of a major city so alive and energetic. At one time, Portland had been going the way of other cities. Its core had begun to decay, and its traffic patterns reflected the chaos that is so routine elsewhere.

Then, the city adopted policies to control growth, and committed itself to light rail, with all rides free inside the borders of downtown. It even demolished a freeway to make way for a three-mile stretch of green, the Tom McCall Waterfront Park. In October of 1980, Ordinance No, 150580 planned for Portland's future. It called for a careful mixture of residence, business, and industry and for judicious control of automobile traffic and parking. It specified citizen involvement. It dealt with air and water quality, and with land resources and noise. It called for ample public facilities.

The city has lived by its plan, and the result has been extraordinary. Portland is one of the most beautiful cities in the country. It also is one of the most successful as a place to live or merely experience. This is not because its location is so breathtaking as, for example, Duluth's, but because its people cooperated to make it that way.

The next morning was Sunday. I had departed from the other Portland on another Sunday also, and had deliberately driven across the country at a leisurely pace, so as to savor it all. In spite of my dawdling and the great distance behind me, the journey, there so near to its end, was beginning to seem too brief.

But I knew the time had come. There were loved ones I wanted to see, obligations I needed to meet, and a living that I needed to earn, so I started the truck and proceeded along the TRIH.

I followed Business Route 30 in on Sandy, which was the original route. Portland does have a Roosevelt Street, but I could find no connection between it and the TR Highway. I turned right on Morrison, crossed the Morrison Bridge, drove straight onto Washington to Broadway, turned left on Broadway to Jefferson, and right on Park. I drove on Park to the statue of Theodore Roosevelt, and had come to the end of the Theodore Roosevelt International Highway.

It was early on Sunday morning, so traffic was almost nonexistent. I parked nearby, and walked to the statue. It is the same as the one in Minot; Dr. Waldo Coe had donated them both.

Roosevelt sits astride his mount as though ready to do battle. The statue is in a lovely park, bounded by Jefferson and Madison Streets on each end, and by Park Avenues on each side (they are one-way in opposite directions). Another fine statue — this one of Lincoln, TR's model as president — stands in the same park some distance from that of TR.

The statue was front-page news in 1922 in the *Oregonian*. Several articles reported on A. Phimister Proctor's sculpting progress in New York, on the selection of a site, on a mini-controversy regarding its base, and on agreement by President Harding, himself, to attend its dedication. The dedication took place on 11 November 1922, but Vice President Coolidge attended instead of President Harding. In 1964, the DAR and a group of TR admirers rededicated the statue, and it has been the subject of several articles through the years.

TR was always news. Edward Miller wrote in the *Oregonian* on the 24th of October 1927 of an incident that had taken place fifteen years earlier, during the Bull Moose campaign. TR was "beaming and smiling" at an early hour when he was "breakfasting on one big cantaloupe, one dish Oregon strawberries, two slices Oregon ham, two lamb chops, one order bacon, four eggs, fried potatoes and two cups of coffee." When he returned to his room, he could not find his prized volume of Hermit

TR Statue, End of Theodore Roosevelt International Highway, Portland, Oregon

Paul's *The Second Roman Republic*. "Concisely stated, the book simply disappeared from the Roosevelt suite in the Oregon Hotel."

The book never surfaced. TR was outraged, went to his address early, spoke to a nearly empty Moose Hall, and was at the station waiting for his train "ten minutes before his Moose speech was slated to start." He was seen through the train's window, reading, as it departed. Obviously, he was reading something else. "The disaster put Roosevelt in such a rage that the Roman Republic crashed the headlines on every newspaper of the Pacific coast."

Viewing the statue, though, one could almost forget that TR had been human. In contrast to the Minot statue, Portland's had a plaque with an effusive eulogy:

HE WAS FOUND FAITHFUL OVER A FEW THINGS, AND HE WAS MADE RULER OVER MANY. HE WAS FRAIL; HE MADE HIMSELF A LION OF COURAGE. HE WAS A DREAMER. HE BECAME ONE OF THE GREAT DOERS OF ALL TIME. WOMEN FOUND A CHAMPION IN HIM. KINGS STOOD IN AWE OF HIM. BUT CHILDREN MADE HIM THEIR PLAYMATE. HE BROKE A NATION'S SLUMBER WITH HIS CRY, AND IT ROSE UP. SOULS BECAME SWORDS THROUGH HIM. SWORDS BECAME SERVANTS OF GOD. HE WAS LOYAL TO HIS COUNTRY, AND HE EXACTED LOYALTY; HE LOVED MANY LANDS, BUT HE LOVED HIS OWN LAND BEST. HE WAS TERRIBLE IN BATTLE BUT TENDER TO THE WEAK; JOYOUS AND TIRELESS, BEING FREE FROM SELF-PITY. CLEAN WITH A CLEANNESS THAT CLEANSED THE AIR LIKE A GALE. HIS COURTESY KNEW NO WEALTH OR CLASS; HIS FRIENDSHIP NO CREED OR COLOR OR RACE. HIS COURAGE STOOD EVERY ONSLAUGHT OF SAVAGE BEAST AND

RUTHLESS MAN, OF LONELINESS, OF VICTORY, OF DEFEAT. HIS MIND WAS
EAGER, HIS HEART WAS TRUE, HIS BODY AND SPIRIT DEFIANT OF OBSTA-
CLES, READY TO MEET WHAT MIGHT COME. HE FOUGHT INJUSTICE AND
TYRANNY; BORE SORROW GALLANTLY; LOVED ALL NATURE, BLEAK
PLACES, AND HARDY COMPANIONS, HAZARDOUS ADVENTURE AND THE
ZEST OF BATTLE. WHEREVER HE WENT HE CARRIED HIS OWN RACK; AND
IN THE UTTERMOST PARTS OF THE EARTH HE KEPT HIS CONSCIENCE FOR
HIS GUIDE.

HAGEDORN

"Hagedorn" was Hermann Hagedorn, a TR scholar and biographer. Among the many
enthusiasts of TR, Hagedorn—as his piece suggests—was arguably the most enthusiastic.

It was over. I had followed the Theodore Roosevelt International Highway for its
full length. There is, or was, another TR Highway in Oregon. The stretch of road along
the length of Oregon's gorgeous Pacific shoreline originally was called the Roosevelt
Coast Military Highway. But it had no connection to the TRIH.

But there is one other thing I must mention. On my way home, I was driving through
Choteau, Montana when I saw a familiar sight. Standing in the window of an antique
store was a black silhouette figure. It was the same as one of those I saw thousands of
miles before in Mooers, New York. It was as if he were made to order, and the truck
had plenty of space.

Charlene named him "Choteau," of course. I placed him, relaxing against a tree, in
our front yard to greet me every time I pulled into the driveway as a welcome reminder
of my journey along the Theodore Roosevelt International Highway.

Chapter Fifteen

APPENDIX: America's Bull Moose

The bellow of the Bull Moose dominated the early years of the twentieth century. America had a president who not only had punched cows, he had punched out a bully in a bar. Not only did the country take pride in its triumph in the recent Spanish-American War, its new president had been a major hero of that war.

The brash new nation stepped into the century and onto the world scene with confidence. To their surprise, its people discovered that their equally brash and most physical president was no bull (or bull moose) in a China shop. TR—for Americans began for the first time to call a president affectionately by his initials—was a skillful political leader, and a smooth and subtle diplomat. These were unexpected qualities in a bull moose, but Bull Moose he remained, of that there is no doubt.

TR, though, was hardly born a bull moose. No one could have predicted, either at his birth—on the 27th of October 1858—or for years later, that he would become one. His frailty as a child combined with such weak vision that he was severely handicapped. Even though he was born to privilege, with love and support from his home, he had much to overcome before he became the youngest person ever to be President of the United States.

On the other hand, Roosevelt did have one physical advantage even as a boy. He was blessed with enormous energy, and with an ability to ignore or overcome fatigue and pain. He also could concentrate intensely and follow a long task through to completion. This required stamina of mind as well as body, and his determination was phenomenal. Without these qualities he could never have become the Bull Moose and thus captivate the imagination of a nation.

Roosevelt biographies are filled with scenes of the asthmatic young "Teedie" gasping for breath. They portray the terror of father and child as Theodore Roosevelt, Sr., would pace the room with the suffocating three-year-old in his arms. Many times he would race through New York's streets in his carriage with little Teedie on his lap bundled against the cold, hoping to force air into his son's puny lungs.

The nineteenth century's best "remedies" made survival itself, let alone recovery, questionable. The last resort, strong black coffee, was the most benign It might even have been helpful. Ipecac, to induce vomiting in a weakened child was bad enough.

Worst of all—in fact, bordering on the unbelievable for any breathing difficulty—was tobacco. Medical opinion held that, during an attack, it was therapeutic to force an asthma victim to inhale the smoke from a strong cigar.

Despite the therapies, Teedie's body survived. His mind actually thrived. The world opened to him as never before, when his father noticed that he had difficulty seeing and bought him glasses. For the first time in his life he could see things more than a few feet away, and gloried in the world's newly-discovered beauty. He had not recognized that he had been almost blind. His vision could be corrected, but there were no corrective lenses to compensate for his lack of physical strength.

Ultimately, when his father said bluntly to him, "you have the mind but not the body," the boy determined to strengthen himself. His father built him a gymnasium, and he began his pursuit of "the strenuous life." It was a long process.

At the age of fourteen, he was humiliated at a camp on Moosehead Lake in Maine. Two boys incessantly teased him until he tried to fight, only to discover that either of them could handle him "with easy contempt." Worse, either could do it so easily as not to hurt him much.

He prevailed upon his father to give him boxing lessons. John Long, a former prizefighter, became his instructor. As one of his biographers, Nathan Miller, described it, he "developed the fighting instincts that were to dominate his character."

The skills did not come quickly or easily, but they did come. He continued boxing even in the White House (the name he bestowed officially on the Executive Mansion), until a blow from a young military aide caused a detached retina, blinding him in one eye. He carefully hid his injury from the public during his presidency.

Thereafter he turned to jiu-jitsu, an art that until decades later, after defeat in World War Two of its Japanese originators, most Americans did not even know existed. His skill and determination earned him a black belt (for this bit of information I am indebted to the late Dr. John Gable, Executive Director of the Theodore Roosevelt Association, who arguably knew as much about TR as anyone alive). Almost assuredly, TR was the only black belt ever to be president; undoubtedly, he was the only one ever to earn it during his presidency!

TR entered Harvard in 1876, but only after considerable preparation for the entrance examinations. For two years, he studied vigorously with the aid of a tutor. In that time he covered three years of work. He had read voraciously for most of his life, and had traveled widely with his family. He read several languages, spoke French and German, and had lived abroad. His interest in nature had led him to become an expert on ornithology and wildlife. But a tutor was necessary because he was weak in mathematics, and in fact had never spent time in a formal classroom. He needed guidance to bring coherence to his broad knowledge. When the time came, he passed each examination easily.

At Harvard, he boxed as a lightweight, wrestled, and studied vigorously. He began his career as a writer, which lasted throughout his life, resulting in dozens of books. Always a prude, he developed also into a bit of a dandy, which made it all the more astonishing that he also came to develop an interest in politics—an activity then considered a dirty business, completely unfit for gentlemen.

Roosevelt's life was shattered when his father died suddenly. He had been closer to Theodore Roosevelt, Sr., than to anyone else. Characteristically, he dealt with the shock of the death by immersing himself even more deeply into his studies. When classes ended, he had won honors in six of his eight subjects, but his grief and rage remained.

That summer he worked them off in intense physical activity. Once he rowed across Long Island Sound and back, over twenty-five miles, in one day. Then, after quarrelling with his friend Edith Carow, he left to spend the remainder of the vacation in the wilds of Maine. His guide, Bill Sewall of Island Falls, was an experienced woodsman.

At first, Sewall thought of TR as pale and thin, with weak eyes and a bad heart. He soon recognized that the appearance was completely misleading; the young man was no typical city dude. Day after day, he found that TR's energy never flagged. He could sleep in the open and tramp through the woods from dawn to dusk, not only enjoying every minute, but always eager for more. Once, sleeping out in the open on a chilly night, soaked in the rain, Sewall was astonished to hear Roosevelt say, "By *Gadfrey* this is fun!" The two became fast friends.

The Maine vacation was Roosevelt's first direct experience with "common people." When he discovered that he enjoyed the company of rough-hewn woodsmen, his class-conscious snobbishness began to fray around the edges. Being in such a different world also helped his grief to diminish, and to restore him. In the years to come, he was to return repeatedly to Maine.

In the meantime, back at Harvard, he met Alice Hathaway Lee and determined that they would marry. "She won't have *me*, but I'll have *her*," he said. The courtship was arduous—with the young Roosevelt fearing that he might have been wrong, and that he would lose her after all—but proceed it did, and according to the stifling conventions of the day. This is not to say that those conventions were difficult for the Victorian and always prudish Roosevelt to honor. The happy couple was married on the 27th of October 1880, shortly after Theodore's graduation in June. To her, he had become "Teddy."

Prior to his graduation, he had written two draft chapters of what was to become his *Naval War of 1812*. He also produced a senior thesis on "The Practicability of Equalizing Men and Women Before the Law," strongly endorsing equal rights. No biographer has been able to document a reason why such a radical topic appealed to the conservative young Roosevelt, but some—including the most critical, Henry Pringle—suggested Alice's influence may have been a factor. Indeed, Pringle noted the "radical conduct" that TR displayed when he once impetuously took Alice to lunch at Harvard's Porcellian Club, "never before polluted by the presence of a woman."

There may be a clue in Edward Renehan's book on TR and his family, *The Lion's Pride*, that hints of an earlier influence. Renehan noted that TR's father had been closely associated in "the reform movement" with George William Curtis, editor of *Harper's Weekly*. Curtis, Renehan pointed out, had been "a tireless advocate for women's suffrage, civil service reform, and improved public education." TR's interest in women's rights may possibly have sprung from his family background. Its roots may have lodged in the same soil that nourished his interest in a merit-based civil service. Miller also suggested that Alice may have been the influence, or that it may have been the reformist views of Roosevelt's father.

This explanation would not have occurred to Pringle, who tried mightily but unsuccessfully to present a balanced account of TR, a figure he manifestly disliked. Pringle believed, unsurprisingly, that "the father of Theodore Roosevelt, like his fellow citizens of the upper middle class, had no particular interest in the movements for social reform which were beginning to get under way in the '60's." Similarly, against all evidence, Pringle concluded that the young Roosevelt's commitment to equal rights was merely a youthful radicalism, and that he abandoned it quickly.

Both Miller, and another biographer, Edmund Morris, recognized TR's lifelong commitment to equality. Miller pointed out, for example, that later, when Roosevelt became a member of the Civil Service Commission, his energy gave the Commission influence that it had never before had. As Commissioner, moreover, Roosevelt saw to it that "for the first time, women were put on the same competitive level with men."

Pringle conceded that TR later did support women's rights, but only "halfheartedly," and only "from time to time." Pringle was even unimpressed by the Bull Moose campaign of 1912 when TR called for women's suffrage while both Taft and Wilson were opposing it. TR, he concluded, had only been a "recent and somewhat bored convert" to the cause. Remember this the next time someone says, "facts speak for themselves."

When he returned to New York after graduation from Harvard, TR enrolled in law school. That year, his 23rd, was especially notable. He finished the highly detailed *Naval War of 1812*, which has remained a standard reference for more than a century. It was the beginning of his lifelong advocacy of a powerful American navy. That year was also the beginning of his political career. He ran for, and on the 8th of November 1881 won, a seat in the New York State Assembly.

Despite being the youngest person in the Assembly, he rapidly rose to prominence. His legislative career was brief—he served three one-year terms—but significant. Before reaching the age of 24, he had become one of the best-known figures in New York politics. On New Year's Day, 1883, the Republicans put him forth as their candidate for Speaker. The following month, he journeyed west to Little Missouri in Dakota Territory where he bought a share in the Maltese Cross, or the Chimney Butte Cattle Ranch. It was a move that was to have lifelong significance.

He did not become Speaker. The Democrats controlled the Assembly and elected their candidate, but Roosevelt's rise had been phenomenal. He did have setbacks, as when he tried again later to become Speaker after the Republicans had taken the majority, and again failed. He learned from his setbacks that, in his own words, he was not all-important. Most vital of all, his legislative experience opened his eyes to the consequences of poverty and the need for reform.

Harvard had contributed nothing to this most important part of his education. Deliberately or not the Harvard education of TR's day carefully shielded students from an understanding of the effects of the economic system upon the workers. It taught that character defects were what generated poverty and degradation—that this was a natural law. Years later, Roosevelt commented that his Harvard education put an unrealistic emphasis on individual initiative; he lamented that it was deficient in not having recognized also the necessity of collective action. He discovered in the legislature something else that Harvard had not taught: judges often knew nothing of life, only of "legalism."

Roosevelt was learning of life at first hand. It was soon to deal him another blow, almost unbearable. On February 12, 1884, while he was away in Albany at his legislative duties, Alice gave birth to a baby girl, later to be christened Alice Lee. The baby was healthy, but the mother was ailing, as was his own mother. Summoned by telegram, Roosevelt returned home as rapidly as he could manage by railroad.

Early in the morning on Valentine's Day in 1884, Mittie Bullock Roosevelt, died. Her children, including TR were at her bedside. That afternoon, in another room in the same house where she also lived, Alice died in her Teddy's arms. She had Bright's disease, a kidney condition, fatal if untreated, for which 19th-century medicine was worthless.

TR and others of the family were to utter that there was a curse on that house. He poured out his heart in a passage in his diary. The myth—romantic, although not completely accurate (as Kathleen Dalton noted in her splendid *Theodore Roosevelt: A Strenuous Life*)—is that afterward he never spoke her name again. What is accurate, is that even though he tolerated it for political reasons, he wanted never again to be called "Teddy," Alice's name for him.

Just as when his father died, he buried his grief in frenzied activity. He completed the legislative session, and threw himself into the 1884 Republican National Convention, where he was among the most active and influential delegates, attracting national attention. He forcefully seconded the unsuccessful nomination of a black delegate from Mississippi to be the temporary chair of the convention, and worked for the candidacy of George F. Edmunds of Vermont.

He was dismayed that the party chose instead the scandal-tainted James G. Blaine to be its presidential candidate. But Roosevelt was a committed Republican. As a delegate, he also had been pledged to support the convention's choice. It was a difficult decision, but he ultimately chose not to join other reformers who did bolt the party to support Grover Cleveland. Cleveland became the first Democrat elected president since the Civil War.

His political career was in doubt, and his grief was almost overwhelming. Roosevelt sold the house in New York and left "Baby Lee" with his sister Bamie (Anna). He already had given up the study of law. Instead of retreating to the Maine wilderness, he returned to the Dakota Bad Lands to become a rancher, this time across the river from Little Missouri to the new town of Medora. Bill Sewall and another Maine companion, Will Dow, joined him as managers on generous terms.

His ranching venture was a financial disaster. Drought was common in the inhospitable land, and that was bad enough. Then, an extraordinarily brutal winter rammed through the territory, freezing to death many of the cattle across the northern plains.

But other things were more important for Roosevelt's development. The loss of money was insignificant when considering the experience as a whole. The Dakota Territory was a place almost literally of rebirth.

It was in Dakota that the Bull Moose was born. Years of exercise had made him strong, but until he went west he still, deceptively, appeared thin and frail. During his days of ranching, he developed the massive frame of the figure who came to capture the excited imaginations of Americans when he wrote articles and books about his adventures in the Badlands. Equally important, he shed the vestiges of his snobbery, and came to value "common people." Late in life he said that if he had never gone west, he could never have become President.

Roosevelt's appearance when he arrived there could hardly have been less suited to the Dakota wilds. His clothes were expensive and tailored. He had a knife, but coming from Tiffany's it did little to endear him to frontiersmen. Above all, he wore glasses. He remarked that Dakotans seemed to think of them as representing a moral flaw.

But his willingness, in fact his eagerness, to work hard along side his ranch hands impressed them. They found his ability to do so—to work harder and longer than anyone else—even more impressive. They may have joked about his command to his men to "hasten forward quickly there," and repeated it so much that it spread with laughter through the territory, but they marveled at his disregard of danger. The nickname "Four Eyes" at first was scornful, but soon it became "Ol' Four Eyes," more a term of affection, and his exploits became the stuff of legend.

Witnesses spread the word of the encounter in Mingus, Montana when a drunk who had been shooting up the bar ordered "Four Eyes" to set up drinks for the house. Roosevelt laughed, treating it as a joke. The drunk then trained his guns on "Four Eyes," and again barked the command. "If I've got to, I've got to," Roosevelt said. He got to his feet, then whirled to plant a sudden right, left, and right to his tormentor's jaw. The thug dropped to the floor unconscious, his guns firing, but not hitting anyone.

Roosevelt had become a deputy sheriff, and was an active lawman. Once he, Dow, and Sewall chased three thieves over a hundred miles through the worst of a Badlands winter. The three had stolen a boat of Roosevelt's. Under the "Code of the West," most frontiersmen, deputies or not, would simply have shot the three on the spot when capturing them. As a good Victorian gentleman, such a thought did not enter Roosevelt's mind. He and his men escorted their captives to Mandan, more than 150 miles distant. They had to take turns watching them at night, because the weather was so cold that the thieves would have frozen if they had been bound. By the time they arrived in Mandan and turned over their prisoners to the local sheriff, the party had journeyed some 300 miles. Never one to waste time, during the perilous journey over land and water through the storms and bitter cold, the young rancher had occupied himself in spare moments by reading *Anna Karenina*—in French.

Roosevelt's assertive courage made him a role model for generations of American youth. He was a "man's man," but cultured as well as courageous; his call for the strenuous life was both intellectual and physical. Expressions of masculinity today often make us uncomfortable, sometimes bringing groans of outright disdain. "Today's insouciant critics," noted John Morton Blum in *The Republican Roosevelt,* "censure as quixotic adolescence or dangerous diversion the intensity of act and feeling they no longer share."

Consider, for example, Ian Frazier's dismissal of Roosevelt's experience in the West. In his otherwise admirable book, *Great Plains,* he wrote flippantly that Roosevelt went west recovering from the death of his wife after having told friends he would never be happy again. But, Frazier sniffed, "Teddy Roosevelt knocked down a man who was mean to him in a bar, and caught three other men who stole a boat from him, and cheered up."

Rejecting macho posturing is one thing. It is quite another to adopt an effete opposition to all things physical, unless they take place in the sports arena or in the manicured environment of a health club. Cheap shots and snide comments tell us nothing. For true insight, consider TR's own comment that "Black care rarely sits behind a rider whose pace is fast enough."

While living the life of a rancher Roosevelt continued his writing and took care to publicize his exploits. He also returned to New York now and then for visits. During one of these visits, he and Edith Carow renewed their acquaintance. During another, they became engaged. For this he berated himself. His Victorian values caused him to disapprove of second marriages—a person should be married and remain true to the spouse, living or dead. Friends heard him in his room condemning himself for lack of "constancy," but when news of their engagement leaked out, he announced that it was true.

When he moved back to New York the Republicans persuaded him to run for mayor. He knew that conditions were wrong and that he had no chance of victory, but he made the race for the good of the party. He was right to hesitate, and came in third.

He did remarry, despite his concern that it demonstrated a lack of character. He and Edith proved to be a perfect match, and "Baby Lee" came to live with them in the rambling home, Sagamore Hill, that he had built in Oyster Bay, New York. During his presidency, TR's friend the novelist Owen Wister chided him that he should control the independent, bright-eyed, and tart-tongued Alice (who did not share her father's aversion to rough language or bawdy jokes). He replied that he could control her or he could be President, but he could not do both. The Roosevelts were to have four sons, and another daughter. Within the family, Alice was not "Alice," but "Sister," to avoid the name that had become so painful to TR.

In 1889, President Benjamin Harrison appointed Roosevelt to the Civil Service Commission. In a position that previously had had little influence, he worked diligently to support a merit-based civil service—often crossing swords with powerful politicians—and to open government jobs impartially to all qualified applicants, including women and blacks. As Commissioner, in spite of his generally jaundiced view of Indian culture, he worked closely with Herbert Welsh regarding Indian rights. Thomas Dyer, in his detailed study *Theodore Roosevelt and the Idea of Race*, wrote that perhaps Roosevelt's "instincts for reform could overpower" his attitudes. In any case, Dyer said that apparently "Welsh believed that Roosevelt had rendered valuable service to the Indian Rights Association." TR's tenure on the Commission was so successful that when Grover Cleveland defeated Harrison, Roosevelt stayed on into the Democratic Cleveland administration. During this time he also was publishing volumes of his massive history, *The Winning of the West*, which received critical acclaim.

While he was receiving praise from scholars, Roosevelt's popular image as a Western hero was growing. Readers devoured his stories and books about his experiences in the Wild West. Among them, his 1888 *Ranch Life and the Hunting Trail*, filled with illustrations by Frederic Remington, enhanced his exploits for a public eager to read more of his adventures.

After six years on the Commission, Roosevelt became restive. He also had financial difficulties, and his salary there was small. On the 6th of April 1895, he accepted an appointment to the New York City Board of Police Commissioners. It not only carried a better salary, but was a post that permitted action—always a requirement for the man who, in Renehan's words, "had always been a bundle of nervous energy: a brilliant man of action—easily bored, rarely satisfied."

Roosevelt threw himself into the position, determined to reform the police force. He made himself the major figure of the time in New York law enforcement. As with every other position he had held, he transformed it into something far greater than it had been before. Miller described it perfectly: "Roosevelt wasted no time in grabbing the Police Department by the scruff of the neck and giving it a good shaking."

His roughly two years as police commissioner easily warranted an entire book. H. Paul Jeffers supplied it in 1994 when he brought forth his penetrating study, *Commissioner Roosevelt*. Jeffers documented Roosevelt's difficulties as a committed reformer who sat on a board of four that required unanimous approval for any action, but he also demonstrated TR's solid accomplishments.

Roosevelt's actions to eliminate favoritism, graft, and corruption brought him into direct conflict with the police force, with its bureaucracy, and with powerful politicians. Conflict flared also with another of the commissioners, Andrew Parker, a loyal agent of Tammany Hall. Time and again, Parker blocked his actions, but Roosevelt did become President of the Board.

Under the circumstances, his accomplishments were phenomenal. He introduced promotion by merit into the police force, and insisted on professionalism. He argued for women clerks to receive equal pay with men for equal work, and caused a stir when he broke tradition by appointing as his secretary (a "girl secretary," according to the astonished press) Minnie Gertrude Kelly. He brought about the creation of thirty-two positions of matron in police stations, so that any time a woman were arrested she would be processed by another woman. He prowled the streets personally in the dead of night to ensure that the police were doing their jobs effectively, and honestly. Page after page of Jeffers's book is filled with his exploits.

The enemies he made are an indication of his successes. In 1896, a reporter from the *New York Times* discovered a plot to oust him. Republican boss Thomas Platt conspired with his Democratic rival, Tammany boss Richard Croker, to remove Roosevelt to clear the way for a return to the days of open graft. "THE REPUBLICAN PLOT TO OUST ROOSEVELT," read the headline in the *Times*, "Political Cowards and Assassins Would Strike Him Down for His Honesty and Courage."

The plot failed, but opportunity accomplished what conspiracy could not. The newly-elected President William McKinley, on the 6th of April 1897, appointed Police Commissioner Roosevelt—the renowned adventurer, naval scholar, and author of *The Naval War of 1812*—to be the new Assistant Secretary of the Navy.

Roosevelt happily accepted the appointment. He left behind him a police force that had been considerably reformed. True, many of his reforms faded as the years passed, but there can be no doubt that New York had a much better force because it had once had Theodore Roosevelt as a member of its Board of Police Commissioners.

Roosevelt's tenure at the Navy Department was as momentous as his service as police commissioner, and it had considerably more national import. In those days before the creation of the Department of Defense, it was a major position. The administration was much smaller than it is today, and had many fewer layers. The Assistant Secretary was the number two person in the department, reporting to the Secretary of the Navy who held a Cabinet position and reported directly to the President.

As a long-time student of naval affairs, Roosevelt in 1890 had reviewed *The Influence of Sea Power Upon History*, by Captain (later Rear Admiral) Alfred Thayer Mahan, for *The Atlantic Monthly*. He and Mahan agreed upon many things, including support for expansion and the importance of a two-ocean Navy. He immediately set about "building up our Navy to its proper standing," and working with Captain Mahan. They pulled together a group of like-minded officials to work for their goals.

Secretary, John D. Long, was content to administer the Department, and rely upon Roosevelt as the master of technical naval intricacies. Nevertheless, the Secretary often found himself distressed by his assistant's pugnacious speeches and the vigorous actions he took whenever he was in a position to serve as Acting Secretary. Comments such as, "He has the backbone of a chocolate éclair," referring to President McKinley's reluctance to become involved in Cuba, failed to endear him to either man although by and large they approved of his actions.

Expulsion of the Spanish from Cuba had become one of Roosevelt's major aims. Although the press, particularly the Hearst newspapers, exaggerated it there is little doubt of the brutal nature of Spanish rule there. It outraged the Assistant Secretary, but it also fit into his desire for American expansion. Superficially, Roosevelt was without question a man of war. He romanticized war and warfare, and saw it as a contributor to heroism and national glory.

Nevertheless, a superficial view rarely is a thoughtful one. There can be no doubt that he wished the country to be ready to fight, and that he was quite aggressive. He did not, however, consider himself a militarist. In fact, he had reservations about a professional military force. He also had no desire for colonies. Miller summed him up perceptively when he concluded "there is no simple, correct answer to the question of whether he as a man of war or a man of peace. Roosevelt was too complex. In truth, he was both."

When war with Spain did arrive, Roosevelt resigned his post as Assistant Secretary in order to go into action. After a year of calling for war, he was determined to demonstrate that he would practice what he preached. His eyesight was weak and he was almost forty years of age, but nothing would deter him. It is difficult to understand today just how momentous TR's move was. We are conditioned in the twenty-first century to accept bellicose leaders who adopt aggressive policies, but who themselves shy away from danger and always ensure their own safety and comfort while sending others to fight and die. Imagine Paul Wolfowitz, for example, resigning as Assistant Secretary of Defense (a position similar to the one TR held) to go fight in the Iraq War that he had partially caused. One can only imagine TR's disgust at his successors.

Secretary of War Russell A. Alger offered TR command of a rifle regiment of volunteers, but Roosevelt replied that he was not yet ready for command. His military experience had amounted to only three years as an officer in the New York National Guard. He thought he could learn enough in a month to command, but a month was too long to delay. He asked instead to be second in command, lieutenant colonel, rather than colonel, and the Secretary granted his request. Col. Leonard Wood, Roosevelt's close friend, became his commander.

He and Wood set out to raise the First United States Volunteer Cavalry. They received applications from all over the country, and selected carefully. Although Wood had the official command, the regiment that resulted was clearly Roosevelt's. With no trace remaining of the snob that he once had been, he melded Indians, cowboys, Harvard men, outlaws, and others into his "Rough Riders."

The war was brief, but bloody. Roosevelt's Rough Riders captured the headlines, and Roosevelt with a promotion became their colonel. As he had done in the west, he worked side by side with his men. He went outside of channels to find them food, he shared the work digging latrines, and he fearlessly exposed himself to fire. Marshalling black and white troops, he personally led the charge up Kettle Hill in the vicinity of San Juan Hill. The documentation of his heroism was so great that it cannot credibly be questioned. Roosevelt, his Rough Riders, and the other troops he pulled together into an attacking force brought the land war to a close.

After the fighting, boredom and disease descended upon the soldiers. In vain, Roosevelt pleaded with General William Shafter and Secretary Alger to bring them home, but nothing happened. Unwilling to see his men wasting with malaria, dysentery, and yellow fever the furious Roosevelt acted on his own. Along with other officers, he signed a round-robin letter to General Shafter, demanding that the troops be evacuated and charging that any official who delayed the evacuation would be responsible for thousands of deaths.

He also sent his own, even stronger, letter. When the leaked contents of his letter appeared in the press, the War Department moved immediately to bring the men back to the States—but, in the understated words of a recent TR biographer, H. W. Brands, Washington officials "didn't appreciate the pressure." Alger's War Department, said Miller, even "emitted veiled threats of a court-martial for Roosevelt."

Major General Joseph Wheeler recommended Roosevelt for the Medal of Honor. So did Major General Samuel Sumner, and Leonard Wood (who by then also was a major general). A host of others in various ranks including junior officers and enlisted men made the same recommendation.

Secretary Alger, though, had his revenge. He blocked the award. At the end of 1998, Congress—belatedly, after the passage of a century—approved a resolution authorizing the President to award the Medal posthumously to Theodore Roosevelt, and requesting him to do so. President Clinton signed the measure, and sought further advice from the Department of the Army. Astonishingly, the Department—which continues to be bound by tradition and to harbor a disdain for volunteer, as opposed to regular, officers—continued for a time to be obstructionist. Finally, however, it conceded. President Bill Clinton made the award shortly before he left office.

Thus, TR and his son Ted are one of only two father and son Medal of Honor winners in American history. Gen. Arthur MacArthur, and his son Douglas, the famed General of the Army during the Second World War, form the other. Ted, who was being promoted to major general during World War Two just as he died of a heart attack, received the award for valor on Normandy Beach. Incidentally, Ted and his son Quentin, II, were the only father and son team on the beach at D Day.

Regardless of the War Department's disapproval, Roosevelt came home a national hero, praising the Rough Riders and the black troops who had fought alongside them. While they were on Long Island waiting demobilization, the enlisted men presented him with a two-foot high Frederic Remington statue, "the Bronco Buster," as a symbol of their admiration.

Even while he was still in Cuba, there had been a Roosevelt-for-Governor groundswell. Upon his return, it became overwhelming. But there was a major obstacle in the form of the powerful Republican boss, U. S. Senator from New York, Tom Platt. Platt wanted officials he could control, and he had no illusions about controlling the independent Roosevelt.

Recognizing Roosevelt's appeal to the voters, though, Platt agreed to a meeting. He emerged from the meeting saying that he and the Colonel had "buried past differences." Roosevelt, he said, had agreed to consult with him about appointments and legislation if he were to become Governor. With Platt's support, the final obstacle vanished.

After a vigorous campaign that included attacks on his integrity, Roosevelt won a narrow victory. His energetic campaigning undoubtedly made the difference. Platt remarked that Roosevelt was the only Republican who could have won the New York governorship that year, 1898. At the age of 40, TR was Governor of the largest and most important state in the country.

Roosevelt, as Platt conceded, was careful to keep his agreement. Platt complained, though, that after consulting him Roosevelt "did just what he pleased." Still, the new Governor made it clear that he was not Platt's enemy. He said approvingly that Platt differed from other bosses in not using his power to enrich himself. In filling minor offices, he usually followed Platt's choices. For major offices, he managed to finesse the appointments skillfully.

For instance, he refused to appoint Platt's choice for superintendent of public works, but then chose four other names, and permitted Platt to choose the appointee from among the four. The Governor thus demonstrated his independence while permitting the boss to save face. Roosevelt was a committed reformer, but he was keenly aware of the realities of practical politics. A political reformer must hold office in order to accomplish anything, and holding office always requires compromise.

The Roosevelt-Platt relationship was never warm, but generally it was cautiously correct. As a result of his skillful treatment of Platt and the legislature, Roosevelt succeeded in securing the passage of numerous reform laws. As a child of privilege, he abhorred radicals, but he was sensitive to the needs of the poor and of labor and he acted accordingly.

He signed a bill strengthening public education and outlawing segregation by local option. He said, "My children sit in the same school with colored children," and that there was nothing wrong with it. He also began to implement one of the foremost concerns that he displayed consistently throughout his executive career, environmental protection.

At that time, the term for New York Governors was still only two years. As his term neared its end, the relationship with Platt fell apart. Roosevelt defied him on a tax measure designed to force utilities to pay what he considered to be their fair share of taxes. Despite Platt's opposition, TR managed to get the bill through the legislature, and he quickly signed it. The Governor feared retaliation. Platt certainly had the power to block his re-nomination.

In spite of his own opposition to "radicalism," many other Republican leaders increasingly feared Roosevelt himself as a "radical." He considered it a distinct possibility that his political career might be finished. He was correct in thinking that Platt might prevent his re-nomination as Governor, but wrong in thinking that Platt would be able to kill his political career—quite the contrary. Against Roosevelt's own wishes (he was under no illusions about the boss's motives) Platt diverted him from the governorship by using his influence within the Republican Party to secure for the popular Rough Rider the Republican nomination as Vice President.

It was, after all, 1900. President William McKinley would be running for a second term, and Vice President Garret Hobart had died in office in 1899, leaving a vacancy. What possible harm could anyone do as Vice President?

McKinley won re-election with no difficulty. His victory owed much to his running mate's tireless, active, and effective campaigning. That running mate, Theodore Roosevelt, won along with McKinley, and became Vice President of the United States. Platt had succeeded in removing him from New York politics.

Not everyone was pleased, though. Another major power in the Republican Party, Senator Mark Hanna from Ohio, had opposed Platt's move and Roosevelt's nomination. He moaned that there was only one life between "that madman" and the presidency. In a letter to McKinley, he said that the newly re-elected President had a *duty* to the American people to *live* four more years from his inauguration.

TR had succeeded in reforming and energizing every position that he had ever held. It is interesting to speculate whether he might have managed to change the vice presidency if he had held the position long enough to put his invigorating stamp on it. As it happened, after his inauguration in March (this was before the 20th Amendment changed the inaugural date to January) he presided over the Senate for only four days. During that time the chamber approved a number of nominations from the President, and then adjourned until December.

TR took an extended vacation, although he digressed to make numerous speeches. He was at Lake Champlain, in Vermont, on the 6th of September while McKinley was attending the Pan American Exposition in Buffalo. A telephone call informed the Vice President that an anarchist, Leon Czolgosz, had shot the President.

TR rushed to Buffalo, but was relieved four days later when physicians informed him that McKinley was out of danger. The President's aides told him that it would reassure the public if he would display his confidence by leaving the wounded President's side. Following their advice, he departed to the Adirondacks, where he joined Edith and his family.

On the 13th, three days after TR departed, McKinley's condition worsened. His aide, George Cortelyou, sent a telegram to the Vice President, who was climbing Mount Marcy at the time. Roosevelt could not receive it until, on the way down the mountain, he met a messenger coming up who brought him the news. Another telegram then came with word that the President was near death.

TR raced in a buckboard forty miles to North Creek where a special train was waiting for him. It was near dawn when he arrived at the station. As soon as he ran into the depot, he received word that McKinley had died during the night.

At the age of 42, Theodore Roosevelt became America's chief executive. Even the young John Kennedy, who almost six decades later was elected at the age of 43, was older. A distraught Mark Hanna was said to have remarked, "Now look, that damned cowboy is President of the United States!"

Despite his irrepressible energy, TR moved thoughtfully and skillfully to consolidate his position. No Vice President who had succeeded to a vacancy in the office had ever been elected to a term of his own. TR had no intention of suffering the same fate.

But if he moved carefully, he also moved firmly. In his view, the President was the power center of American democracy, not a mere administrator carrying out congressional policy. His "stewardship theory" held that the President had the authority to take any action for the benefit of the country unless the Constitution or the laws forbade that action. TR remarked in his *Autobiography* "I have a definite philosophy about the Presidency. I think it should be a very powerful office, and I think the President should be a very strong man who uses without hesitation every power that the position yields; but because of this very fact I believe that he should be sharply watched by the people, held to a strict accountability by them, and that he should not keep the office too long." It was, as he described it, the Jackson-Lincoln theory of the presidency, in contrast to the Jeffersonian, which he rejected.

True to his belief in a merit system, he made every effort to appoint the best people to public office. As a partisan Republican, all other things equal he appointed Republicans. When he was unhappy with the quality of the Republicans available, however, he appointed Democrats without hesitation.

Shortly after he took office, he invited the prominent black educator, Booker T. Washington, to the White House. There they dined and discussed policy toward the South. Word leaked out that the President had dined with a black man, and many Southern whites were furious at this affront to their racist views. Miller quoted the Memphis *Scimitar* as having said that the dinner was "the most damnable outrage ever." Many other comments from the South were even worse. TR said simply that he had dined with a good American whom he respected, and that he regarded the attacks with "contemptuous indifference." He expressed sadness, though, that such feelings should exist.

A few years later as his time in the White House was drawing to a close, Annie Riley Hale, a bigoted writer from the South, wrote a book, *Rooseveltian Fact and Fable* (1908) viciously attacking almost everything about TR and his administration. Surprisingly, she condemned him less for the dinner with Washington than for most of his actions. She almost excused it, in fact, because she concluded that TR was a "Yankee," who simply knew no better. It was nevertheless a terrible thing, she thought, because the President had used "the people's house" for something which "the people" disapproved—the dinner had therefore violated the principles of democracy.

Regardless of his attitudes on the race issue, TR was a practical politician. He did not repeat the Washington dinner, nor did he campaign for civil rights. Had he done so, given the climate of the day, it is likely that he would have been driven from politics.

John Gable was absolutely correct when he wrote in *The Bull Moose Years* that "Roosevelt did not think that any race was inherently or biologically inferior or superior to any other. But he was anthropologically and philosophically provincial in his views of culture and 'civilization'." As a result, he considered their history of oppression to have kept American blacks as a group behind American whites as a group socially and culturally. On a personal basis, he operated on his "Great Rule of Righteousness," which said that every person should be treated solely on his or her merits. As a politician he was keenly aware of the attitudes and prejudices of his country. He recognized how little he or anyone else at the time could accomplish regarding civil rights. The topic therefore was not on his agenda, even though in private he condemned Southern prejudice and bigotry.

Roosevelt's record does reflect one instance of enormous injustice that his critics believed to be racist. In 1906, he sanctioned discharge of a group of black soldiers because of a disturbance in Brownsville, Texas in which some of them may have been involved. He was always sensitive about the issue, and always denied that race had been a factor in his decision. He said that it would have made no difference if the soldiers had been white.

This probably is true. His action reflected his own definition of integrity, and the strict "honor code" that he believed had to apply. He was disturbed that no one would divulge information about anyone else, and acted accordingly. Such honor codes continue to exist at the service academies at Annapolis, Colorado Springs, and West Point. Roosevelt probably did in fact base his decision on strict military discipline, and not on race—but there is no denying that it was unjust, whatever the reason. Combined with his typical reluctance to admit any chance that he might be wrong, this episode is probably the least attractive of any in Roosevelt's presidency. It becomes all the more noteworthy when considered against the outstanding nature of his record as a whole.

On the 1st of December 1901, in his first message to Congress, TR called for mild reforms, but he also sounded a warning that hinted at what he was to become—the Progressive Movement was under way, and he would be a great Progressive President. There was serious evil in the rapidly-expanding trusts. He called for a Department of Commerce with a Bureau of Corporations that could compile information on the trusts and their activities which the Department of Justice could use for anti-trust prosecutions. Congress took no action on his suggestions until 1903, when it created the Department of Commerce and Labor (Labor became a separate department in 1913).

As a good Republican, TR had no quarrel with bigness in business. He welcomed it, accepting bigness as necessary. It must be remembered that one of his idols was Alexander Hamilton.

He did very much have a quarrel, though, when business used its enormous power in ways that damaged the public. He railed against those whom he later called "malefactors of great wealth," and, astonishing Wall Street, he moved. Foremost among the "malefactors" was the formidable J. P. Morgan and his Northern Securities Company, a holding company put together to control the major railroads in the West. On the 18th of February 1902, Roosevelt's Justice Department brought suit to dissolve Northern Securities, charging the Company under the Sherman Anti-Trust Act with restraint of trade. Morgan was jolted. Roosevelt was from his own class, and had moved against him without warning.

Regardless of his class, TR recognized that huge concentrations of wealth in private hands could lead to oppression as much as any government tyranny. In fact, of all tyrannies, he considered that of mere wealth to be the "least attractive and most vulgar." He was the first President to recognize that in the complex modern world, only government had the potential to protect the people from oppression by huge concentrations of private power. He pointed out in speech after speech that there was nothing sacred about corporations, they were creatures of the state and the state had not only the authority but also the duty to control them when necessary.

Morgan, for his part, in the complete absence of government regulation had always done as he pleased. When TR threatened him, he reacted accordingly. Meeting with the President in the White House, he said, "If we have done anything wrong, send your man to my man and they can fix it up." Roosevelt sent Morgan packing, letting him know that it was not business as usual, he was dealing with the President of the United States. TR later complained that Morgan thought he could treat the President as though he were a mere business rival.

Morgan lost. The case made its way to the U. S. Supreme Court, which upheld the decision to dissolve the company. The young upstart President had won a major victory. The Bull Moose had become the Trust Buster.

In May of 1902 the United Mine Workers struck against the coal mines in eastern Pennsylvania. They were protesting working conditions, low pay, and the 12-hour a day six-day a week schedule. The strike dragged on. George Baer, representing the owners, refused negotiation. When winter neared, disaster threatened. Most of the country heated with coal, and the supply had dwindled. The owners were confident that when the situation became too severe, the government would do what it had always done, intervene to crush the strike.

Roosevelt at first, reflecting his background and his rejection of "radicals," was wary of the union. Nevertheless, he considered the public good to overshadow the rights of either party. Accordingly, he invited representatives of both to Washington hoping that they would listen to reason.

He was pleasantly surprised by John Mitchell, UMW President. Mitchell had previously pleaded with the strikers to avoid violence, and he was completely cooperative, offering to accept arbitration. Baer, on the other hand, was haughty and arrogant. He resented being dragged to meet a criminal, he said, even by the President of the United States. He demanded an injunction to crush the strike, and if necessary to end it, the use of troops.

TR later remarked that Mitchell was the only person in the room who conducted himself like a gentleman, including himself. Baer had been so insolent that he had lost his temper. If it had not been for the dignity of his office, Roosevelt fumed, he would have seized Baer by the nape of the neck and the seat of his pants and thrown him through the window.

If Baer wanted troops, TR decided, he would get them. He informed the owners that if they did not agree to arbitration, he would send in the army and run the mines himself. The owners buckled. They agreed to a commission consisting of a mining engineer, a military officer, a businessman, a federal judge, and "an eminent sociologist." They refused to have a union representative, but TR in a brilliant stroke, appointed E. E. Clark, president of a railroad union, as the "eminent sociologist." The owners accepted, the strike was settled, and Theodore Roosevelt became the first President ever to use federal power to intervene in a labor dispute on behalf of the workers, rather than the owners.

In 1904, TR became the first Vice President who had succeeded to the presidency to go on and win a term of his own. This first makes his great majority that year even more impressive. To settle the fears of critics who accused him of thirsting for power, he promised that he would not run again in 1908.

He also was the first President to thrust the United States into the middle of world affairs. Miller noted perceptively that TR brought the same attitudes to the world stage that he had demonstrated as a young reformer in Albany, New York City, and Washington. "Then," Miller wrote, "he had fought with righteous zeal against corrupt politicians and businessmen. Now, he projected a mixture of nationalism and practical idealism into global affairs. America, he believed, had the moral obligation to overawe international bullies, maintain order, and uplift backward peoples."

His extraordinary efforts on behalf of peace brought the Russo-Japanese War to a close in 1905, and won him the Nobel Peace Prize in 1906—making him the first American Nobel laureate. He succeeded in securing the Panama Canal for American security and for international commerce. However high-handed his methods may have been, there is no doubt that ultimately they provided great benefit worldwide. He was the first American President to submit a dispute involving his own country to the Court of International Justice at The Hague.

He greatly strengthened the Navy, and sent the "Great White Fleet" on a cruise around the world. This was not mere bravado. TR recognized that the Navy had fallen behind the technological curve, and considered the cruise vital for its practical value.

One result among many when it returned fourteen months later was that the "Great White Fleet" would be painted white no longer. In those pre-radar days, gunners located their targets visually, and white ships made excellent targets. Another was that the cruise with its intense firing practice brought vast improvement in naval marksmanship, which had been lacking, as well as in techniques of maintenance. Many authorities had thought it impossible for a huge fleet to complete a cruise around the world. TR demonstrated not only the possibility, but the practicality of such a venture. Covering a distance of some 40,000 miles, there had been no major breakdown.

Roosevelt's keen insights into international affairs led him to predict many of the actions of the Japanese and the Russians decades later. Concern about Japanese power was one of the factors that had convinced him that the cruise was necessary. Without belligerence, it demonstrated American power to the Japanese. There is reason to believe that it delayed Japanese-American hostilities for many years.

Congressional opposition to the cruise had been strong for several reasons, especially the great expense. Members of Congress, tending to be parochial in their interests and understandings, rarely if ever had (or have) TR's grasp of international affairs. When he proposed the cruise, congressional sources threatened to cut off funds. TR was not to be thwarted. He exercised his authority as commander-in-chief to send the fleet on its way using funds already appropriated. *Then* he approached Congress for the additional funding needed to bring it home. It was a proposal the members could hardly refuse. They could not very well leave the American fleet stranded somewhere far from its base. TR had injected the energy into the presidency that it required to function effectively in the twentieth century.

Presidents generally have a freer hand in international than in domestic matters, but TR succeeded in becoming the leader in domestic policy as well. After his victory in 1904, he called for a wide range of consumer protections: meat inspection, a pure food and drug law, supervision of insurance companies, restrictions on child labor, an Interstate Commerce Commission with the authority to regulate railroad rates, and much more. He also announced suits against companies benefiting from rebates on rail costs.

TR signed both the Meat Inspection Act and the Pure Food and Drug Act into law on June 30, 1906. Some two weeks earlier, he had signed the Hepburn Act providing power to the ICC to regulate railroad, pipeline, and warehouse rates. His boldest actions came with regard to conservation and the environment. In 1905 he named Gifford Pinchot to head a powerful Forest Service now in the Department of Agriculture, and he named a conservationist, James Garfield, Secretary of the Interior.

TR's commitment to the environment was surely the most consistent and sincere of all his strongly-held positions on public policy. Yet even on this topic he has been misunderstood and thus misrepresented. Brands, for example, in his lively biography, *TR: The Last Romantic*, wrote that TR was a conservationist, but "hardly a preservationist." In no way could he compare to Thoreau, who "valued wilderness for wilderness' sake." To be sure, TR was a use-conservationist—one who desired to reclaim land for productive human use. This, however, was only one aspect of his approach to the environment.

John Gable presented a fuller picture in his review of *The Last Romantic* for the *Theodore Roosevelt Association Journal*. "TR was, of course," Gable wrote, "*both* a preservationist, like his friend John Muir, and a use-conservationist, like his friend Gifford Pinchot. The Newlands Act of 1902, which gave Theodore Roosevelt Dam to Arizona, involved irrigation and reclamation, was use-conservation, while the National Monuments Act of 1906, which saved Muir Woods, the Grand Canyon, and other natural treasures, was preservationist." Gable demonstrated clearly that TR's approach to nature was balanced: "Of his federal bird preserves, TR wrote: 'Birds should be saved for utilitarian reasons; and, moreover, they should be saved because of reasons unconnected with dollars and cents'."

TR had the authority, under an 1891 law, to create "forest reserves" from federally-owned lands to protect them from exploitation. In the decade before he became President, his predecessors had reserved some 50 million acres. TR moved much more rapidly, and had reserved another 150 million acres. In addition, his administration had moved to indict numerous westerners for land fraud, including some powerful figures in his own Republican Party. Oregon Senator Charles Fulton accused the federal prosecutor of conducting a political vendetta, and demanded that Roosevelt fire him. TR shot back that the senator's "wrath should be reserved not for him but for those Republicans who have betrayed the party by betraying the public service and the cause of decent government."

In retaliation, Fulton in 1907 drew up a measure forbidding the President from creating any new forest reserves within six western states or adding to existing reserves without Congress's express approval. He attached the measure as a rider to an appropriation bill for the Department of Agriculture that it was important for TR to sign. Before signing the act that would strip him of his authority to create additional reserves, TR ordered Pinchot to identify the most important federal lands still outside the reserve system. He then, on the 2nd of March 1907, signed an executive order reserving sixteen million additional acres. Two days later—only after having created the additional reserves—he signed the new law that stripped himself of the authority to do so.

TR's critics, of course, were enraged. This was a much bolder step even than President Clinton took when he moved to place a significant, but much smaller, amount of federal land in Utah under protection. Utah officials blasted Clinton for his "high-handed" action. But the definition of "high-handed" depends upon one's perspective. Brands criticized TR's move as having added "16 million midnight acres. Roosevelt defended his move as reflecting 'the utmost care and deliberation'," Brands wrote, "but he fooled no one. It was patent that, Congress having outmaneuvered him he was fighting a spirited rearguard action, using his power before it vanished."

Well, yes, but Miller described it quite differently. If TR had vetoed the bill, the entire Agriculture Department would have "come to a standstill; if he signed it, the Forest Service would lose control over millions of acres of public lands considered essential to the national reserve. But Roosevelt," he wrote, "was not to be so easily thwarted."

It is *reasonable* to ask which party was the one outmaneuvered: Obviously, the President won, and Congress lost. It is *important* to ask what were the fundamental motivations involved: Just as obviously, TR acted not out of selfishness or thirst for power, but in pursuit of his view of the public good. It is *vital* to ask what were the results: There can be little doubt that the public today is better off than it would have been without TR's order.

Miller saw the executive order as "snatching some sixteen million acres out of the outstretched hands of would-be exploiters." His overall record on conservation, Miller believed, was TR's "great legacy to the American people." This legacy included broadening the notion of conservation to include coal and mineral lands, oil reserves, and power sites in addition to forests and wildlife. It included thirty irrigation projects, eighteen protected national monuments including Grand Canyon and Niagara Falls, and it included five new national parks and fifty-one wildlife refuges.

Brands saw the order as a "rearguard action," and complained because TR was "using his power before it vanished." That hardly seems to be a damning indictment—power can only be used "before it vanishes"—and without doubt, however much the incident reflects conflict with Congress, President Roosevelt was within his legal rights to do as he did. That, one should remember, is the way the system works. It is refreshing in this instance to see it working to benefit the public.

In 1908, about a year before TR's term ended, Henry Ford began producing the Model T. The Good Roads Movement had not been a significant force in TR's administration, but the new flivver was a harbinger of the flood of automobiles that was just over the horizon. Farmers, who previously had accepted isolation as inevitable, began to recognize that the new machine could expand their lives—but only if there were roads.

That was also election year. TR had promised not to run again. As a man of honor, he lived up to his promise. It was a promise he wished he had never made. He loved the office, hated to leave it, and could easily have been re-nominated and re-elected. Instead, he threw his support to his friend and associate William Howard Taft, who handily defeated William Jennings Bryan in Bryan's third run at the presidency.

After Taft took office in March 1909, TR went on an extended safari to Africa. He wanted to take himself out of the picture, and not interfere with the new President. The more news he received of the new administration, however, the more unhappy he became. Taft was anything but a fiery Progressive, and entertained a Whig philosophy of the presidency—the President essentially should be an administrator, carrying out congressional policies.

In 1910, TR gave a fiery speech in Osawatomie, Kansas. One of his finest biographers, Kathleen Dalton, said that it was the most important speech of his career. Before some thirty thousand listeners who flocked to the small town, he outlined his "New Nationalism." America needed social security, a graduated income tax, an inheritance tax to put "swollen fortunes to public use" (this is the tax that his Republican successors a century later foolishly call the dreaded "death tax"), and a removal of special interests from politics.

Dalton's 2002 study examined TR's career after his presidency in much more detail—and with much more perception—than any previous biography. The Roosevelt literature, though, until 2005 continued to lack an entire volume devoted to Roosevelt's highly significant life and career after he left office. That year, Patricia O'-Toole remedied the lack with her excellent *When Trumpets Call: Theodore Roosevelt After the White House.*

By 1912, TR had become thoroughly disillusioned, as were his Progressive supporters. He again threw his hat into the ring, and declared his candidacy for the Republican nomination. Although he overwhelmed Taft in the primaries, party leaders still controlled the majority of the delegates to the National Convention, which selected the nominee. They had been delighted with the relatively passive Taft, so much more conservative than the exuberant TR, that they threw their influence his way. Taft was the Republican nominee for re-election.

Believing that he had been robbed of the nomination, TR responded to pressure from the Progressives to run a third-party campaign. He felt as "strong as a Bull Moose," he thundered, and his Progressive Party became the Bull Moose Progressives. Surely, that strength was there. On his way to a speech in Milwaukee, a would-be assassin shot him in the chest. A thick folded paper and his glasses case in his pocket slowed the bullet, which lodged near his heart. He insisted on making the speech, as scheduled, before going to the hospital where surgeons concluded that the bullet could not be removed. He carried it the rest of his life.

His courage again struck a responsive chord with the people. They flocked to his support, but a third-party candidate in the American political system has little chance at the national level. He came in considerably ahead of Taft, who carried only Utah and Vermont, the only time when a third-party candidate for the presidency came in ahead of a Republican or a Democrat. But the winner was the Democratic candidate, Woodrow Wilson.

The Bull Moose Progressive platform of 1912 went far beyond TR's actions as President. With its call for women's suffrage, regulation of industry, rights for workers, concern for health and social justice, social insurance, and the like it was the most wide-ranging program ever put forth by a major presidential candidate—despite his third-party status, he was a major candidate as his second-place finish indicates. TR anticipated much that came later in the New Deal, and in fact to some extent went beyond it.

In October 1913, with the campaign behind them, TR and Edith went to South America. The governments of Argentina, Brazil, and Chile had invited him for a series of lectures. They journeyed extensively, and he was received with great enthusiasm. While there, the former president was invited to join a party to explore the River of Doubt. He said he had to do it. It was his "last chance to be a boy." Edith returned home in December. In January 1919, TR and his son Kermit joined Brazilian explorer Colonel Candido Rondon on the Paraguay River at the Brazilian border.

Two months later the party re-emerged, after having been given up for dead. TR in fact, almost did die. The group had endured the most terrible conditions. At one point, he jumped into the river to save a boat of supplies, injuring his leg severely. His other leg had never fully recovered from an injury in 1902 when his carriage collided with a streetcar.

The new injury, soaked as it was in river water in those pre-antibiotic days, became infected. It got worse, and he became delirious with fever. Collapsing, he insisted that the party abandon him. Kermit refused. Even if his father died, he said, he would insist on carrying him out. So TR pushed on. When the party returned to civilization, it had mapped the entire distance of the river, an enormous length of 1,500 miles. TR had lost fifty-seven pounds. Brazil re-named the river Rio Roosevelt, popularly called Rio Teodoro, in TR's honor. In 2005, Candice Millard's *Theodore Roosevelt's Darkest Journey: The River of Doubt* chronicled the harrowing Brazilian trip with a degree of detail never before attempted.

TR remained active in public life. He was concerned about the Wilson administration's lack of military preparedness, and wrote and spoke out forcefully criticizing the

President. Sometimes his charges, said his critics, descended into demagoguery. He rejected nomination by the Progressives to run for President again in 1916. There also was some talk within the Republican Party of nominating him, but many things worked against it. There was continuing resentment of his Bull Moose campaign, and he simply refused to campaign for the nomination.

When the World War did come, as he had predicted it would, he appealed to President Wilson to be permitted to raise a division and go to fight. Despite the bitterness between the two men, Wilson remarked later that he had been charmed by TR's personality. "There is a sweetness about him that is very compelling," he said. "You can't resist the man."

But resist him, he did. He refused TR's request to enter the service, saying that he would rely entirely on conscription and professionals. Even though TR offered to go in a lower position and not as commander, even though he was surely as qualified as some of the generals who did go, even though French Premier Georges Clemenceau urged Wilson to send TR as a great morale builder, Wilson refused to send his old rival.

The refusal crushed TR. It was one of the greatest tragedies of his life. He urged his four sons not only to enter the service, but to get into combat. Each did. Even Ethel, his daughter, went abroad as a nurse with her husband, Surgeon Richard Derby. Quentin, the youngest, an Army Air Corps pilot, was killed in battle. TR could hardly bear the grief, especially knowing that he bore much of the responsibility for Quentin's death. "Poor Quenikens," friends would hear him mutter to himself.

His popularity, however, had resurged. The Wilson Administration had become increasingly unpopular, and prominent Republicans, including Will Hayes the Republican National Chairman were pressuring him to run again in 1920. Hayes was certain he would be the nominee.

This was not to be. TR died in his sleep on the 6th of January 1919. Many factors combined to weaken his previously powerful, but prematurely aged, body. He had never fully recovered from the effects of the fever that he had contracted in the Amazon. He likely suffered also from lead poisoning as a result of the bullet that had remained lodged in his chest. Added to this was the grief he bore from the loss of his youngest son. At TR's death, his son Archie summed it up in a cable to the others: "The Old Lion is Dead."

Had he lived, the chances are that the first three-term President would have been Theodore, rather than Franklin, Roosevelt. Since Warren Harding, the eventual nominee, had been virtually unknown, yet won by the greatest popular vote landslide to date, it is even more likely, that the colorful and popular TR would again have been President.

America has been blessed with many heroes, but it has never seen anyone else quite like Theodore Roosevelt. John Milton Cooper rhapsodized about his presidency in his comparison of TR and Wilson, *The Warrior and the Priest*. TR's "catholic interests and intellectual and aesthetic tastes led him to exploit the varied dimensions of his office to a degree that has never since been fully matched, he wrote. In redecorating and renaming the White House, he "foreshadowed an interest in governmental promotion of the arts that had not existed since the 1820s. In 1904 and 1905 he directed the Treasury to redesign American coins, and he commissioned his friend, the leading sculptor Augustus Saint-Gaudens, to do the work. He thereby gave the country, he later boasted, 'the most beautiful coinage since the decay of Hellenistic Greece'."

Cooper noted TR's support for scientific and cultural projects, particularly research and exploration by the Smithsonian, and the establishment of the National Gallery of Art. He wrote that TR set an example for the public by inviting leading writers, painters, sculptors, and scientists to the White House and publicizing the guest list. Despite rather conservative tastes, "he defended Edgar Allen Poe's reputation, and promoted the career of Edwin Arlington Robinson." Moreover, "Roosevelt based his cultural views upon wide cultivation and genuine reflection." Cooper quoted the novelist Owen Wister as saying, "For that once in our history, we had an American *salon*," and the historian Jacob Burckhardt as saying that the Renaissance political ideal was "the state as a work of art." That, Cooper concluded, "was the ideal Roosevelt pursued during his presidency."

Could there be better praise for a national leader than to say that he pursued the state as a work of art? Can we wonder that such a figure captivated the imaginations of Americans? John Morton Blum said that Roosevelt sought to use positive government to "promote national strength and to assure to each individual unfettered opportunity for realizing the dignity and the satisfactions of honest work. Whatever his shortcomings," Blum wrote, TR's "habit of action had enduring value. He made a virtue of dutiful vitality applied in an age of vigor and confidence. In a more troubled time the world learns painfully again the need for deciding firmly what is right and laboring assiduously to achieve it."

I look at this spirit, and then at our national spirit today, and experience a sense of loss. The more significant memorials—Mount Rushmore, Theodore Roosevelt Island in Washington, D.C., the Theodore Roosevelt National Park, and many others—work to keep alive that spirit that TR gave to his country. This is not true for the largest of the memorials, the Theodore Roosevelt International Highway. It, sadly, has almost entirely faded from memory.

TR had no direct connection with the Highway. It was conceived as a memorial after his death, one that would benefit the country and its people, and honor its most vigorous President. Its brief existence as a named highway helped the country make the transition from a localized, rural, series of communities to a mighty industrial state bound together by communication and transportation that few if any in TR's day could have envisioned.

How fitting it would be if Congress and the states through which the once mighty Highway went would re-recognize it in his honor, much as the Interstate System bears the name of President Eisenhower. The Theodore Roosevelt International Highway once again would proudly carry his name across the Continent, at the top of the 48 states.

Index

DATE DUE